INTERNATIONAL COLLEGE
LIBRARY – FT. MYERS

DEMCO

BACK TO MISSISSIPPI

INTERNATIONAL COLLEGE
LIBRARY – FT. MYERS

BACK TO MISSISSIPPI

A

Personal Journey

Through the Events

that Changed America

in 1964

MARY WINSTEAD

An Imprint of Hyperion
New York

Copyright © 2002 Mary Winstead

Excerpt from "Letter from Birmingham Jail" reprinted by arrangement with the Estate of
Martin Luther King, Jr., c/o Writers House as agent for the proprietor, New York, NY.

Copyright © 1963 Dr. Martin Luther King Jr., copyright © renewed 1986 Coretta Scott
King

All rights reserved. No part of this book may be used or reproduced in any manner
whatsoever without the written permission of the Publisher. Printed in the United States of
America. For information address: Hyperion, 77 W. 66th Street, New York, New York
10023-6298.

ISBN: 0-7868-6796-5

Hyperion books are available for special promotions and premiums. For details contact
Hyperion Special Markets, 77 West 66th Street, 11th floor, New York, New York, 10023,
or call 212-456-0100.

FIRST EDITION

Design by Abby Kagan

10   9   8   7   6   5   4   3   2   1

To Wilbur Collins Winstead

Acknowledgments

I WOULD LIKE TO EXPRESS MY GRATITUDE first to Mrs. Carolyn Goodman, Andy Goodman's mother, for her indomitable spirit and personal integrity, and her generosity in sharing her time and her experience of having lost a son to murder. I also thank Stanley Dearman, recently retired editor of the *Neshoba Democrat*, who provided me with a fearless and compassionate insider's perspective into how Neshoba County has grown and changed in the thirty-eight years since the murders of Goodman, Schwerner, and Chaney. A thank-you to Phil Dray, coauthor of *We Are Not Afraid: The Story of Goodman, Schwerner, and Chaney and the Civil Rights Campaign for Mississippi*, for sharing with me his resources and expertise and for his book, which provided me with valuable historical documentation. To Jerry Mitchell of the *Jackson Clarion-Ledger* for his research, time and perspective on the subject, I offer much appreciation.

A thank-you to Professors Valerie Miner and Arthur Geffen from the Department of English at the University of Minnesota for their support of this work and for their ongoing professional encouragement. Thanks to Maureen Gibbon and Carlen Arnett for reading and commenting on early drafts and for moral support when things got painful with family.

Thanks to family and friends in Mississippi, Georgia, Oregon, New York, California, and Minnesota and especially to my father, who never yielded in his support of my telling the truth. I owe a special debt of gratitude to my husband, Peter Blewett, for his intellect, warmth, and love. Thanks to my kids, Sam, Joe, and Sarah Breckenridge, for being proud of me.

Many thanks to my agent, Angela Miller, who believed in the project from the beginning, and to my editor at Hyperion, Leslie Wells. Thanks go to Jared Santek at The Loft Literary Center in Minneapolis, and to the McKnight Foundation for their financial support. Finally, I acknowledge the Virginia Center for the Creative Arts in the foothills of the Blue Ridge Mountains for providing me with the environment I needed to turn my manuscript into a book.

Contents

The excursion is the same when you go looking for your sorrow as when you go looking for your joy.

—EUDORA WELTY, "THE WIDE NET"

PROLOGUE

Memphis, Tennessee, December 1982

M Y FATHER AND I LOVE MAPS. On a low-flying Airbus from Memphis to New Orleans, an atlas of the United States lay open between us, propped up on our bent knees. We pored over the maps together, tracing highways and rivers with our fingers as though searching for a pulse. We recited the names of cities and towns until the words began to sound like the names that connect the generations in the Bible. "First there's New Orleans, then Slidell through Picayune into Hattiesburg, to Laurel and Stonewall and finally Meridian," my father said.

We were traveling a thousand miles south, from Minnesota to Mississippi, to introduce my infant daughter to aunts and uncles and cousins on my father's side. Sarah was slightly feverish, asleep against my shoulder. Her cheeks were flushed, her pink coat unbuttoned, her hat hanging down her back from a limp satin ribbon. Seated beside us my father slowly turned the pages, carefully studying one map after another.

All my life I've listened to my father tell stories about his childhood. The son of a Mississippi sharecropper, he filled my own child-hood with vivid pictures of the poverty and hardships that marked the rural South of the 1920s and 1930s. Because of his stories I got to know grandparents I'd never met. In my mind Daddy Bob was very much alive, trudging up and down cotton rows behind a mule-drawn plow; and Grandma Ora still lived, yoked to her sister, lug-ging dinner pails into cotton fields under the midday sun, so that stopping to eat wouldn't mean stopping the work.

My father, whose nickname is Windy, just celebrated his eighty-first birthday. After a lifetime of smoking, his lungs are weakened from emphysema, and he now wheels a small tank of oxygen behind him wherever he goes. But from the depths of his remarkable mem-ory he still tells his stories and seasons them with southern charm and colorful details. He also loves a good joke. With an eye that has always twisted an event around so that he finds the humor in it, his wit can range from corny to self-effacing to bawdy to down-right crude.

Yet the closeness he maintains with his past and its intimate details makes my father an elusive man. His physical presence draws everyone's attention and his basso profundo voice fills a room, but his heart is often elsewhere. On the sultry summer evenings of my Minnesota childhood, our neighbors gathered on the front lawn of our south Minneapolis bungalow to listen to my father talk about growing up in Neshoba County, Mississippi. His stories described an era that was rapidly vanishing with time, progress, and technol-ogy. In 1996, I began to record them for my teenage children so that the world their grandpa grew up in wouldn't be lost from memory.

When I began this book, I tried to locate those places that took my father's mind far away from us in Minnesota, where he has lived for fifty years. Sometimes I went with him, as on our trips to Mis-sissippi to see his brothers and sisters. Sometimes I tried to bring him back, with questions about the places that nobody else but he could go: behind a mortar at Guadalcanal in 1943, in a boxcar with his family in 1929.

To add important background to the stories, I decided to investigate the family's history. From Mississippi to Virginia, our deep Scotch-Irish roots stretch back through the Carolinas, where I found vestiges of the Winsteads' stopping-off points in the names of restaurants, real estate agencies, and on street signs in small towns. And in the family churchyard in Neshoba County, the names on the headstones reveal their final resting place.

Our relations are now scattered throughout Mississippi. My father was the youngest of five. Having recently lost his older sister and brothers, his closest Mississippi kin now include one sister, several nieces and nephews and their brood of kids and grandkids. In the North, his own family of five children has expanded, and now our family gatherings in Minnesota include sons and daughters-in-law, significant others, and nine grandchildren.

Even before I began to look into the family history, I'd suspected that my father had told us only part of the story. I wasn't surprised, then, when I followed the thread of racism that had made its presence known in the slurs that he had woven through his speech, and in the culture we'd seen on our infrequent visits to Mississippi.

Our first trip took place in 1966 when I was thirteen years old. Unlike friends and neighbors who drove their kids every summer to Mount Rushmore or the Wisconsin Dells, we were never able to afford family vacations. Other than weekends at the lake homes of my mother's more prosperous sisters in Minnesota, this was the only vacation our family ever took.

During that memorable visit, I experienced the warmth and acceptance of aunts, uncles, and cousins whose loyalty toward kin formed the very foundation of life. I saw a deep respect for a day's work, as well as religious convictions and a lifestyle based on resourcefulness and economy, no doubt born in hard times and sustained by the will to survive. I learned to savor the dual southern delights of a home-cooked meal and time afterward to sit and visit. I listened to the grown-ups tell stories that rose from a devotion to family history that was colored with humor, tempered by sorrow, and strengthened by faith.

In this context I also experienced a landscape that was entirely different from my own, peopled as it was with ethnic differences. I witnessed a system of patronage that dated back centuries, where black people worked as domestics and tenant farmers, remnants of a culture that had been based on slavery. I listened to the adults discuss issues like integration of the schools and voting rights that back home in our own segregated community were merely philosophical, but that for our southern relations were very real. I saw for the first time the squalor of rows of shacks on unpaved roads in the black neighborhoods. Before this, my awareness of racial issues was limited to what I saw on television. Back home, I'd had no firsthand contact with anyone of color in my life.

I didn't return to Neshoba County until I had young children of my own. In 1980 and again in 1982, I took them to Mississippi with my father. He drove us along the rutted clay roads he'd walked as a child, and his stories sparked memories of my own childhood visit. Though the schools were now integrated and public services extended to the black neighborhoods, vestiges of the social hierarchies and economic differences between the races still made their presence known. And despite the differences in our lifestyles and the distance that separated us, I felt the familiar warm welcome I'd received years before from my Mississippi kin.

In 1997, my research into Dad's family came upon the events in Neshoba County during the Freedom Summer of 1964, and my investigation took a disturbing turn. What had begun as a search through the family history became a painful journey that led me, discovery by startling discovery, to the roles that certain kinfolk had played in the murders of civil rights workers Andrew Goodman, Michael Schwerner, and James Chaney, and the consequences I'd face if I chose to write about it. I uncovered secrets that had distanced us in Minnesota from the truth about kin who were members of the Klan and the denial that had constructed an idealized version of history that would protect both beloved family members and the family outcasts that nobody wanted to claim.

I had discovered parts of family history that everyone would just as soon forget. And yet it was in the very attempt to forget that the most serious issues emerged. I would enjoy the full and open co-operation on the part of my southern kin when it came to remembering my father's Neshoba County childhood. But when I discovered that his cousin Preacher Edgar Ray Killen was involved—indeed is alleged to have masterminded the murders—the doors would close and communication would stop.

There were stories to tell that nobody was telling, and my father was caught in the middle, between the family he loved in Neshoba County and the reasons he'd left Mississippi in 1940. He'd rejected the isolation, poverty, and lack of opportunity he'd grown up with, but he found that he'd carried the Neshoba County ethos to Minnesota with him nonetheless. It showed in his attempts to balance loyalty to his roots with loyalty to his offspring, and the emotional barriers that would come between us as a result.

More than thirty years after one of the most spectacularly brazen crimes in the history of the civil rights movement, a pivotal moment in our nation's history, we were just discovering evidence in our own family of involvement. Even then, the details would only emerge from the fragments of information I was able to piece together from my research, spurred forward by two questions: *How could this have happened?* and *Why didn't we know?*

It would have been much easier for me to leave the shameful aspects of the story unspoken, and I'd have safely adhered to the unwritten family rule that the worst crime anyone could commit would be to say anything that would place kinfolk in an unflattering light. But against the wishes of most members of Dad's family, I have decided to include that story in this book. "I don't want my name associated with any book that has to do with civil rights," an aunt told me. "We have to live here, in this community, and you don't," a cousin wrote. "You can't be responsible for what your kin does," another cousin said. In thirty-five years nobody has ever spoken out. Doing so would mean hurting somebody, or risking that other people might say ugly things. And that would be painful.

It was a wire service photograph that caused me to change my mind: a photograph of Andrew Goodman's anguished mother watching a coffin bearing the remains of her middle son being lowered from an airplane. She didn't have a choice; her family was forced to suffer. Here was an historical event of profound significance that had something to teach me personally. I'd always confined my compassion to family and friends, but it wasn't too late for me to break through the lifetime of limitations I'd placed on love.

Then came a comment from family members. No, two comments. One, that after all this time it still hadn't been proven that the three decomposed bodies found buried in a dam six weeks after their disappearance belonged to the civil rights workers. From my research I knew that the three had been positively identified using dental records, what was left of their fingerprints, and ID cards that were found in the pockets of their blue jeans when their bodies were discovered.

Finally came an uncharacteristically harsh judgment from a relative whose gentleness is heralded throughout the family: that the three young men had been trash.

It was then that I decided to meet Mrs. Goodman, who welcomed me into her home and graciously shared with me a mother's experience of losing a child to murder. During the course of several conversations, Mrs. Goodman made it abundantly clear that these young men had come from hardworking, educated, and loving families who'd encouraged their sons to make a difference in the world.

Mine was no longer a simple question of whether to include the story, but of whether to break a family rule and speak out.

As a mother, Mrs. Goodman's testimony became an essential element in this story. I wanted to know Andy and his companions, not as mythical figures from the civil rights movement, but as human beings whose loss has been painful and real. Their deaths resulted in profound changes on the national level, but I had a more immediate goal in mind: I wanted their deaths to matter to us. I wanted their deaths *to hurt*.

Writing about Preacher Killen was a trickier matter. As with other civil rights murders whose perpetrators have only recently been tried for homicide, this case will likely be tried soon, and Mississippi's attorney general has named Edgar Ray Killen as the state's main suspect. So Preacher Killen isn't talking. Not that he has been open about the murders; in fact, he has denied his involvement ever since he was dropped off at a Philadelphia, Mississippi, funeral home by the lynch mob on the night of June 21, 1964.

I have written about him, using the testimony of witnesses during the 1967 trial, people in the Neshoba County community, and those writers and reporters who have covered his activities over the past fifty years. Everything that appears in this book regarding Preacher Killen and his activities has been documented extensively in numerous written texts over the past four decades. My sources appear in the acknowledgments and bibliography.

But I've written about him for more personal reasons. Everyone has disowned Edgar Killen, outcast and renegade that he is. But I discovered that by claiming the monster in our midst, I uncovered the monsters in myself.

Even though my blood ties place me inside, my decision to write about this will brand me as an outsider. Outsiders from the North often find it far easier to express outrage, at dinner parties and in conversations, at the villains in white hoods "down there" in the South. Yet the outrage too often focuses exclusively on these more visible signs of racism, which keeps us from taking an honest look at ourselves. It's far easier to demonize, point our fingers, and assign blame.

We live in comfortable houses in segregated neighborhoods and work for companies whose executives reflect the racial makeup of our communities. And in our isolation, we rest on a set of beliefs about our own racial virtues that have rarely been tested; beliefs that, if challenged, would likely reveal a darker side we'd rather not face. And it is this unchallenged set of beliefs, this absence of direct confrontation, that leads to the passivity that makes it so difficult for real change to occur.

Does this erase the blot upon my family's name that was placed there by those who, when tested, failed utterly to do the right thing? Of course not. But I've come to see firsthand that evil exists neither "out there" nor in a vacuum, and that to deny it is to deny that it often flourishes in a community of busy and good-hearted people who cannot, will not, or simply do not address the depravity of those who are bent on harming others. As Dr. Aaron Henry, a black Mississippian on the front lines of the drive for voting rights, said to an assembly at Queens College in the spring of 1964, "The thundering silence of the good people is disturbing."

Set in opposing times and places, the stories my father tells form the heart of this narrative, while the other parts of the story unfold outward, in contrast and comparison. I've looked at cultural norms that we followed so diligently, for instance, that made it easy for us to leave the problems of civil rights in the hands of others. Then I placed them side by side with the activism of Andy Goodman, J. E. Chaney, and Mickey Schwerner and against the activities of Preacher Killen and the Klan, all of which lead up to the moment of the murders on June 21, 1964.

As a result of my research, I've acquired the sense that if an event like this was going to happen, it was likely to happen in a place like Neshoba County. I see more clearly how my family's involvement in culturally entrenched systems enabled this event to occur. But larger insights emerge when I begin to see the broader implications of the crime in relation to its time and place: this event took place in Neshoba County because up until this point, the rest of the nation had ignored what was happening there for more than a century.

My book does not attempt to justify the unjustifiable, to remove the responsibility for the crimes from those who carried them out, or to explain what cannot be explained in human history or in human nature. I also try to refrain from the self-righteousness that characterizes many of the accounts of the murders that have been written by people like me, who live in the North. I attempt to explore the roots of hatred, fear, and ignorance that caused people to commit the unthinkable in the context of a family, a community, and even a nation that didn't want to admit that it was happening.

"It's a clash of cultures," my father will tell me. "I've lived in the North and the South, and b'lieve me, I understand 'em. They bury everything." In spite of everything, however, I will claim my father's family as my own; his story as the prelude to my story; his road the road that led to mine. I may be an outsider, but my roots remain, if only as part of the soil upon which my father walked as a child, if only as a place my children can locate in the stories I've written.

But this is all in the future. Right now my father, my baby daughter, and I, ears popping, descend into the Mississippi Delta. Sarah nurses, my father hands me a stick of chewing gum, and I close my eyes and swallow. If I could, I'd erase all of the painful things I'll discover in my family and in myself. But that would make us less than human, and would allow us to remain as comfortable as before.

My father closes the atlas and the plane lands. We set foot on southern soil and the story begins.

PART ONE

A Family of Storytellers

CHAPTER 1

Meridian, Mississippi, 1997

I T'S THE MIDDLE OF FEBRUARY, the middle of the night, and I don't know what time it is. I haven't known what time it is for five days. Maybe two weeks. From the foldout couch in the family room, my father's snoring rattles through his sinuses like a ripsaw. Unable to sleep, I open my door and cross the room in my nightgown, breaking through waves of sound that vibrate at frequencies varied enough to confuse a heartbeat.

The room is full of antique clocks: grandfather and grandmother clocks, school and mantel clocks, each pendulum ticking out its own metronomic pulse. I search their faces for the right time but don't find what I'm looking for. One of the clocks strikes four. Across the room another chimes six. Half an hour ago, it was midnight. When time becomes disjointed, it interrupts my sleep and interferes with hunger. It has even confounded the onset of menses: my monthly cycle is all fouled up.

I've never been much of a sleeper, so the rhythms of this temporal dissonance seem almost natural. I often wake at odd hours from recurring dreams of houses, water, and crying babies. I wander the house in the middle of the night, doing household chores other people take care of during the day: washing dishes, folding laundry, dusting the coffee table. Which means I've learned to snatch fragments of sleep when I can: my head on the desk at work, catnaps on airplanes, stretched out on the sofa with a book open across my chest. My father does this too. He pulls the car over in the middle of the day, locks the doors, and closes his eyes, falling asleep with his mouth open, his head leaning back against the headrest.

When I was little, I'd crawl into bed with him, making myself as small as possible, straight and still on the narrow strip between his broad sleeping back and the edge of the bed, unable to fall asleep for trying not to fall onto the floor.

I loosen the dead bolt and slip out the door to sit on the front step. Camus wrote that even though all is not well under the sun, history is not everything. In Mississippi, family history comes together bit by bit, from a past that reveals itself to me in fragments: photographs, papers, interviews, and the mother lode of my father's memory. But there is a reservoir behind the wall of consciousness that informs my instincts, like a blind girl feeling her body with her fingers and discovering another world.

THE CLOCKS belong to Auntie Lu, my father's sister, whose full name is Allma Lumiere (pronounced *loo meer'*). Uncle Ed collected them after he retired from his job driving a Coca-Cola truck. He plundered old barns and haunted collectors' fairs. He found them at auctions and in junk stores. He usually got them for almost nothing. Only he could see the beauty in the disparate parts: the polished oak, delicate hands and stern but helpful faces beneath the layers of grit, broken glass, and warped, yellow varnish. Often he brought them home in pieces, then replaced the springs and cogs in the clockwork until they kept perfect time.

For thirty-five years, Ed drove U.S. Highway 80, "Ol' 80," my father calls it, the only good road connecting Jackson, Mississippi, and Meridian before construction of the interstate in the 1960s. Uncle Ed lugged wooden cases of wavy green bottles into the road-side restaurants that today stand vacant along Ol' 80, now a little-used frontage road that lies in the shadow of the elevated freeway.

This afternoon, I'm in Lumiere's kitchen, reading a newspaper article about Ol' 80, looking at four-color photographs of the dilapidated buildings that once were lively with people stopping along the road for a snack and something to drink. There's the old Nelva Courts, where you could order all the fried catfish you could eat for a dollar, and a dead-tired roadhouse without a name, just the word CAFE stenciled in big letters across the side.

Not everyone could stop there, however. In a snapshot over a sidebar about the slow death of Jim Crow thirty-five years ago, the WHITES ONLY signs hang weathered and lopsided over the boarded-up rest rooms.

Auntie Lu is at the stove, putting the finishing touches on my father's favorite dishes. A platter of crusty fried chicken—the crisp-iness comes from cornmeal—waits at the sideboard. There's sweet potato pecan pie for dessert. The table is set with my grandmother's pink rosebud china. "I'm own tell you the truth, Mary," she says, fishing out a piece of boiled bacon from a saucepan and placing it on top of a steaming bowl of black-eyed peas. "Don't anybody like sittin' on a toilet when they don't know who's been they before."

I put the newspaper away, butter a wedge of hot corn bread, and put a forkful, moist and crumbly, into my mouth. Auntie Lu explains about the clocks. She points to a small, hump-backed time-piece that sits at the center of the mantel. It wears a black enamel coat that's crazed and chipped. It has a yellow face and delicate, openwork hands. "This little ol' bitty clock was listed in *Ripley's Believe It or Not,*" she explains. "Grandma Collins carried it out of five burning houses."

I ask about the houses the family grew up in, but it's hard to tell how many. There's the big white house, long vanished, with tall pillars across the front that my father draws in pencil on a page in my notebook. He sketches seven rooms and a porch with a swing at each end. "The closest we ever came to antebellum," he says. After the stock market crash they lived in a boxcar, then in their grandparents' cabin. During cotton season, it was a series of two-room sharecropper shacks.

I HAVE COME BACK to Mississippi with my father to dig through boxes of old photographs, to drive along remote clay roads in scrub pine forests, to listen to my aunts and cousins while we sit in the kitchen and chat. And eat. There's always food on the table. Lumiere's banana cream pie with crushed vanilla wafers for a crust. Pearl from across the street has brought her Christmas fruitcake, even though it isn't Christmas, because she remembers that it's my favorite. Cousin Darla brings okra from her garden. Cousin Troy stops for chicken. We eat and talk. Rather, we eat and they talk. I listen.

I discover aunts who love me so much that at times I question my capacity to return it in kind. I find cousins who welcome me with affection, though we really don't know one another at all. At home, we don't seem to get as close. Auntie Lu invites intimacy. I tell her how lonely I am, so many years after my divorce, and she takes my chin in her hands. "Y'all so pretty, Mary. It's gonna take somebody truly special to win your heart again." Her voice melts like heavy syrup all over me. Later I sit on the back steps and wonder if I've ever learned to love.

To discover the truth here, a person has to do some digging: a dark path leading through time. I piece together the fragments I've gathered. My great-grandfather watches General Sherman march along the Pine Grove Road in February of 1864. In a shoebox full of old photos from a cousin's closet there is a sepia-toned daguerreotype of a mixed-race family, taken sometime after the Civil War. Aunt Ruby once pulled from her top dresser drawer a tiny pair of brown leather driving gloves that belonged to her mother-in-law, Miss Effie Lester, whose husband, Mr. Matthew, owned much of Neshoba County in the early part of the twentieth century, my father says. And I visit sharecropper shacks from the 1930s and 1940s, where I find, beneath the rotten shingles of a caved-in roof, pages from my great-grandmother's Bible.

And in all of these fragments, I find my father. Linked to the stories of his grandparents, who were eyewitnesses to the burning of Meridian, the fall of Vicksburg, the emancipation of the slaves. Who watched the overseers weigh the cotton of the black sharecroppers while the white pickers just tossed their bags onto the truck. Who remembers his mother yoked to her sister as they carried ten-gallon dinner pails to the fields at noon beneath an August sun so hot it kept the chicken pan pie bubbling beneath the crust inside the metal buckets. Who traveled from lumber camp to lumber camp with his mother and brothers and sisters after his father lost everything in 1929. Who listened to his mother sing opera ("she was classically trained," my father says) as she stood in the wind to pull greens from between the railroad ties to cook for dinner. Revival tents. Uncle Spike's still. Missing a year of school because he didn't have shoes. Names that sound funny at first to the northern ear, like twin cousins named Wilber and Milber—and a distant cousin that nobody claims.

For most of my life, Mississippi was a scrapbook of sepia-toned photographs collected in my father's memory. There was no one in Minnesota to confirm or contradict his stories, and the images always pointed to the end of his childhood and the end of an era, of which leave-taking there was no specific destination. But this is a story of generations, where nothing is ever finished, where endings become beginnings and the stories go on forever.

I finish my black-eyed peas. I've become witness to a century in a rural Mississippi county so quiet you'd think that nothing ever happens here. But there's history waiting to be discovered, buried beneath decades of interpretation, as if a roof had collapsed and covered over everything.

CHAPTER 2

Fishin' for Chickens

I COME FROM A FAMILY of storytellers. We've got dinner table sermonizers, ribbon-cutting speechmakers and stand-up comedians. We've got cussers, complainers, and mythmakers. We are poor listeners and interrupters and embellishers of the truth. For a family of storytellers, an ordinary life isn't good enough; it has to be *special*. Unfortunately, the neighborhood where I was raised tried very hard *not* to be special.

I grew up in south Minneapolis in the 1950s and 1960s, where elm trees that had been planted forty years before met in a leafy arc over the street in July, and in January brushed their bare branches together against the gray winter sky. The streets had been graded in the 1910s and 1920s so that the three- and four-bedroom bungalows were built into the sides of a hill that curved alongside a narrow creek. Most had two stories, sloping roofs, and a front porch that ran half the width of the houses.

My mother was a Minneapolis native whose only foray from home had been a four-year stint in Washington, D.C., during World

War II. She'd enlisted in the navy and worked with the intelligence corps. This was where she'd met my father, who was in Washington to recover from malaria after twenty-seven months in the Solomon Islands. My parents were married in 1947 and decided to settle in Minneapolis, where they raised my three sisters, my brother, and me.

We lived in the middle of the block, in a green house with a green picket fence. My mother kept a card table on our front porch, where in the winter she stored Christmas cookies in five-pound coffee cans and in the summer she served us family dinners. Seven of us sat on chairs we'd pull around that small table from all over the house, eating picnic-style from paper plates.

She prepared simple meals, mixing together canned tuna, peas, boiled macaroni, and Miracle Whip into a salad that she chilled in the refrigerator and plopped onto iceberg lettuce leaves that curled on each plate like an upturned palm. She poured potato chips into a basket that was lined with a paper napkin and then placed at the center of the table. We drank iced tea from dented metal glasses that came in primary colors and had begun to sweat on the outside, and were thus slippery and hard to hold.

Afterward my younger sister Ann and I cleared the table, and my mother washed the dishes in our small kitchen. Beside her, Liz stood on a stool with a dishtowel tied around her, drying the wooden spoons. Liz was not quite three years old. My two older siblings were orbiting out of the center of the family picture: my brother Gene, who was fourteen, found yet another excuse to keep from helping, and had disappeared with his friends into the shadows across the street. Linda was in the bathroom, ratting her hair into a bubble, getting ready for a dance at the Knights of Columbus hall. Linda was sixteen going on twenty-one, my mother said. My father went upstairs to change his clothes.

My father had his own sense of time, which means that he ignored deadlines and moved to an internal clock that seemed to tick at half the normal speed. He paced himself so slowly, in fact, that

Grandma Lind, my mother's mother, always said that if he went any slower, he'd go backward.

My father was a natural-born salesman, and needed a job that would provide him with an audience. From the floor of the carpet department at Dayton's Department Store, he won people over with stories, jokes, and a politeness that caused him to call his customers "sir" and "ma'am," in a way that brought to mind his southern upbringing. He disliked anyone telling him what to do, and hated it when someone in authority got in the way of his making a sale or exercising any of his freedoms, for that matter.

He also liked to push the boundaries of propriety, just to get a rise out of people, and he often slid eyebrow-raising comments into the texture of general conversation so that they appeared as part of the fabric of his colorful discourse.

Just that evening at dinner, he'd told us about how his manager had hollered at him in front of the other salesmen when he'd made a house call to measure for wall-to-wall carpet and missed another staff meeting. "That jerk couldn't sell a hooker in a lumber camp," he said disdainfully.

"Windy," my mother admonished from across the table. Gene snorted. Linda rolled her eyes, and I felt stupid for not really understanding what everyone was reacting to.

Mostly he entertained people and made them laugh. He drew crowds to him, no matter where he was. So as the sun went down on the warm and humid summer evenings of my Minnesota childhood, our neighbors gathered on the front lawn of our two-story bungalow to listen to my father talk about growing up in Neshoba County, Mississippi.

It would be almost eight, and I'd have stationed myself on the front stoop. From the backyard next door came the muffled roar of Mr. Franz's power mower. A slight breeze carried the smell of popcorn from our kitchen through the open window and mingled it companionably with the summertime smells of freshly cut grass and gasoline. From down the street a wooden screen door slammed. Old Mr. Farmer sat on his front porch and lit a cigarette.

Dave and Elaine Rahm had arrived, and behind them Irene and Chuck McConnville. Of all the neighbors, the Rahms and McConnvilles were my favorites: they were young and lively, and they laughed easily. Pretty soon more than half a dozen people from up and down the block were arranging their folding lawn chairs around my father, who sat shirtless in his plaid shorts, up to his navel in the cool water of our blue vinyl wading pool.

From somewhere above him, like a choir hidden in the dark and leafy elms, came the hum and chirp of locusts and crickets. "It's going to be hot again tomorrow," my mother said from the kitchen. As the sun went down behind me, this became the evening sanctuary from which my father entertained the faithful.

From this place, I watched the dusk fall around us and darken the yard, the sky still light above the houses and the trees. The stories he told carried me raftlike down the Mississippi River, from our town all the way to the delta. Each one brought me closer to a world that existed a thousand miles to the south. It was a world I'd never seen, and the relatives who lived there seemed more like characters in a story than flesh-and-blood relations.

"Did I tell you about the time my brother Arby'n me went fishin' for chickens?" he asked. His father, Daddy Bob, was a sharecropper, who moved his family from place to place during the Depression while he looked for work. For a long time they lived with Pappy and Donie, my father's grandparents.

Sometimes Ann would stick around for a while. Sometimes she'd head off with the neighborhood kids to play kick the can. I didn't want to join the other kids but preferred to stay behind and listen quietly from the front step, where the concrete, warm against my legs, had baked in the sun all afternoon and still held its heat.

"So we'd perch on the roof of Pappy's henhouse with a coupla fishin' poles, see," he began.

He reached down into the pool for one of the bottles of Kingsbury beer (the kind that he and Mr. Schmidt from three doors down bought by the case and shared), that he'd placed under water to keep cool. He opened the bottle with a church key that hung from a chain around his neck along with his Marine Corps dog tags. As he spoke, his voice slowly picked up the drawl he'd lost from seventeen years of living with a Yankee woman, as he called my mother.

He rambled through each story, as he rarely saw any reason to rush. It allowed Judge Stone to shift in his seat to get more comfortable, and Grace Galvin to squirt a dab of mosquito repellent into her palms and smooth it onto her forearms.

"Pappy was ornery. He'd whup a boy's hind end if he caught him messin' with his chickens. We learned to stuff the backs of our overalls with the *Neshoba County Democrat*," he said.

The neighbors—teachers, a carpenter, a district court judge—sat transfixed around my father like ants around a melted Popsicle. They'd arranged themselves into a circle with my father in the middle, where they sat into the night talking, smoking, and swatting the mosquitoes that rose up in clusters around their ankles. When one of the little kids, like Ruth Anne Schmidt, got tired of playing, she crawled up into her mother's lap and slept, her sweaty hair matted on her forehead as she fell back heavily against her mother's shoulder.

"Bring me a cigarette, Spook," my father called over to me. When he saw me hesitate, he said, "Don't worry, I'll wait for you." I ran into the house, scooted upstairs to my parents' bedroom, and fished the red pack of Pall Malls from the breast pocket of the short-sleeved blue dress shirt from Montgomery Ward that he'd worn to work that day. It lay in a crumpled heap at the end of his bed. My parents slept in narrow twin beds pushed together—Hollywood beds, like Rob and Laura Petrie in *The Dick Van Dyke Show*.

At eleven years old, I got to light his cigarette myself in full view of the neighbors, and hand it to him. Then I took my place on the step and listened some more, picking sweet bits of tobacco from the tip of my tongue.

He reached down and tore a sheet from a roll of paper towels in the grass beside the pool, dried off his hands, and smoked.

"So we're sittin' on the roof, each of us holdin' a fishin' pole," he said. "We used willa' switches, the kind Pappy chased us around with. Then we tied bits 'a corn to the ends of our fishin' lines and threw the lines over the edge. One by one, those dumb chickens took the bait. They swallowed the corn, fishhooks and all."

He smiled, paused, took another sip from his beer, and surveyed the ring of faces around him. Elaine Rahm put a handful of popcorn in her mouth. Her husband, Dave, lit up a Marlboro. They both sat very tall in their chairs, their long legs crossed. Then they leaned forward. Satisfied that everyone was paying attention, he continued.

"We started haulin' more chickens up to that roof than we could count with our fingers and toes. Feathers flyin' and chickens shriekin'. Would've gotten 'em all up there, too, if somebody hadn'ta stopped us.

"When she heard those chickens squawkin', Pappy's colored woman screamed." He squints his eyes a little and chuckles to himself at what he sees in his mind's eye. "That woman could scream like a panther."

At this, everyone shook their heads and laughed: as much at the slow and syrupy unfolding of my father's tale as at the story itself.

"Then we hear Pappy. 'Can't stand no nigger screamin',' he'd always say. Pappy moves out onto the back porch with Daddy Bob's shotgun and puts a hole in the henhouse the size of a silver dollar. ' 'Cept when them drotted boys is messin' with my chickens.' You didn't know who got off that roof faster, the chickens or my brother'n me."

Our neighborhood was completely white; the only colored people I came close to existed in my father's stories. I would have been surprised to learn that someone in my neighborhood had behaved badly toward someone of another race; we thought of ourselves as kind and decent people. But we went through our ordered and predictable lives on a little island of privilege. Not privilege in any monetary sense; our neighborhood was solidly middle class. Rather, it was the privilege of being white. We walked the streets comfortably without somebody questioning our presence there. White mothers and fathers did not worry about buying a home on our street. The merchants at the corner stores didn't watch us when we cruised the aisles after school for candy and bubble gum. At our neighborhood school, flesh-colored crayons matched the color of our skin. And in my family, we didn't often venture off the island; we didn't get our hands dirty in other people's business; we didn't take those kinds of risks.

My father did pepper his speech with racial epithets, however. Sometimes he'd use the word *nigger* without even blinking. And while using this kind of language was true to the telling of his stories and added to their authenticity, it didn't take away the jarring sound of it. "Oh, Windy," Irene McConnville would probably say.

It was late June of 1964. A thousand miles to the south, the world of my father's childhood was about to explode. Three young men, two from New York and one a Mississippi native, had helped to plan Freedom Summer, during which college students from all over the nation would conduct voter registration drives for black citizens in Mississippi. There hadn't been a great deal of publicity surrounding the project, although both the civil rights organizations sponsoring it and those in Mississippi who opposed it had been preparing for the influx of volunteers. Although now the newspaper headlines reported that the three had just disappeared from Neshoba County and a massive manhunt had begun.

This was not the stuff of my father's stories, however. He went off on a tirade from time to time, but someone—usually my mother—always put him back on track.

"What the hell do they want?" he asked, his voice rising. "George Wallace has it right, dammit. Integration is gonna ruin this country."

His face grew tight, and the fist that wasn't holding the beer slid under water, where he opened and closed it, causing a small disturbance on the surface of the pool.

My mother's eyes rolled up a little in the direction of the late-night sky. With her elbow resting on the plastic arm of her chair, she took a drag from her cigarette and blew the smoke out through her nostrils. She twirled her hand around at the wrist so that the glowing red cinder on the end of the cigarette looped around in the dark, like a lariat on fire in a gesture that said, *enough already.* "Windy," she broke in.

He stopped a moment and looked at my mother. "What're *you* talkin' about?" he said. "Your daddy, right here in liberal, Hubert Humphrey Minneapolis, bought the house next door to keep the colored from moving in."

She shrugged and held her palms upright in a gesture of casual helplessness. "You're right," she conceded. My father shook his head and laughed again, a hiss that blew through his teeth like a whistle.

"Listen," he said. "They just don't know how to handle it. Instead of hirin' tutors to bring the colored children up, the white children are goin' down." Whenever he said this, I'd picture a school playground full of seesaws, with black children on one end and white children on the other, each going up and down with the weight and thrust of the other.

"Anyways, where was I? Oh yeah. Pappy was so mad at us, we headed for the woods and stayed there till suppertime, when my daddy come home and switched us but good."

It would be midnight before he got to the end of his story. He'd have gotten out of the pool, dried off, and pulled a white cotton T-shirt over his head. He joined the neighbors then, as they sat in chairs that circled the pool, their bare feet in the tepid water, which by then was floating with grass clippings and drowned bugs. Then everyone got up, stretched, and folded their aluminum chairs. When they walked away into the darkness, red crisscross marks were etched into the backs of their legs.

———

THIS WAS THE STUFF of my father's stories: from time to time he pulled out a battered black-and-white snapshot of his mother lying in her open casket. Grandma Ora died in 1943 of breast cancer. She was fifty-four years old. Cracked and wrinkled, the photograph showed a heavyset woman who looked like she was asleep in a white lacy dress. Her eyes were closed, her mouth stern, her hands folded, as if in prayer. Her thick black hair ("auburn," my father said) framed her face, which had the puffy look of the cancer that took over too fast and too soon. Around the casket stood my grieving aunts and uncles. Uncle Maurice had a round face and thinning hair. His hat was in his hand. Ruby had small children around her and was buxom in a dress that buttoned down the front. There was Lumiere, pretty with shiny dark hair the color of her mother's. Beside her, Arby looked astonishingly like my father: tall, large-featured, a shock of wavy black hair.

I always wanted to make the taking of photographs of the dead into a kind of strange southern quirk, but in truth it was Ruby who insisted upon the photographs, mostly for the purpose of sending them to my father, who is missing from the picture. He'd joined the Marine Corps before Pearl Harbor and was on active duty in New Guinea. When he got the telegram that his mother had died, he requested leave to go to the funeral, but his leave was denied. "I got so crazy I went AWOL," he said. "I couldn't b'lieve Mama was dead and that I couldn't be with her."

Later Auntie Lu will tell me that Grandma Ora died holding his Marine Corps portrait over her heart, and I will find the portrait on a dusty shelf at Ruby's house, two years after Ruby's death. It will be the hand-colored photograph of a serious young man with large features and auburn hair. He's wearing a gray sweater with an *M* across the front. The photograph is faded, dusty, and water-stained, but not so much that you cannot see that he has written his childhood nickname in brown ink across the right-hand corner: "Chub."

In the funeral photograph, a dozen or so black people stand at a distance behind the family. A grove of trees in full leaf crowns the picture, just beyond. "Sharecroppers," my father said. "Worked alongside 'em all m'life. Worked with my mother too. And Pappy."

Most of the black women wear going-to-church dresses and hats. One has a scarf tied tightly around her head, and she looks straight at the camera, squinting. One holds a hand over her eyes to shade them from the sun. Hats in hand, heads bowed, the men's faces are shadowed.

"What were their names?" I asked after many years and many showings of the funeral snapshot.

"Mostly they lived on the farm," my father said. "McCormicks and Thames, I b'lieve." But he couldn't remember anybody's first name.

CHAPTER 3

Aunt Jemima and Uncle Ben

U NLIKE MINNESOTA, where spring begins in late April with the snowmelt and ends three weeks later with the arrival of the mosquitoes, Mississippi enjoys a real springtime. As early as February, the redbird returns, the magnolia begins to bud, and the breeze through the screen door is soft and mild and carries with it the rich smell of the damp earth that will soon be ready to turn over with a garden hoe.

On just such a day, in late March of 1964, Edgar Ray Killen, a sawmill operator and part-time Baptist preacher who lived in rural Neshoba County, paid a visit to a friend he'd grown up with, but who now lived in Meridian. Preacher Killen stopped by the police station and found his friend Wallace Miller sitting behind a desk. Wallace had been an officer on the Meridian police force for fourteen years. The two chatted for a few moments before Preacher began to describe a "strong organization" that had recently started up in the area that opposed communism and integration. But Wallace was on duty, and the two couldn't really talk. So Preacher Killen waited until Wallace got off duty at eleven that evening, and followed him home from work, where the two men resumed their conversation.

Preacher felt comfortable being candid with Wallace. The two had been good friends for a long time. They'd gone to high school together. When Wallace got married, the wedding took place in Preacher's home. When two of Wallace's children died, Preacher performed the funerals.

Wallace's wife had welcomed Preacher Killen into their home on several occasions. Some people in the community thought Preacher a little odd: a bit reclusive, something of a braggart. At age thirty-seven, he still lived at home with his parents. His face looked severe, his black hair slicked back with an excess of Brylcreem. But to Mrs. Miller, he was almost like family, and with family, you don't let things like that get in the way.

Wallace's fellow police officers knew him as easygoing, a nice guy you couldn't help but like. At police cookouts he held forth at the barbecue grill and was famous for his chicken and catfish.

This evening, Preacher Killen began to describe the organization. It was very patriotic, he said, political and orderly. He added that "better" men and citizens belonged to it, including doctors, lawyers, and peace officers. Wallace finally asked his friend to come straight to the point. "Are you talking about the Ku Klux Klan?"

"Yes," Preacher replied. Perhaps he felt a moment's concern. Wallace was, after all, a police officer. "Still interested?"

Wallace said that he was interested. Preacher then administered the Klan oath in the dining room, where friends and family often gathered for formal occasions.

On the night of Saturday, April 4, 1964, wooden crosses wrapped in burlap and soaked in diesel fuel burned across Neshoba County: six in the black section of Philadelphia called Independence Quarters, and one on the lawn of the courthouse in downtown Philadelphia.

The following week, the sheriff was quoted in the local newspaper as saying that the fires had been set by outsiders who sought to disrupt the good relations enjoyed by all races in the county.

EARLIER THAT SUMMER, my father had come home from work one evening with a plastic faucet, painted silver, that had a sharp, threaded end. The idea was to screw the faucet into something and fool people into thinking that water would come out of it. So he screwed it into the side of his briefcase. I opened the package for him and held the briefcase against my lap while he used his drill to start the hole where he'd screw in the spigot.

"Y'know," he said, huffing a little as he turned the U-joint of the drill, "I used to set on the steps of Pappy's front porch, whittlin' a stick with my brother's pocketknife."

I held the briefcase as still as I could. We were sitting on the front steps. I sat a step higher than he did, to keep us level.

"Mama and Mammy Donie'd be washin' the dishes inside. They used a metal wash pan that was a bathtub too, on Saturday nights before church. I could hear their voices talkin' together through the screen door."

He picked up the spigot and began to twist it into the hole he'd made with the drill in the middle of his briefcase.

"Mammy's colored woman'd lug the water in buckets from the well and heat it on the stove after stokin' it with a coupla logs from the woodpile my brother'n me kept stacked."

He turned the spigot until it fit tightly against the vinyl. It really did look as though water could come out of it if he turned the handle. He picked up his briefcase and looked closely at his work.

"My hound dog'd set rockin' himself in one of the chairs 'til Daddy Bob'd come out and chase him off the seat and over next to me. Then he'd set down where the dog'd been keepin' the seat warm, take a plug a chewin' tobacca, and fill his lower lip with it, ever' once in a while spittin' into an empty tuna fish can. Pappy'd come out from the kitchen and set down beside 'im.

"That old man hated everything. My brother'n I would tease him somethin' terrible, just to watch 'im pitch a fit. Like the time we strung the geese together."

"What did you do?" I asked. I didn't want him to stop talking. I knew that he was dying to take his briefcase next door to show it to the neighbors.

"We tied dried food to a string: corn, beans, anything we could find that they couldn't digest, see, and fed it to one of the geese. We'd wait for the goose to shit out the whole bean, still tied to the string, then we'd feed it to another goose, and so on, till half a dozen of 'em was strung together, walkin' single file in the chicken coop." And then he'd laugh, his tongue between his teeth and his shoulders shaking, soundless except for a little hiss, like air escaping from a balloon.

Then he got up and went next door. The faucet that he'd attached to his briefcase looked so authentic that two nuns passing by our house on their evening walk asked him if it really worked.

RECRUITING STUDENTS for Freedom Summer took place in early 1964 on college campuses all over the North. The speakers were activists whose detailed testimonials from the front lines of the civil rights movement in the South were intended to incite privileged and comfortable kids from the North into action.

Most students who attended the meetings were familiar with the racial climate in the South. Most had followed the media coverage of the integration of the Little Rock schools, the Montgomery bus strike, the lunch counter sit-ins, and the riots at Ole Miss. But what struck them about the descriptions they heard about Mississippi were the ways in which the state, over the past century, had isolated itself from the rest of the nation. Built into a racial hierarchy that pushed black people to the bottom of the political, social, and economic order, discrimination had become embedded into the local culture. Through a structure of laws and customs that set it apart from the rest of the country, Mississippi emerged as a separate nation-state that was not accountable to a higher authority. So systematized was the racial infrastructure in Mississippi that it even distinguished itself from the rest of the South.

The speakers' graphic descriptions showed the reprisals blacks faced when trying to register to vote: one had narrowly escaped being shot to death on a deserted highway a year before. Another was choked to unconsciousness on a courthouse lawn before a crowd of at least fifteen jeering white bystanders. Some were kicked and beaten until their assailants tired and stopped. Others had been pistol-whipped and threatened and their families threatened. A few had been murdered.

In April, a meeting took place at Queens College in New York. Among the students who came to listen was twenty-year-old Andrew Goodman. The rhetoric of social activism was familiar to Andy. He had participated in equal-rights demonstrations in New York, at the Thirty-fourth Street Woolworth, and at the 1964 World's Fair. His interest in the Mississippi summer project had been sparked earlier that month when Allard Lowenstein, a student organizer, had introduced the idea on campus. "Hundreds of students from across the country" would converge on "the most totalitarian state in America," he'd told the crowd.

Andy came by his interest naturally. The son of progressive parents, he had attended Walden School on Manhattan's Upper West Side, receiving an education at home and at school that had prepared him for activism. A naturally sensitive young man, his upbringing would fuel his inbred desire to organize against injustice.

"The thundering silence of the good people is disturbing," said one of the speakers Andy listened to that week. Aaron Henry, a black pharmacist from Clarksdale, Mississippi, had delivered a powerful message, one that indicted both those who used violence to maintain the racial status quo, and those who stood by and did nothing. "This is a family problem," he went on, excluding no one in his call to action. "And there are no outsiders."

Perhaps these were the words that moved Andy to volunteer.

Michael Schwerner had come to Mississippi in January of 1964 with his wife, Rita, to prepare for the influx of volunteers who'd arrive in the summer to start freedom schools, where black citizens would receive education and support to participate in the voting process.

That spring, the Schwerners had established the Meridian Community Center, with a library of more than ten thousand donated books, a game room, and meeting space. Twice weekly, Mickey taught a voter registration class. Rita solicited donations and taught sewing. One of the locals who'd volunteered to help set up the community center was twenty-year-old James Chaney. Chaney, known to his friends as J. E., had become a full-time civil rights worker that winter. In the spring, J. E. and Mickey began a series of trips to the community of Longdale in Neshoba County, to find black churches whose leadership would be interested in forming freedom schools. Their trips did not go unnoticed by Neshoba County law enforcement, which began to monitor their movements.

IN MINNEAPOLIS, my father's briefcase with the faucet in its side became one of his signature jokes, and he carried that briefcase to work with him all summer long. That fall he held it in one hand when he took us trick-or-treating at Halloween. In the other hand, he had an empty martini glass. At each door, the neighbors laughed and poured my father a drink.

We stopped at the home of my friend Eileen, who lived across the street and a few houses down. Their house was usually dark, but tonight a jack-o'-lantern was lit on the front stoop and a welcoming light burned on the front porch. There was something different about Eileen's family, a refinement that stood out in the neighborhood. Her father was a college professor and did not sit outside with my parents and the other neighbors on summer evenings. Their living room was full of books—floor-to-ceiling collections with leather jackets whose gold titles glowed when Eileen's father and his friends sat in the firelight, their hands cupped around snifters of brandy.

Unlike the walls in our living room, where my mother had hung botanical prints she'd clipped from magazines and framed herself, on their walls hung real art. Over Eileen's mantelpiece was a bucolic English landscape in oil. Architectural lithographs hung from the walls in the alcove off the living room, where they kept a grand piano, upon which Eileen was often called to play for her father's friends.

Eileen had a beautiful dark-haired sister who was about to marry a mysterious man who was much older than she. He was there one afternoon when I was visiting Eileen. She stopped playing when he arrived and busied herself sorting the sheet music that her father stored in the piano bench. Seated beside her while she practiced at the grand piano, I took a sheet and hid my face behind it: one eye on the scales, one eye on him.

This man was terrifying. His ragged gray whiskers were long enough to cover his neck, and thick black glasses sat on his wide, pocked nose. His yellow-stained fingertips held a cigarette and a glass of something that looked like iced tea. Instead of speaking he growled, and when he opened his mouth he revealed teeth as brown as the living room carpet and, from my vantage point, about as fuzzy.

From time to time he rose up from the chair, waved his arms, and shouted, "Joyce!" and "Pound!" so loud that I almost fell off the bench. When he lifted his arms, an aroma like a wet dog filled the room, and I lowered my head back behind the sheet music. Eileen resumed her playing.

Years later his picture was on the front page of the *Minneapolis Tribune*. He was a humanities professor at the University of Minnesota and a Pulitzer prize–winning poet. He had jumped to his death into the Mississippi River off the Washington Avenue Bridge.

I wonder what Professor Berryman must have thought about my

parents. While he was pacing the length of Eileen's living room that Halloween night, talking with her father about modern English poets, Ann and I were at the front door, dressed up as Aunt Jemima and Uncle Ben, costumes my mother had made. When Eileen's sister opened the door, Berryman stopped talking with Eileen's father on the sofa in front of the fireplace, arched his eyebrows, and glared at us.

In blackface and head scarf and a housedress and apron, plumped up with pillows, I looked like the round-faced woman on the box of pancake mix. And in a butler's jacket, bow tie and a white-fringed wig whose bald pate my mother had blackened with charcoal, Ann looked like the man on the box of instant rice. My father came with us to the door, his vinyl briefcase with the fake faucet in one hand, his empty martini glass held out when we opened our pillowcases for the candy.

It was the only house on the block at which I felt that something about our costumes wasn't right, and one of the occasions during which an outsider in our midst would make me feel ashamed. The embarrassment was momentary, however, and I pushed it away from me as soon as we stepped back into the darkness, taking our places alongside kids who were dressed like the characters in comic books: Superman, Popeye, the Lone Ranger and Tonto.

CHAPTER 4

The Wonderful Tar Baby

IN THE FALL OF 1960, my father brought home a John F. Kennedy campaign poster. For two months before the election, Kennedy's face smiled out onto York Avenue from one of the picture windows on our front porch. Dad's admiration was short-lived, however. In four years he would support Barry Goldwater and after that George Wallace, telling anyone who would listen that Kennedy was the only Democrat he'd ever voted for, and one of the biggest mistakes he'd ever made in his life.

Like many of his southern compatriots, my father directed his anger toward the civil rights activists—the vast majority of whose demonstrations were peaceful—and toward the Kennedys. "It was anarchy back then," he said. "Those idiots were tearin' up the South and the Kennedys did nothin' to stop 'em."

At the beginning of the Kennedy administration, the Klan wasn't as strong in Mississippi as it was elsewhere in the South. Up until this point, Mississippi had successfully established a framework of

governmental and cultural institutions that had protected the s
order and kept segregation firmly in place. It was the power of these
institutions, like local laws that made it difficult if not impossible
for black citizens to vote, that pushed the civil rights movement
harder and harder into Mississippi. It was the power of the elected
officials who supported these institutions that, to a great extent, kept
federal intervention at bay. And while over time my father would
on the one hand speak out against the Bilbos and the Vardamans
in Mississippi's past, he would also blame those who tried to change
the system for the violence that ensued.

Carrying the tradition into the 1960s was Ross Barnett, governor
of Mississippi. Barnett, like the demagogues who preceded him, used
the Bible and his own theories of racial superiority to maintain the
status quo. "The Negro is different," he was fond of saying. "Because
God made him different to punish him. His forehead slants back,
his nose is different. His lips are different and his color is sure
different." Barnett wasn't about to allow the civil rights movement
to take hold in bus stations, on the campuses of state universities,
or in the voting booths.

The early 1960s however, ushered in changes that even Barnett
could not have predicted. In 1961, Freedom Riders had begun their
attempts to integrate public facilities, and by 1962, James Meredith,
a twenty-nine-year-old air force veteran, had successfully won ad-
mission to the University of Mississippi. So when reports reached
Mississippi that a campaign was being planned for the summer of
1964 that had the potential to allow black citizens to register to vote,
the Klan took its cue and began to mobilize.

The White Knights of Mississippi had splintered off from the
Louisiana Klan in late 1963, under the leadership of Sam Bowers, a
small-business owner from Laurel who'd appointed himself grand
wizard of the new organization. Bowers was alarmed about the summer program, which he characterized as an invasion of Communist
workers into the state, and began looking for a solid recruiter who

would help the Klan bolster its membership. He also had his eye on a troublesome young man named Michael Schwerner who'd moved to Meridian in January of 1964 with his wife, Rita.

Schwerner was just the kind of young person that Sam Bowers despised: educated, liberal, from New York, and Jewish. Schwerner's blue jeans, boots, and goatee scared Bowers, who saw him as a beatnik who'd come to change the values of the clean-cut whites, and make friends with the blacks. He began to refer to Schwerner as "Goatee." It wasn't long before he had decided that Goatee was a menace and had to be stopped.

Bowers had been moderately successful in starting a klavern in Meridian, but what he needed was a rural community where he could get the support of local law enforcement and small town government, and a group of the citizenry who would carry out a newly hatched plan to get rid of Mickey Schwerner. He'd tried several of the outlying counties: Kemper, Winston, Newton, and Clarke, but nobody had emerged who'd been willing to organize a klavern with the kind of local infrastructure Bowers needed.

Then he tried Neshoba County, and met a local sawmill operator and part-time preacher whose name was Edgar Ray Killen.

ON ELECTION NIGHT 1960, after a hiatus from pregnancy for six years, my mother, who wasn't ready to stop having babies, became pregnant again at forty. While much of the nation celebrated Kennedy's victory as a hopeful step toward a more progressive era in American political life, my parents had apparently celebrated it as a victory for the romance of youth, vigor, and sexual energy.

It is this time that I return to when I need to see my parents as I want them to be: happy and playful. It is during the cocktail hour, and giggling like a couple of teenagers, they decide to dress up like a bride and groom. My father is tall, dark, and slim; my mother is petite and eight months pregnant with Liz. My mother's belly balloons out from under her wedding gown, which of course, she can't button up the back. My father totes my brother Gene's Davy Crockett shotgun as they march next door to demand that Judge Stone marry them and make an honest woman of my mother.

The August evening that Liz was born, my sister Ann and I sat on the living room floor watching *The Loretta Young Hour.* Loretta floated down an open staircase wearing a floor-length strapless gown with a full diaphanous skirt. We watched her every Tuesday night and the following morning would argue about who got to be Loretta that day.

I was eight years old. Ann was six. My mother dressed us alike, and in a Polaroid snapshot of the two of us that night, we are wearing identical shorts and striped T-shirts, hers blue and mine pink. Irene McConnville was staying with us. "Look into the camera, girls," she said, waving her free arm to get our attention. When we turned away from the television set, she tripped the shutter, and a flash of light blinded us for a moment. While we rubbed our eyes, the camera made a whirring sound and the photo slid from a door that opened just beneath the lens.

She held a black square in her hand so we could watch our faces emerge from the oily emulsion. There was Ann, sitting beside me smiling, her hair a tangle of walnut-colored curls. I was scowling, my black hair cut too short in a style my mother said made me look like a pixie. For a little girl who had difficulty falling asleep at night, worried about whether there really was a God, a haircut intended to make me look perky was an insult. "Mary, what kind of a face is that?" Irene asked, handing the picture to Ann.

"An unhappy face," I said.

The next morning I sat on the toilet seat holding my father's cigarette while he shaved. "What's the matter now, Spook?" he asked. "I think your hair's real cute."

"Not you too," I said and handed him the cigarette in exchange for the razor. "Are you *really* excited about the baby?" I asked.

He was silent for a moment, drew heavily on his cigarette, and gave it back to me. "Aren't you?"

I was sort of excited about a new baby, but I suspected that I was the only one who had reservations. I felt that things in the family were changing, and I didn't like how I felt.

For as long as I could remember, Ann and I shared a small yellow room at the back of the house on the second floor. We played there in a trapezoid of sunlight that fell across our bedroom carpet. We were each other's antidotes. Her sunny personality buoyed me up so that I could see the good things, and my melancholy brought ballast to her happiness and thoughtfulness to her face.

At bedtime we'd crawl into bed with each other to scratch backs and fall asleep, or to look out the window at the moon that hung over the roof of the garage. Sometimes my father would stand at the doorway, his face bathed in the reddish glow of sunset, and tell us Uncle Remus stories about Brer Rabbit and Brer Fox. My favorite story was "The Wonderful Tar Baby."

> " 'Didn't the fox never catch the rabbit, Uncle Remus?' asked the little boy the next evening.
>
> " 'He come mighty nigh it, honey, sho's you born—Brer Fox did. One day atter Brer Rabbit fool 'im wid dat calamus root, Brer Fox went ter wuk en got 'im some tar, en mix it wid some turkentime, en fix up a contrapshun w'at he call a Tar Baby, en he tuck dish yer Tar Baby en he sot 'er in de big road, en den he lay off in de bushes fer to see what de news wuz gwine ter be. En he didn't hatter wait long, nudder, kaze bimeby here come Brer Rabbit pacin' down de road—lippity-clippity, clippity-lippity—dez ez sassy ez a jay-bird.' "

We didn't understand all the words, and my father's accent, which had thinned in the twenty years since he'd lived in Mississippi, took on a quality I heard nowhere else. His voice rose and fell as though he were singing, and his shoulders shook up and down when he laughed at a picture that the words, so strange to us, created familiarly in his mind. For us, our father was speaking a foreign language that only became decipherable over time, when repetition would stamp the stories in our memories. And the stories, for their very inscrutability, became the indelible markers that he used to move us closer to the childhood—so long ago and so far away—that he revisited as he read. It was as though he bypassed the barriers of our conscious understanding and traveled easily on the back roads of imagination and emotion. So we felt sad as he read, with a longing we didn't comprehend, and happy with a feeling of connection that transcended time and space.

> "Brer Fox, he lay low. Brer Rabbit come prancin' 'long twel he spy de Tar Baby, en den he fotch up on his behime legs like he wuz 'stonished. De Tar Baby, she sot dar, she did, en Brer Fox, he lay low.
>
> " 'Mawnin'!' sez Brer Rabbit, sezee—'nice wedder dis mawnin',' sezee.
>
> "Tar Baby ain't sayin' nuthin', en Brer Fox he lay low. Brer Fox, he sorter chuckle in his stummick, he did, but Tar Baby ain't sayin' nothin'."

And we waited to hear what would happen next, not realizing fully what had happened before, but peaceful and secure in the sleepiness of our father's voice as it rose and fell like a lullaby. We didn't need to understand. All we needed was his presence in the door and his voice in our room. This was everything. This was the fullness of childhood—his and ours—and we fell asleep as if rocked in his arms or soothed by the sound of a train whistle, held fast in a moment that we believed would last forever.

"You kids are everything," he'd say to us. But I sometimes wondered if it was true. From time to time he'd call his sister Ruby in Mississippi, and would pass the phone around to each of us. But I never understood what anyone said, would just say "hi," when they said, "Hey, Mayree, ha' doin'?" and quickly pass the phone to someone else. When he spoke with them his voice softened to a whisper and took on a heavy sweetness that dropped the ends of words and slurred the syllables together, talking about people with foreign-sounding names, like Lumiere, Miss Effie, and Uncle Dink. After these calls he'd get in his car and drive away, and I wouldn't get to sleep until he'd come home, long after my mother had gone to bed.

I carried his homesickness like a stone in my chest, and tended it so carefully that an abiding sense of loneliness became part of my own personality. I wanted nothing more than to make him feel better. So I looked for ways to please him, like fetching his coffee or beer or changing the channel on the television so he wouldn't have to get up, things like that. I bought him soap on a rope for Father's Day (as did my brother and sisters, until we looked in his top dresser drawer once and saw that it was full of red boxes of soap on a rope, all full and unopened) and rode my bike to the corner store with a quarter in my pocket and a note he'd written for a pack of Pall Malls. I brought him the sports page on Sunday morning, and weekdays got up early to curl up on the sofa in the living room and watch him do his paperwork at the dining room table.

We didn't talk much; rather, I followed him around like a puppy with a pair of slippers in its mouth. He was a big man, took up a lot of space and seemed to require a great deal of elbow room. So instead of being helpful, I was a pest. Being in proximity to me wasn't going to make him happy or want to stay home.

He spent a great deal of time in his car, working late and driving from house to house to measure the floors for wall-to-wall carpet. But this didn't stop me. I asked him to take me with him, pulling at his elbow until he waved me away like a fly he wanted to shoo, but once or twice he said yes. When I got in the car, I sat tall by the passenger window. It was rare for just me to share the front seat with my father, since someone else was usually riding along. If I could have, I would have rolled down the window and waved like Princess Kay of the Milky Way in the annual Aquatennial Parade.

He liked to whistle when he drove, and once we made up a

game. He picked out a song, whistled a few bars,
me to guess the name of it.

"Okay, Spook, you'll never guess this one."

He whistled four familiar notes. " 'Old Man R.
He thought for a moment, puckered his lips and whistled again.
" 'I'm an Old Cowhand from the Rio Grande.' " He was toying
with me. He looked at me sideways.

"Well, you've got me beat," he said.

"Wait, wait," I begged. "Just one more."

So he began "Zip-a-dee-doo-dah," but I pretended not to know
the name of the song so I could listen to him whistle it the whole
way through.

IN THE 1920S of my father's childhood, the Klan had undergone a
revival of sorts in Neshoba County. They held secret meetings in
the Masonic lodge, burned crosses, and under cover of darkness
gathered in hoods and gowns on the low scrub hills of the country-
side. The revival was short-lived, due in part to an absence of an-
tagonists (Philadelphia's population included one Jew, one Asian,
and a few thousand Negroes and Choctaws, most of whom kept to
themselves). In the 1930s the Klan abandoned the Masonic Lodge
for a livery stable on a side street where their discussions, according
to Clayton Rand, editor of the *Neshoba Democrat* at the time, revolved around "the irregularities of nonmembers." Like many of the
residents of the county, Rand spoke out against the Klan, describing
them as "an outlaw organization going about its work behind masks
and in clown suits."

There had been other voices of opposition. Albert "Ab" Deweese,
also unafraid to challenge the 1920s-era Neshoba Klan, had wanted
to protect the black employees of his lumber company from intimidation. Legend has it that one evening he forced his way into a
Klan meeting and said, "We're not going to have the Klan in this
county, boys, so put up those hoods."

Forty years later, in preparation for the influx of Freedom Summer volunteers, Preacher Killen's clandestine recruitment of Klansmen in both Neshoba and nearby Lauderdale counties had resulted in more than seventy new members. While the sudden resurgence of Klan power in their local community may have taken many of the white residents by surprise, the black citizens of Philadelphia had known for a long time that there were white people in their midst who were to be feared.

One of the most infamous perpetrators was Neshoba County sheriff Lawrence Rainey. Before becoming sheriff in 1963 (winning handily over Preacher, who also ran but came in a distant eighth), Rainey had served on the Philadelphia police force for four years. During that time, Patrolman Rainey was alleged to have shot and killed several black men. One of them, Luther Jackson, was from the area but had moved to Chicago and was back in town visiting friends and family. No witness could contradict Rainey's story that shooting "the Chicago nigger" was self-defense, and he was cleared of any wrongdoing.

There is also evidence that Rainey shot another black man shortly afterward, when he was deputy sheriff. He and Sheriff "Hop" Barnett had responded to a call from a black home where a twenty-seven-year-old epileptic had gotten out of control. Barnett and Rainey handcuffed the young man, put him in the backseat of the patrol car, and promised to take him to the state mental hospital at Whitfield. Barnett had refused to allow the young man's father to accompany them.

Later, Sheriff Barnett testified that the epileptic man, handcuffed, ill, and seated in the backseat of the patrol car, had attempted to grab a gun in the glove compartment and had to be shot dead. Many believed that Rainey had pulled the trigger despite Barnett's claim that he had shot him. Many believed that the sheriff had lied in order to soften Rainey's growing reputation for unnecessary brutality.

It didn't come as a surprise to anyone in the black community that Preacher Killen had been so successful in recruiting local whites into the Klan during Rainey's tenure as sheriff. What came as a surprise is the extent to which the white community claimed that it did not know.

OUR HOUSE was bustling with life, in preparation for the arrival of a new baby. My mother had placed the crib in the alcove beneath the sloping ceiling in our room. "I'm going to need you to help me," she said. Soon there would be three in our tiny room, across the hall from where my parents slept. At the foot of the stairs were Linda's and Gene's bedrooms.

Gene was the only boy in a family of sisters. He was a mechanical wizard and was frequently called upon to fix things. He'd rigged up an electric eye at his bedroom door, and when anyone came through, a buzzer would sound. Often he walked home from school with a toaster oven that had overheated or a radio with a frayed cord that the nuns had asked him to repair.

You'd sometimes wonder about whether my father was really raised on a farm, because he didn't know a Phillips screwdriver from a crescent wrench. As a result, my brother was called upon to keep the house in working order. Before he was ten years old, Gene was repairing the plumbing when the kitchen sink backed up and replacing the motor on the washing machine. "I've been fixin' to do that," my father would say when the lawn mower broke down or the screen door came unhinged. "Well, I'm fixing it now," my brother would reply.

Perhaps he resented it that we depended so much on him to keep the house together. I don't know. But I do know that he had a bad temper, and that it was a good idea to stay out of his way when he was in one of his moods. He teased and taunted and tickled you until you cried. From time to time he'd sneak into our room and put a pillow over my face. Ann would leap from her bed, forty pounds of pit bull in a white flannel nightgown, and she'd beat on his back while I suffocated. When he let up, I gasped for air; my head filled with a silvery, starry pressure that only went away when my breathing returned to normal.

Nobody ever said anything to Gene about it, but my mother must have told my father, because he found me behind the garage after work a few days later, where I'd gone to hide and read. "What are you doing back here, Spook?" He sat down beside me, pulled a cigarette out of the pack he kept in his pocket, and stretched out his long legs.

"Don't let Gene bother you," he said. "It's just the pecking order." I turned my face to him and showed him my black eye and swollen lip.

"He told me I was ugly and hit me with his fist," I said.

"That's a pretty good shiner," he said. And we walked together into the house. But nobody commented about my face, and I never knew whether he talked to Gene, because it wasn't the last pretty good shiner I took at the business end of his closed fist.

In addition to my brother's daily reminders, the kids at school also taunted me about my looks. My skin was sallow, my face long and narrow, and my nose too prominent. My eyes were a dull green and my hair thin and black and baby fine. To make matters worse, my sister Ann was round-faced and lively and cute. Once she and I got our hands on a harem outfit, and she pulled me around the block in our wagon, telling people that I was Fatima, her cousin from India.

I was skinny and short. The neighbor ladies called me Little Mary. The fourth and fifth grade boys called me Hose Nose. I often asked my mother if my nose would grow to match my face. When I did, she'd sigh and say she didn't know.

I didn't like going to school, or to the corner, the small shopping area just two blocks away where my father sent me for cigarettes. I preferred to stay home.

Grown-ups, even complete strangers, were always telling me to smile, but I didn't feel like it. One Saturday morning, in the parking lot at the Food Lane, on my way home with a small bag of groceries, a group of older boys called me over to where they stood by the wall that was painted with a big DAD'S ROOT BEER sign. I stood there for a moment and looked at them in silence. One of the boys began to laugh.

"Hey, she's really ugly," he said to his friends in a loud voice.

I didn't stay to listen to them snicker. "I know," I said with all the earnestness I possessed, and walked across the parking lot toward home. After that, at recess I hid behind an air duct on the playground. At home, I spent more and more time in my room.

I also spent a good deal of time in church, much of it praying that God would change the way I looked. I had come to believe that there had been some kind of cosmic mistake: little girls were supposed to be cute, adorable, and protected. Little girls were supposed to have big eyes and rosy cheeks and curly hair. They were supposed to take dancing lessons and have recitals where their parents snapped pictures and beamed with pride and took the whole family afterward for ice cream. Little girls were supposed to grow up pretty, get married, and find the security that came from being loved.

In short, I had begun life on the wrong trajectory. For a female, I wasn't what I was supposed to be; I didn't know where I belonged or where I should go. So I spent far more time in church than was healthy for a child. While the other kids were outside playing kick the can and learning to play the piano, I was saying novenas, rosaries, and Stations of the Cross. Praying for God to make me pretty was hard work, the hardest work I'd ever done, and the most ineffective. It didn't matter how hard I tried; God didn't change the way I looked. So I doubled my efforts and added daily mass and communion to my routine. It never occurred to me to ask God to stop people from teasing me; I was certain that as long as he had made me this way, torment was my due. The only solution was to pray for the miracle of physical beauty.

It also never occurred to me to ask God for the power to stand against it: to protect myself and my worth no matter how I looked. Nobody I knew was reading *The Feminine Mystique*, and if they were, they kept it to themselves. Women talked about hairstyles, makeup, and clothes. They talked about dating and getting engaged and being married. They talked about babies and children and keeping their houses clean.

THE YEAR AFTER I WAS BORN, the state of Mississippi passed a constitutional amendment by a vote of 75,488 to 15,718 designed to eliminate black voters by tightening the restrictions that allowed a citizen to register. Not that the existing requirements were open and inviting: the black citizen in Mississippi had been effectively disfranchised since 1875. In fact, the state constitution had been rewritten in 1890 to legalize black disfranchisement by implementing the poll tax and a requirement that any prospective voter be able to read or interpret Mississippi's constitution.

In 1957, the Mississippi legislature passed an amendment to further narrow these restrictions. Its effect was widespread and debilitating, drastically reducing the number of black voters. Statewide, the 22,000 blacks that voted in 1952 had plummeted to 8,000 by 1958. In Neshoba County, the circuit clerks reported that between 1948 and 1960, no more than eight black citizens had registered to vote. In response to *Brown vs. Board of Education*, voters in the state of Mississippi had passed another constitutional amendment, this time to abolish the public school system if it seemed that integration was inevitable. In Neshoba County, the amendment passed by a vote of 1,722 to 292.

As whites freely abused the political process to shift the power to become educated and to have a voice in government away from black people, they also depended upon the tactics of militant locals to enforce the law, which included, of course, intimidation, violence, and if necessary, murder.

In the late 1940s, black citizens in the Longdale and Poplar

Springs communities of Neshoba County had begun a local chapter of the NAACP. One of the leaders received an anonymous letter saying, "You niggers better stop having those meetings in the school house." One Neshoba County black citizen, a landowner from the Mount Zion community, had tried and failed to register every year from 1952 through 1964, and only succeeded after President Johnson signed the Voting Rights Act of 1965 and the attorney general sent federal marshals to oversee registration in county courthouses that were known as trouble spots. Another Mount Zion resident reported being told by a local white that the Negroes should stop pushing to integrate the schools and to vote. There would be bloodshed, he was warned, and the blacks were "not going to get help out of us like you used to." Suddenly black loans at white banks became due, black schools were denied necessary funding, the local school board was abolished and black teachers were fired.

In late May of 1964, Mickey Schwerner had met with Mount Zion elders to ask if they would permit him to use their church as a voter registration site for blacks. Two weeks later, the Klan burned the church to the ground.

These enforcement techniques were all sanctioned and carried out across the state by the local Citizens' Councils, a series of groups of white citizens that exerted control over their communities with the goal of maintaining segregation in every facet of life. From their inception in 1954 until 1965, the Citizens' Councils had succeeded in prohibiting integration in Mississippi schools, workplaces, public and private facilities, neighborhoods, and at the polls. And while many whites opposed the philosophies and tactics of the Councils, membership was powerful enough to silence those who dared speak out, thus extinguishing any hope of change at the local level.

The Councils also supported the appropriation of tax dollars to create and sustain the Mississippi Sovereignty Commission. In theory, the Mississippi Legislature had created the commission in 1956 to "protect the sovereignty of the State of Mississippi and her sister states" from federal government interference. In practice, it worked behind the scenes to preserve a segregated society and to oppose school integration.

Outwardly, the commission ran an effective propaganda campaign that extolled racial harmony. Internally, the commission was secretly paying investigators and spies to gather both information and misinformation. It went so far as to report on the activities of performers like Harry Belafonte, Joan Baez, and Elvis Presley. It investigated others who performed in Mississippi and those who supported civil rights. In the course of its efforts, the commission purposely targeted civil rights leaders and workers for defamation, accusing them of alcoholism and of having a venereal disease or extramarital affairs. The commission also spread rumors that maligned the character of those who were involved in civil rights activities, successfully using—among other tactics—name-calling campaigns, racist advertising, newspaper editorials, and leafleting.

When woven into the fabric of daily life, the exertion of power over those who cannot attain it becomes the dominant theme, the unspoken expectation, the norm. The acquiescence of those who are powerless becomes a virtue, a knowing of one's place and a willingness to stay there in order to avoid the harsh consequences of breaking free.

The problem, then, ceases to be the structure that binds people, but the attempt to change it. And everyone pays a price. Those who create and protect the system spend a lifetime robbing others of their freedoms. Those who challenge the system risk the reprisals of its architects and caretakers. And those who do nothing enable the suffering to continue. All end up in a kind of prison, whose walls may look secure but are in reality only fear transformed into the illusion of safety. Nobody is ever out of harm's way.

I'D FOUND OUT my mother was pregnant with Liz the Thanksgiving before, from my cousin Missy. Ann was downstairs with Mom in the kitchen, standing on a chair stirring the gravy. My father hadn't told us yet—in fact, he never told us outright—that he had just lost his job, and he sat in the living room with Uncle Ray, watching football.

Missy sat at the edge of my bed, brushing my Barbie doll's blonde ponytail. "Aunt Ginny is going to have a baby, you know," she told me.

"No, she's not," I said, thinking of the white apron tied around my mother's narrow waist.

"You know how it happens, don't you?" she asked. She looked up from Barbie's hair, which was an impossible tangle of shiny, spun vinyl.

"Sure," I said, explaining what I'd heard from Sister Rosarita, that married people prayed for a baby, then God made the woman pregnant. Missy threw the Barbie to the floor and laughed. When she told me the truth I was shocked. "My parents don't do that," I insisted.

"Oh, yes they do," she said as I rescued Barbie from the floor. Her hard, cool body was familiar and reassuring in my hand.

To think that my parents did that! My parents, whose only conversations in front of me involved where my father was going to take my mother on his day off. She'd never learned to drive, and they only went to Dr. Meader's office and to the grocery store, to church, and to my grandmother's apartment to pick up the mending.

What else did my parents do behind closed doors? One of the curses of not being able to sleep at night was that I heard them argue, sometimes about money, in voices that made me feel like the floor below me was going to give way.

A doctor had once told my mother that she'd never have children, so she and my father had planned to travel, perhaps someday adopt.

"I never wanted this deal," I heard him say to my mother from behind the door.

They argued in hushed tones, using words that they never intended anyone to hear. I didn't know what happened next, and whether there were whispered words of apology or physical expressions of regret. All I knew was that I felt as though the bottom was falling out.

So for the rest of my mother's pregnancy, I felt protective of her and watched her closely as her belly grew. In addition to doing whatever I could to make my father happy, I now tried to be extra helpful to my mother.

In a neighborhood of clean houses, ours was the cleanest, and even on the hottest summer days I helped her move the refrigerator from the kitchen wall so she could wax the floor underneath. She ironed everything: sheets, pillowcases, and underwear. I learned to sprinkle my father's good shirts using a 7UP bottle, filled with water. Into the mouth of the bottle my mother had placed a red plastic stopper that she'd found in one of Aunt Billy's catalogs. The water came out in delicate droplets from tiny holes in the domed top, as if from a watering can, and when the shirt was sufficiently damp, I ironed perfect creases into the white cotton sleeves from the shoulder to the cuff.

One Sunday morning, weeks before Liz was born, my mother and I were leaving the house for mass. My mother, huge in a black and white maternity dress, caught her heel on the welcome mat and fell down the steps. I stood at the top and grabbed for her, but my hands did not reach her in time. She fell forward and twisted her torso to the side, her knees taking the force of the fall. Her pregnant belly slammed against the pavement like a wrestler pushed to the mat. Her skirt went up around the globe of her abdomen. The cement tore tornado-shaped holes in the knees of her stockings, and the white garters holding them up unsnapped and slapped her thighs like slingshots. A man in a black suit and a woman in a red dress rushed across the lawn to help her. As the man helped her to her feet, the woman looked up at me from the bottom of the stairs, and I felt strangely implicated. As if a little girl in a pink princess dress and black patent leather shoes could keep her mother from falling.

CHAPTER 5

A Lind Girl

M Y FATHER told his stories before a captive audience, but my mother and her four sisters saw interruptions as an essential component in the storytelling process. At one point, in preparation for a visit from the Lind Girls, my father began to tape a poster from the film *Jaws* to the front door of our house.

From the way my father told it, the storytellers in his family needed a front porch, a sliver of shade, or a baby on the floor with a circle of grown-ups gathered around it. On the other hand, the storytellers in my mother's family needed a Thanksgiving turkey picked down to its bare rib cage, several packs of cigarettes, and an ample supply of bourbon. They loved to linger at the dinner table, talking. The other kids had finished eating and gone into the living room to watch *The Wonderful World of Disney*, but I liked to stay at the table with the grown-ups, sitting quietly so that they wouldn't notice and tell me to run along.

My mother and her sisters were drinking coffee spiked with Old Grand-Dad and chattering: everyone at once and nobody listening to anyone. The leftover lettuce grew limp in my mother's milk glass salad bowl, and the candles burned down to a nub in her matching candlesticks, but nobody noticed. Bursts of laughter punctuated their chatter, which grew louder and faster until it began to resemble a food fight in the school cafeteria, the words flying around the room like so many peas and carrots.

Most of the time, they weren't even aware of my presence. I liked being invisible; besides, it was to my best listening advantage to remain unseen.

Usually they talked about whoever was missing from the table. They were talking about my mother, who was in the kitchen, slicing the pumpkin pie. They all had cigarettes between their fingers, and as I listened the smoke rose up to the ceiling and swirled around the dining room chandelier like cirrus clouds around the moon.

"Well, I was behind her on the lawn and saw the whole thing," Aunt Sophie began, picking up the thread of a conversation they'd left dangling before dinner. She reached across the table for Grandma Lind's silver coffee service. "It was just after she'd come off duty. Coffee, Louise?"

Aunt Louise lifted her cup and saucer toward the coffeepot and nodded to Sophie. "What was the name of the hotel? I didn't really visit back then, did I?"

In Washington, D.C., during the war, apparently my father and one of his marine buddies made bets on the weekends to see who could get the most girls to wait for them under a tree. My mother, who was in the navy, shared an apartment with Aunt Sophie, who was a marine. On my father's invitation my mother had waited for my father under the tree, as had half a dozen other young women.

Louise looked down at me for an instant and sighed. "In those days I shopped at John W. Thomas," she said in a half-whisper. Aunt Louise was married to a surgeon who came from old Minneapolis money. During the war he'd practiced medicine in the army. "I remember one Saturday afternoon I was standing on the corner of Ninth and Nicollet in a black silk dress. Someone whistled at me from a passing car."

Sophie rolled her eyes and put down the coffeepot. "What has that got to do with anything? Besides, *I* was the one with the outfits," she said. Aunt Sophie had moved to New York City after the war and now prided herself on the beautiful clothes she wore to work every day at the offices of the Ponds cold cream and cosmetics company. She then called out to my mother, who was still in the kitchen. "I really was a stunning bride, wasn't I, Ginny?"

"I wasn't at your wedding, Sophie," my mother answered from the kitchen. She measured a teaspoonful of vanilla extract into the bowl and began whipping the cream with her hand mixer. "But you've seen my wedding pictures," Sophie said. "I sent you all a picture."

Aunt Billy began rummaging through her purse.

"See?" Sophie cried triumphantly. "Billy has one in her wallet."

"Oh, stop it, Sophie," Billy said. "Since when do I carry a wedding picture of you in my purse? I'm looking for the Lillian Vernon catalog." Aunt Billy never left the house without a mail-order catalog.

Aunt Billy and Uncle Tom had eight children and lived in a lovely white house in the country club district. Their kids got new clothes for Christmas and birthdays, and every season she sent the things they'd outgrown to my mother and Aunt Jane.

Jane got up from the table. Aunt Jane and Uncle Ray lived in our neighborhood. I got invited to my cousin Missy's birthday parties. Aunt Jane was my mother's best friend. At the kitchen door, she turned to the rest of her sisters. "Ginny is no dummy," she said. "How could she not have known about the bet?"

"Ginny, how could you not have known about that bet?"

Aunt Billy followed Jane into the kitchen. From her purse she'd pulled out a small mail-order catalog, which she was leafing through. "Y'know, Ginny, there's this battery-operated whisk on page twenty-three," she began.

At that moment my father wandered in from the living room, looking for a piece of pie. "Whattaya need all that junk for?" he asked, sticking his finger into the bowl of whipped cream.

"Billy, put that thing away," Louise said. "It's tacky."

Billy flipped through the catalog and stopped, pointing to something on a page. "Tacky? I just ordered three sets of percale sheets for the price of one," she said, her finger on a photograph of folded white linens.

"People I knew wore sheets," my father said.

Aunt Jane's jaw dropped and her eyes opened wide. Aunt Louise looked disgusted.

"Didn't have clothes," my father replied.

Marrying my father may have been the most courageous decision my mother ever made. As a northerner who gave herself airs (but wouldn't admit it) about her upper-class urban upbringing, choosing him meant trouble that she probably never anticipated.

During one of their dinner table conversations, Aunt Louise had criticized my mother for marrying beneath herself. "Sharecroppers, Ginny," Louise had said. "He had no business marrying a Lind Girl."

It didn't bother me so much that Aunt Louise had money; it bothered me that she lorded it over everyone. It also showed me that having an education didn't necessarily mean that a person was no longer ignorant.

I am endlessly fascinated by the virtue that people assign to certain stations in life. At any given time at the dinner table, for example, a person might have heard any number of virtues pulled out from some great cosmic treasury. Perhaps the Good Lord chose some people to receive the blessings of wealth and status, or hard work and determination could raise a person's fortunes. Maybe obedience to the rules would secure a respected place in the community.

The extent to which the distribution of the world's privileges depended on luck, history, or social and geographical context didn't often enter into the conversation. Rather, it was discussed in terms of God, merit, or subservience. Prosperity was clearly a reward for virtue.

By definition, then, poverty took on the appearance of vice. Aunt Louise must have measured out the relative assets that each of my parents brought to the union and found that the Lind side tipped the scales on the side of goodness.

My father left home in 1940. A year and a half before Pearl Harbor, he declined a basketball scholarship to Neshoba Central Junior College and signed up instead for the marines. "I wanted to get away from farming," he said. "The service was the only way a boy could get away without being a traitor."

A traitor may have overstated the status of his leave-taking, but certainly his decision was met with concern. Wanting something more, however undefined, must have puzzled kinfolks who found deep contentment in staying close to home and caring for one another.

A child of the Depression, my father left Mississippi because he could no longer face the kind of suffering he and his family had experienced. "By 1935, Lumiere, Maurice, and Ruby were married and gone," my father said. "They had no idea what my brother'n me went through."

I couldn't fully comprehend it either. The harshness of his childhood would not touch me emotionally for another two years, when he would take us to Mississippi for the first time. I lacked the real-life experiences that would transform existence in rural Mississippi into something tangible. I didn't know how it felt to be hungry and to have to wait until tomorrow for something to eat. I didn't know the humiliation of staying out of school for a year because there weren't clothes to wear. I didn't know what it was like to work in suffocating heat and humidity. To work under a sun that seared the skin through shirts so worn you could see through to the sunburn. To lie in bed protected from the weather by sheets of newspaper that covered the cracks in the walls and ceiling.

This was the family Aunt Louise felt was beneath her. To tell the truth, my father wasn't crazy about Aunt Louise, either. He'd wanted to borrow money from Uncle Frank a few years earlier, to start a small carpet business. Uncle Frank had promised to under-write the venture but never made good on his promises, and left my father with a failed business and a mountain of debt. Not every Lind Girl had married a financially successful husband, and my father never forgave Aunt Louise and Uncle Frank for reminding him of it.

A Lind Girl was one of five sisters who grew up in a three-story Tudor home in south Minneapolis during the first half of the cen-tury. She didn't work outside the home (except for Aunt Sophie, who had married an artist, so naturally she *had* to work). A Lind Girl sewed curtains and picked out upholstery fabric and wallpa-pered the dining room. She was the den mother and the Brownie leader, the keeper of the family dental records and immunization schedules. A Lind Girl kept a rosary and a missal on the bedside stand. She went to mass on Sundays and Holy Days of Obligation. She prayed to Saint Anthony when the paperboy was at the front door and she couldn't remember where she'd placed her purse, and to Saint Jude when pacing the floor in the middle of the night with a feverish baby.

A Lind Girl kept Christmas like nobody else: she baked more cookies, hung more ornaments from the tree, and left no room free from boughs of holly, spray-flocked wreaths, or little slope-roofed wooden stables with the blond-haired ceramic baby Jesus inside. Even in the bathroom the toilet wore a fuzzy slipcover with a laugh-ing Santa on the seat, and the toilet paper was printed with candy canes.

A Lind Girl wore cinnamon-colored hose and white gloves when she took the bus downtown to spend the day shopping, eating lunch at Dayton's Sky Room, and seeing her obstetrician in the Medical Arts Building beside the Foshay Tower.

This was the family my father married into. Most of the Lind Girls had married well. They didn't have financial struggles and nobody drank too much. Husbands were never unfaithful to their wives, and the kids didn't give anyone much trouble. And when everyone was talking at the same time, and nobody was listening to anybody else, it didn't seem to matter much whether these things were 100 percent the case.

Unlike the funeral photograph of Grandma Ora, the images of my mother's parents were not so much taken out from time to time and looked at as they were prominently on display. Their more visible presence in our everyday lives set the tone and established the priorities in our daily lives. Looking down on us from the walls in our living room, hallway, and in my parents' bedroom were wedding photographs of Grandma and Papa Lind, a charcoal drawing of Grandma Lind when she was five years old, and framed collages of each of them from various stages in life. There was Papa Lind at the Calhoun Beach Club, smoking a cigar and playing cards, and Grandma Lind in a veiled hat, holding a china cup and saucer in one hand, and in the other a silver teapot.

MINNESOTANS often take issue with those who look upon the Midwest as little more than a flyover space, a kind of vast no-man's-land where nothing is new and change occurs in imitation of last year's East or West Coast innovations. And yet Middle America might be better understood as the place to find people like me, who find safety in the center. In Minnesota, half a continent in every direction keeps us from the dangers of the edge. We have no San Francisco earthquakes, no World Trade Center twin towers, no Hurricane Hugo or melting Arctic snow mass. We believe ourselves to be protected, surrounded as we are on all sides by a cushion of land.

Growing up in New York City in the late 1940s and early 1950s did not necessarily mean that a boy would find himself immersed in edgy ideas, or guarantee that life would be lived in contradiction to the great groundswell of post–World War II conservativism. But for Andy Goodman, it meant exactly that. Raised in the Upper West Side neighborhood of his father's boyhood, he was surrounded by people who believed in challenging the status quo. Raised by a mother whose drive to organize emerged early in her own childhood, he was given a role model whose liberal values helped shape his own.

Early on, in elementary school, Andy became known for his fairmindedness. One incident, his mother told me, involved a kid who was known as a real pain in the neck, "a provocateur," as Mrs. Goodman characterized him. A gang of kids had jumped on top of this boy on the playground and Andy had stepped forward in his defense. "He's a pain," Andy had said to the other boys. "But fair is fair. One at a time, not all of you at once." Andy was also a regular kid. He played baseball and the clarinet (once while practicing, Andy turned on the television to watch the Dodgers play and swung his clarinet like a baseball bat, in imitation of Jackie Robinson, only to break a lamp in the living room). He acted in school theater productions and liked girls his parents weren't so sure about.

Andy's mother, Carolyn, was born in a Long Island suburb to parents who supported the independence of their bright, ambitious daughter. She started her first movement at ten years old, when she felt that the man who did the family's gardening wasn't earning enough money. Organizing came naturally to Carolyn, and by the time she was an undergraduate at Cornell in the 1930s, she had become active in many liberal causes, including the struggle for democracy in Spain. She joined the League Against War and Fascism, organizing American sympathizers to "adopt" a Spanish family or child, victims of the Spanish Civil War. Then she met Robert Goodman, a peace-minded poet and student activist who had won an oratorical award for a speech entitled "A Plea for Active Pacifism." After they married, the Goodmans moved to Manhattan's Upper West Side, into what was arguably the largest progressive community in America. This was where they raised their three boys: Jonathan, Andrew, and David, and where they introduced them to the liberal causes that were to become part of the fabric of their family life.

For Michael Schwerner, whose social consciousness was also nurtured by activist parents, growing up in New York City meant that he and his brother attended excellent private and public schools. Mickey's father, Nathan, was a partner in a wig manufacturing company that had been in the family for three generations. His mother, Anne, had taught high school biology. Both of Mickey's parents had been involved in liberal causes, and Nathan was a member of the War Resisters League.

Mickey, the younger of two boys, was an athlete (he played golf and once drove a ball through a school window, which he paid for out of his weekly allowance). He loved animals and thought for a time of becoming a veterinarian. He dabbled in dramatics and sold ads for his high school yearbook. By the time he reached college, Mickey had changed majors a couple of times, deciding finally to focus on rural sociology. His friends remember that he'd led a successful campaign to pledge a black student into his fraternity.

Mickey enrolled in a graduate program at the Columbia School of Social Work in New York City after graduating from Cornell in 1961. He soon grew frustrated with the school's apolitical approach to social work, which did not address racism and other root causes of poverty. A year later, he dropped the program and took a job as a social worker at a settlement house on Manhattan's Lower East Side.

Mickey had met Rita Levant the summer before his senior year at Cornell, and the two had clicked immediately. Rita had just completed her freshman year at the University of Michigan, and the following year they kept in touch. Rita transferred to Queens College for her junior year, and in July of 1962 the two were married in the Schwerners' home.

James Chaney was born in Meridian, Mississippi, to parents who sent him to the best school available to black children in the city—St. Joseph's Academy, Meridian's Catholic school for Negroes. His mother had worked as a domestic but took a job closer to home as a lunchroom helper in a white school. His father worked as a plasterer, and was often away for long stretches, working at plastering jobs across the state. James, or J. E. as he was called at home, took on the role of man of the house in his father's absence, helping his sister with chores, and protecting his mother. He was a fast runner and a good baseball player who also terrorized his little sisters but had everything in order when his mother got home from work.

The Chaneys, like most black families, had stories to tell of relatives who had tried to stand up for themselves and had paid for it with their lives. A cousin in Alabama disappeared in the early 1940s, after complaining to his white boss that he hadn't been paid. His mother's step-grandfather had been murdered trying to protect his property from the white neighbors who'd wanted to buy it and had threatened to burn it.

In his immediate family, J. E. and his sisters had experienced the threat of violence. They walked to school through a white neighborhood, and often had to run from dogs set on them. When the son of a white bill collector once referred to her father as "Ben," J. E.'s sister Barbara demanded that he call her father "Mr. Chaney." For that infraction of the social code, the white bill collector told Mr. Chaney to beat his daughter for being sassy.

When J. E. decided to be apprenticed to his father as a plasterer, he experienced firsthand the indignities of Jim Crow in rural and small town Mississippi. Traveling by bus, he and his father noticed that police routinely boarded in small delta towns known for being especially tough on integrationists, to make sure that the black people rode at the back. There were certain towns where they simply would not stop, and Mr. Chaney made sure that they stayed in private homes where the meals were provided, since few restaurants and fewer motels would provide them with food and shelter.

J. E. was recruited into civil rights work in October of 1963. At first it was thought that his interest was personal: there was a young, attractive black female on staff. But J. E. showed up ready to work, and with his intimate knowledge of Meridian and the back roads in the surrounding communities, he soon became a valuable asset in getting out word of the movement's activities to those in outlying areas.

The lives of these three young men came together in June of 1964 during a training session for summer volunteers held in Oxford, Ohio. The lessons they'd learned early in life had brought them to this pivotal moment, and they were preparing themselves for a head-on challenge unlike any they had faced before. Each had been given the desire to reach beyond himself and help others, even if it meant his own peril.

BY THE 1950s, our south Minneapolis neighborhood was mostly peopled with second- and third-generation Scandinavian and German families. As a Lind Girl, my mother fit in with the hard-working women who defined the neighborhood norms. Mostly what that meant for this generation was that they knew how to keep the place clean. Women volunteered to sweep and dust the church sanctuary, the priests' residence, and helped one another with spring and fall housecleaning. Life was neatly ordered, and each day was lived within a small circle of housework, chores, and child rearing that was rarely broken by interferences from the outside world. Our mothers kept us home from school during the Cuban missile crisis and mourned when President Kennedy was assassinated, but they worried about pregnancies and miscarriages and paying the doctor bills.

It was an insular world run primarily by women. Few of the mothers had cars; everything they needed was within walking distance or could be delivered to the house. During the day, the neighborhood was empty of men, except for those in uniform who delivered mail or milk or brought cardboard boxes of groceries to the back doors. The fathers were salesmen, carpenters, policemen, butchers, and bus drivers. In the morning they took the family car to work and left their wives behind, some of whom rarely ventured from the neighborhood, a few of whom didn't venture out of the house.

For some women, this kind of conformity gave each day definition and purpose. Following the example of those around them and staying within the boundaries the church had set for their station in life made for a sheltered existence that warded off the ambiguities that existed in the outside world. "An apple pie is a very important thing," my mother was fond of saying (though most of her pies were of the Mrs. Smith's frozen variety).

There were other women, however, for whom the inability to deviate from this structure made the neighborhood into a kind of personal dead end. Across the street from us, Mrs. Macalester stayed inside with the shades drawn. But from time to time she walked over to our house in her black stretch pants and gold lamé slippers with jewels in the toes. Wearing sunglasses and holding a lipstick-marked glass of something in her hand that smelled like bourbon, but that my mother insisted was iced tea, she'd circle the dining room table and go back home without saying a word. If she spoke, it was to tell us in a sad, watery voice that she had the "creeping crud."

"She's a highly intelligent woman," my mother would say when we asked her what was wrong. "And very unhappy," she concluded, in a way that made intelligence sound like a serious liability.

Besides, the standards for keeping a house clean were so high that there was neither time nor energy to engage in business that extended beyond the small, enclosed yards.

My mother took great pride in her canning and preserving and from time to time would make a special trip downstairs to the store-room just to admire the colorful fruits and vegetables that shone through the clear glass of the quart jars. The shelves were stacked with home-canned dill pickles, stewed tomatoes, rhubarb preserves, and applesauce. Often when she was preparing dinner, my mother would ask me to fetch something from downstairs.

I had developed the habit of daydreaming, which allowed my mind to vacate the room whenever I felt vulnerable. Because of this, I was often withdrawn. So when I pulled the chain on the bare bulb in the ceiling of the cobwebby storeroom, I just stood there as if newly wakened, knowing I'd been told to do something, and completely unaware of what it was.

I blinked at the shelves of sparkling glass jars whose edible contents were arranged by color, labeled and dated with black Magic Marker on strips of masking tape. I may not have remembered the errand I'd been asked to run, but I knew one thing for certain: this was the foundation of my mother's life. I was surrounded by the security that she had built using Depression-era tactics of hoarding the essentials, just in case. As long as her storeroom was full, she knew she could provide for her family.

There were other objects on the shelves that my mother saved, broken things that had been sitting idle for years. But it wasn't so much another thrifty carryover from hard times as it was a sign of hope that my father would eventually fix something.

Beside my mother's storeroom was a tool room that we said was my father's but which stood perpetually idle. The wooden workbench with its empty drawers had become home to generations of spiders and centipedes. To walk on the floor meant to crunch over the calcified shells of deceased water bugs and dead flies, so that you never went into the basement in bare feet. It was a scary room: deserted, dark, and dirty. Had I reached back, my hand would have touched a damp stone wall whose green leaded paint was peeling away in chips the size of my fingernails.

I thought about my father's middle-of-the-night comment and wondered what parts of the deal he didn't want. There must have been comfortable associations with home and gardens and children or he wouldn't have chosen that life, would he? Were there other kinds of men who made other kinds of choices? He'd grown up on a farm, but had left it behind, and I sensed a no-win restlessness as he both appreciated the world that women like the Lind Girls created for their families, but also refused to stay completely within the lines they drew around them.

He was not a father who spent his weekends oiling the wooden handles of handsaws and U-shaped drills. He didn't repair the fence posts when they became loose, or replace the missing shingles that caused our roof to leak. Ours was a house full of broken things waiting to be fixed, usually by my mother with Elmer's glue and cellophane tape or by my brother.

My father built the infrastructure of our family life using words and images that came from his ability to notice, to remember, and to interpret. We learned to step outside an event and become its critical observer, watching carefully for the humor in it, the irony, or the absurd. Yet in our own basement, the workshop stood idle while the walls crumbled, poison leached from the paint and asbestos lined the furnace pipes. We looked for the folly in others and often missed it in ourselves.

But we put a good face on it all. Behind the battlements of my brother's handiness and armed with her credit cards, my mother covered up any visible cracks that may have appeared on the domestic front. Her efforts won for her family the Lind Girl Seal of Approval.

My father's family, therefore, mostly absent from center stage, came to us in story form. Perhaps he'd start talking from behind the wheel of our hump-backed 1954 Chevrolet, one hand driving and the other resting across the length of the seat back that divided us. Like a stagehand, he painted the colorful backdrop against which our lives were played.

" 'Round about August, there was nothin' to do but watch the cotton grow, so we lay the farm by," he said. It would have been an impossibly hot and muggy Minnesota afternoon, and we'd have stopped for ice cream after a trip to the beach. So while he told his story, the ice cream would be melting down the cones, onto our chins and over the fronts of our bathing suits. But we would have vanished from the sphere of his awareness.

My father had gone back to Mississippi, where there were no kids in the backseat with sticky pools of ice cream between their bare thighs. "August was when the travelin' preachers come through. Tent shows. Snake oil. That type a thing. I guess I was about ten, and Arby twelve or so. There was a revival that came through that summer. Preacher's name was Railroad Spinks. We was all gonna be saved. People come from ever'where. Farm people from the counties all around. Let's see. Winston, Lauderdale. You know, too far away to see but once a year when the revival pitched a big tent just outside Philadelphia.

"We eat good too," he went on. "Picnic baskets fulla ham, corn bread, chicken pan pie, coconut cake, watermelon, and butter beans. And after dinner everyone'd set down on blankets and chairs under the tent to listen to the preacher. At the end they come forward to be saved."

Though it happened forty years ago, I can imagine the tent show and the preacher, I can still feel the thick and sticky coolness of that ice cream between my thighs, and I can remember the look on my mother's face when she turned around and saw what was happening in the backseat. She took a stack of napkins from the glove compartment and passed them out as fast as a blackjack dealer, her body bent in two over the front seat so that her hands were mopping up ice cream in the back while her feet had left the floor in front. With each bump in the road, her head jerked and she looked as though she'd catapult, headfirst, into the backseat with us.

My father was oblivious to all of this, of course, and kept on talking while my mother shot him an irritated look.

"We didn't dare mess up Daddy's Packard with ice cream," she said to us in her primmest Lind Girl voice. "We ate fast or we knew what we'd get when we got home." Papa Lind was dead, and I sometimes thought he sounded mean, like he had scared people into goodness.

The backseat would soon be littered with wadded-up napkins and my mother's lips would disappear as she pressed them together and drew her mouth into a straight line, the way she always did when she wanted my father to shut up and give her a hand.

"That preacher was shoutin' at ever'one about the end of the world. My brother 'n' me wasn't about to be saved, so while the preacher paced the stage like a foamin' dog, we snuck out of the tent and back behind. Parked back there was dozens 'a wagons. An' we saw that lots of people had left their babies to sleep in the backs of the wagons. 'Let's switch babies,' Arby whispered to me from behind the tent.

"I don't know what come over us, but we decided then and there to move the babies around from one wagon to the next. Mix 'em all up. 'Course nobody notices that they have the wrong baby till they get home, and nobody has telephones back then. Wasn't until the next night that they got their babies back."

He let his breath out slowly as he laughed. "Nobody ever knew that it was my brother and me done it," he said. "If they had, Pappy woulda chased us halfway 'cross the county with a strap." He shook his head. "The way we tormented that old man," he said, pausing a moment, as if to make a mental note of the next story he would tell us. "I'm glad he didn't catch us that time."

CHAPTER 6

Sinkin' Spells

IN MY FAMILY, the Catholic church was our primary connection to the outside world. Television's influence, still so new, took a distant second to the church, which interpreted events, doled out truths, and formed our values. From the pulpit, in the confessional, and in the classroom, Catholics were given guidance about what to think, how to behave, and a Catholic's place in the hierarchy of salvation.

The nucleus of our mostly Catholic neighborhood was Christ the King Parish. Not unlike a military compound, the church, school, playground, rectory, and convent took up most of the block just north of us. In religious studies, the sisters taught us that we belonged to the One True Church. We took up collections of nickels and dimes for pagan babies in Africa. We asked the Blessed Virgin Mary to intervene in times of trouble. We prayed for the forgiveness of sins and the communion of saints, but the communion of saints was strictly circumscribed: we were warned that to enter a church that wasn't Catholic was highly dangerous to our faith.

"I was the only Lind Girl who married a non-Catholic," my mother said. "Papa Lind was very upset and had to consult with Father Fenlon before giving his consent."

Though he hadn't been baptized, my father was raised in the Baptist Church. He converted to Catholicism after he married my mother. He always insisted that it wasn't because the church frowned upon mixed marriages, but because the Baptists were agin' everything.

He told me that the family in Mississippi wasn't too sure about his salvation, either. "Ruby was always gettin' after me," he said. "She was scared I was goin' to the devil. 'Am I growin' horns?' I'd ask her, and she'd quiet down for a while."

These accounts confused me. I wondered how his sister could think that those who belonged to the One True Church were going to hell, when I was being taught exactly the opposite. To tell the truth, the One True Church in which I was being raised was a scary place. It was full of eternal damnation and souls in Purgatory and babies in Limbo. It was also full of imperious nuns and angry priests who could go toe to toe with any Baptist preacher when it came to being agin' things, I was very sure.

Devout parents rigidly followed *Canis Connubii*, the encyclical on Catholic marriage that Pope Pius XI had written in 1930, which paid careful attention to all aspects of a Catholic's sexuality. In meticulous detail, the pope had spelled out the Catholic Church's divinely inspired directives to the faithful on such harrowing moral questions as impure thoughts, unclean images, marriage outside the church, infidelity, divorce, and masturbation. The use of artificial birth control was strictly banned.

For my parents, this meant, of course, that my father would convert and that he and my mother would welcome as many children as the Good Lord would bless them with. It also meant that when Dr. Meader wanted clues as to why my mother was having so many miscarriages, the semen sample from my father could only be collected after intercourse (and after several Manhattans, they told the neighbors), which took place, naturally, on an examination table in the doctor's office.

Now Paul VI was pope, and his *Humanae Vitae* galvanized the encyclical of Pius XI and reinforced the parameters of a Catholic woman's life. When the weather was warm, pairs of nuns in their sweeping black habits strolled arm in arm up the hill from the convent and past our house. They surveyed us with eyes that had almost disappeared into their faces, which were puffed out from the starched white headpieces they wore beneath their veils. I often had the feeling that they looked with satisfaction at the large Catholic families: boys mowing the lawns, the girls washing windows with ammonia and newspapers, and the fathers kissing the mothers hello when they came home from work.

Inside, the small houses teemed with children. Most were one-toilet houses with a bathroom door that was loose on its hinges from kids fighting and pushing to be first in line to take a pee. Two, three, and sometimes four kids were crammed into each bedroom, often tiny and likely to smell of wet diapers. At least a third of the mothers were expecting another baby.

Our dining room table had to be cleared of the snow-capped mountains of folded sheets, towels, underwear, and diapers before the seven of us could squeeze around it at dinnertime for a meal of meat loaf and canned corn and shoestring potatoes. My mother was living the life the Church had taught her to live. She wore an expression of perpetual fatigue on her face and had hands that were rough and knuckly from hot water and detergent.

The fatigue deepened as the weather changed. On winter days, when the sunlight had vanished by four-thirty in the afternoon, the snow looked even colder for being shrouded in deep blue shadows. In the dark, my mother fell asleep in front of the television set after dinner.

To cope, she kept a stack of prayer books on her nightstand. The crisp pages, worn thin almost to transparency, were edged with gold and opened to her favorite passages with silk bookmarks in red, blue, purple, and green that had been sewn into the binding. These were the pages she turned to and read each morning before she got up to begin her day.

In 1963, with the deaths of President John Kennedy and Pope John XXIII, Catholics had lost two of our most promising beacons. One was youthful and made being Catholic seem like something vigorous and alive. The other promised to open the windows and let fresh air into the Church. Both represented the kind of hopeful energy that might have spared the faithful from an obsessive terror of mortal sin. But in the year that had passed, the Church was still teaching us to set ourselves above others and to spend vast amounts of time saying the rosary, attending mass, doing Stations of the Cross, and praying before statues of the Blessed Virgin and the saints.

For the most part, Catholic kids went to Catholic school, and all the others went to public schools, which divided my mind into neat, opposing factions: the Catholic of my mother's side of the family and the Publics of my father's side. It also helped me divide the world up into other convenient columns: black and white, North and South, them and us.

The world was small and therefore easy to fit into categories. The nuns herded us into the basement of the school for civil defense drills once a month, but the threat of nuclear attack wasn't real. Dying and going to hell after eating a hamburger on meatless Fridays was very real. President Johnson would sign landmark civil rights legislation, but the teachers in my Catholic school would not bother us with it.

We memorized the *Baltimore Catechism* word for word, doctrine for doctrine. The people in our textbooks were a reflection of us: American and white and middle-class and Catholic. All across the globe, Those Who Are Not Us were placed into the category of Those Who Need to Be Converted to the One True Church, and Catholic missionaries had been dispersed to evangelize and baptize. Entire cultures were disappearing because of it, but that didn't come up. It would have raised questions the sisters couldn't answer. We learned that the Catholics had gone to the Crusades to save the world from the scourge of heathenism, but we didn't learn that they had tortured and murdered a generation of people. Christopher Columbus was a hero.

In September of 1963, when four young girls were killed in the bombing of the Sixteenth Street Baptist Church in Birmingham, Alabama, Mickey Schwerner made the decision to apply to the national office of CORE (Congress of Racial Equality) and asked to be posted somewhere in the South. His wife, Rita, would graduate in January, which would free them both to relocate.

In his application when stating his desire to be involved in the movement, Mickey used words that expressed an almost religious conviction, except that he placed his beliefs outside the constraints that people often place on God.

"As a social worker I have dedicated my life to social ills," he wrote. "However, my profession, except in isolated instances, as yet has not become directly involved in the most devastating social disease at the present time—discrimination. I also feel that the Negro in the South has an even more bitter fight ahead of him than in the North and I wish to be part of that fight. In essence, I would feel guilty and almost hypocritical if I do not give full time for an extended period.

"The vocation for the rest of my life is and will be to work for an integrated society," he went on. "I plan to do this work primarily in New York City where my roots are, but I feel it is important that I have a firsthand understanding of how people in other sections of the country specifically are affected by prejudice and how discrimination is being dealt with. I want to know and work with 'people,' not just read about situations or take someone else's subjective view. I want to be there firsthand."

The Schwerners received their acceptance as CORE staff workers on Thanksgiving Day in 1963, just days after President Kennedy had been assassinated. They moved to Mississippi six weeks later and for the first few nights slept in a black church and in the homes of black families, who soon received threats and had to ask the young couple to find housing elsewhere. Virtually no white churches would have anything to do with them. When a lone white minister showed the courage to invite the Schwerners and two black friends to attend a service, an editorial appeared in the *Meridian Star* the following Tuesday:

LET'S WAKE UP

We Southerners are prone to put all the blame for our racial troubles on outsiders. The truth is that while outsiders indeed cause a great deal of our difficulties, we ourselves are partly to blame for our woes. . . .

If members of another race invade our Southern churches, what do we do about it? Even though most of these people come not for the purpose of worship, but merely to cause trouble, many of us do nothing whatsoever. We don't avail ourselves of peaceful, legitimate means of protest. For example, we don't bother to register a protest with church officials. We don't even vote with our feet by walking out on the invaded service.

If we want to preserve segregation, why don't we wake up and do something about it (*sic*).

Rita later wrote a report to CORE's national office, in which she explained what Mickey had done in the editorial's aftermath. "Mickey telephoned the minister to express our concern for him," she wrote. "But also to make clear that we believe in the moral rightness of our action. The minister appeared to appreciate the call and said that he, too, believed that the action had been correct and that the congregation would have to learn to accept integration."

MY FATHER wouldn't fit neatly into any of the clearly defined categories that the Church had set out for him. He existed somewhere in between North and South, Protestant and Catholic, Them and Us.

He'd even told my mother when they were dating that he was part Negro, just to see what her reaction would be. "Two things came to my mind immediately," she said. "The first was, 'How will I ever tell my father?' the second was, 'What does this mean for our children?' " After realizing her distress, he quickly denied any Negro in his heritage.

Depending upon the circumstances, my father often took surprisingly disparate points of view. For instance, he was a Bomb-Them-Back-to-the-Stone-Age advocate for crises elsewhere in the world, while at home he showed great compassion for his neighbors. One of his brightest moments took place one summer with one of the Franz boys, who lived next door. Mrs. Franz played the organ at church and gave piano lessons in an alcove off their front room; each day a steady stream of kids came in and out of their front door carrying sheet music under their arms.

The four Franz boys, slightly older than Linda, were handsome, smart, and had a reputation for being the life of the party. From time to time, in the middle of the night, the neighborhood would waken to shouts from their upstairs bathroom because one of the boys had come home drunk and Mr. Franz was giving him a cold shower.

This summer, one of the Franz boys had been driving a car that crashed into and killed a young woman who was about to be married (at the wake she was laid out in her wedding gown). He was sixteen or seventeen years old, and spent the entire summer sitting alone in a lawn chair in the Franzes' backyard. Ann and I watched him from our bedroom window, and every day it was the same: he sat alone and stared at the side of their garage.

When my father came home from work, he would take a lawn

chair over to the Franzes' backyard and sit next to him. Sometimes they spoke, sometimes they were silent. I never knew what my father said to him, nor could I imagine what there was to say. But he sat beside him, sometimes for ten minutes, sometimes half an hour. Then my father would get up, place his hand on the boy's shoulder, and come home for supper. Mr. Franz said afterward that my father was the only person who had reached out to his son that whole awful summer.

I wished at times that my father had reached out more to me. By age nine, I started having, as my father called them, "sinkin' spells." You get a little dizzy, the edges of your vision blur, and you're all at once so tired you can't keep your eyes open. From time to time I'd black out but remain conscious. It was as though the nerves in my eyes shrank for a few seconds and blocked out whatever it was they didn't want me to see. The time I remember most vividly was at church.

I'd had sinkin' spells before, when, overcome with fatigue, I'd had to lie down in the middle of the day. But never had my eyes failed me. I'd gone to mass on a weekday morning, when only a couple of dozen people—old ladies and businessmen, mostly—sat here and there among the otherwise empty pews, making the church seem darker and more lonely than it did on Sunday mornings when the sanctuary was full of people. But this morning there was nothing to distract me from the darkness of the semilit church. And so, when I got up after kneeling before the priest and taking the communion host on my tongue, everything went black. I didn't pass out, but wish that I had, because I groped my way to the side exit of the church, hands before me like Patty Duke as Helen Keller in *The Miracle Worker*. Lucky for me that I spent so much time in church, because I could gauge from memory how far it was from the center of the communion rail to the double doors that led to the exit.

Once outside, I leaned against the cool brick wall of the building while slowly my vision returned to normal. It took me a couple of decades to realize that nobody had rushed forward to help me. The men in their navy blue business suits. The old women with lavender pillbox hats on their heads and veils over their faces. Everyone watched me grope my way toward the door and did nothing. Oddly, the next day one of the sixth grade boys asked my why I acted like I was blind in church.

It seemed to me that in those days, we slept through the bad things or looked the other way. It was useless to talk about it. I didn't tell anyone about the blackouts; it didn't occur to me to say anything. I prayed about it, however, at daily mass and communion and in front of my dressing table shrine to the Blessed Virgin.

For more than a century and in countless ways, the Klan had blighted the state of Mississippi, and in the name of Christianity had desecrated many of its cherished traditions. Especially heinous was the Klan's disrespect for the way in which Mississippi families lay their loved ones to rest. There is no greater contempt for human life than an act of premeditated murder, and no greater ignominy than to hide the remains in some remote spot intended never to be found. There is no greater insult than an unmarked grave.

Yet this is exactly what the Klan was planning, on a Sunday in early May of 1964, when Preacher Killen and his friends met in the Boykin Methodist Church just south of Jackson. In its small church-yard lay those who had founded the community, and the murderers passed their headstones as they gathered in the sanctuary.

The Klan had scheduled this meeting to plot in secret the fate of the students who were soon to arrive in Mississippi. Their main concern was how to stop Mickey Schwerner, whom they'd watched since January and whose elimination Klan leadership had approved.

The Klan had gathered that night to plan the murder, and opened their meeting with a prayer.

"Oh, God, our heavenly guide," began the Klan's spiritual advisor, known to Klansmen as the Klud.

"As finite creatures of time and as dependent creatures of Thine, we acknowledge Thee as our sovereign Lord. Permit freedom and the joys thereof to forever reign throughout our land. May we as Klansmen forever have the courage of our convictions and may we always stand for Thee and our great nation. May the sweet cup of brotherly fraternity ever be ours to enjoy, and build within us that kindred spirit which will keep us unified and strong. Engender within us that wisdom kindred to honorable decision and Godly work. By the power of thy infinite spirit and the energizing virtue therein, ever keep before us our oaths of secrecy and pledges of righteousness. Bless us now in this assembly that we may honor Thee in all things, we pray in the name of Christ, our blessed Savior. Amen."

There was a pause. Preacher Killen bowed his head. "Amen," he answered with his fellow Klansmen in chorus. "Amen."

Low-flying planes were circling overhead, watching the roads for any signs that the meeting might be disrupted. Armed men who knew the secret password were stationed along the road to intercept outsiders who might try to get past them.

Inside, Preacher's good friend Sam Bowers walked into the pulpit. Sam was the Imperial Wizard; his orders to recruit enough troops to fight the battle ahead. Before a gathering of more than three hundred Mississippi Klansmen, Bowers spoke.

> The military and political situation as regards the enemy has now reached the crisis stage. Our best students of enemy strategy and technique are in almost complete agreement that the events which will occur in Mississippi this summer may well determine the fate of Christian civilization for centuries to come. We will, of course, resist to the very end the imposition of martial law in Mississippi by communist masters in Washington. Members of the White Knights would be justified in killing any civil rights workers caught outside the law.

You'd have thought he was talking about Red China, the North Vietnamese or the Soviet Union, but Bowers' enemy consisted of college kids. With its military overtones and patriotic calls to action, Bowers' bellicose language must have impressed Preacher Killen and those with him in the church that day. Using Klan standards as his guide and with his faith to fuel his ardor, Preacher Killen must have been aroused, for he carried from the meeting the urgency of what he was about to do.

Two weeks later, in the middle of the night, the Neshoba Klansmen firebombed the Mount Zion Methodist Church in Longdale, in an attempt to lure Schwerner back into Neshoba County. Mount Zion's congregation had agreed to allow Schwerner to use the church for a voter registration site.

A few days after the bombing, Mickey drove with Andrew Goodman and James Chaney to Neshoba County to investigate the ruins of the church.

AUDEN WROTE that this is the way it always happens: people go about the work of their lives while all around them other people suffer . . . "how it takes place while someone else is eating or opening a window or just walking dully along. . . ." They aren't bad people, they're busy people, ordinary and unremarkable people who pray and go to church and trust that God is taking care of things. People who vote and trust that their government is taking care of things.

We were taught to put our families first and to place the welfare of our intimate circles at the center of our lives. As a result, we lived with the knowledge that fathers were working to feed us and to make sure we had a home and clothing. We knew that mothers would prepare the food, keep the home clean, and care for us. We also learned to care for our friends and neighbors. The idea was that if each community cared for its own, our efforts would ripple out into a peaceful world.

We didn't know that outside the circumference of our inner circles decisions were being made that would make our prayers impossible to answer. We didn't know that while the priest prayed in Latin for peace there were people who were planning war. While he prayed for justice, elsewhere people were asking God to bless their plans for murder. Men were saying those hateful prayers in a community of people who were busy and ordinary and unremarkable, who voted and went to church, just like we did. And in the war of prayers that was fought in June of 1964, those men succeeded.

CHAPTER 7

The Patron Saint of Lost Causes

M Y FATHER rarely professed his love for my mother out-right, which worried me so much that I continually watched them for signs of affection. "Do you really love each other?" I asked again and again, so often that finally Grandma Lind told me to stop asking because my parents were getting upset.

My father made it sound as though my mother chased him to the altar, for instance. "One minute we were on a date, the next minute her friends were buggin' me to call her, the next minute her mother was takin' the train from Minneapolis to Washington to meet me," he said. This was his way. Rarely an agent in his own destiny, he always claimed that he'd been hoodwinked, missed a lucky break, or that someone had talked him into something against his will. A series of business opportunities came and went: a Jacuzzi dealership and his own carpet business never got off the ground. But an instinct for gambling that he and my mother tried to hide from us carried him through these disappointments and satisfied his entrepreneurial desires.

Nervous to the point of dizzy spells, my reaction to his passivity was to increase the diligence with which I looked for signs that my parents loved each other. A peck on the cheek when my father came home from work in the evening was worth half a night's sleep. Calling each other "Honey" or "Dear" meant that perhaps I could get through the morning without biting my nails. I needed to know that we were going to be all right, and I walked through the house with my ear cocked as I passed doors where my parents stood on the other side, talking.

While my mother was pregnant with me, for example, she and my father had been married for six years and lived in a two-story prefabricated Cape Cod–style house on a suburban tract of land southwest of Minneapolis that boasted few hills and fewer trees. Just south lay a farm that five years later would be cleared for the development of the first enclosed shopping mall in the United States. This was where my father would eventually sell carpet for twenty-five years to the people who built split-level prefabricated homes on the flat, treeless landscape that once had been the farm.

My parents struggled financially around the time that I was born, and my father had gone to Mississippi for three months to find work. While he was away, my mother sent him black-and-white snapshots of Linda and Gene dressed in Halloween costumes and me, a baby with a fright mask over my face. My father was upset when he received those photographs in the mail because he wanted to show us off to his relatives, but our faces were hidden behind masks of Tom and Jerry and the Frankenstein monster.

But he came back from Mississippi broke, jobless, and defeated, a kind of one-man Gettysburg: a Southerner coming in from the North and a Northerner coming in from the South. When he returned, he sold pharmaceutical goods to drugstores in small towns all over Minnesota. He worked on the road, and when he came home, he slept for long stretches, snoring and grinding his teeth.

I'll never know whether he really wanted to go back south and couldn't, or made a show of wanting to go back and wouldn't. One thing I feel certain of: my mother would never have gone. At least, not happily. My mother wanted to raise her family the way her mother and father had. She wanted him to be the breadwinner. She wanted to stay home and raise children.

But it was more than a question of roles. It was also a question of familiarity. Minneapolis was a place where my mother recognized everything. Upon this terrain she stood surefooted, her life bound on four sides by place, tradition, family, and religion. She knew that she could board the number six bus on Xerxes Avenue and that northbound it would take her to Grandma Lind's house in Linden Hills, or downtown to Dayton's and to Doctor Meader's office. Southbound she rode to Southdale Mall in Edina, where my father worked and where fast-food restaurants and strip malls began to spring up, familiar in their sameness along the edge of town.

She'd always said that she was glad we'd never had to live north of Lake Street. While Lake Street was an ambiguous marker of class and social standing (many of Minneapolis's oldest and most beautiful homes were in the Kenwood neighborhood, which lay north of Lake Street, as did the Philips neighborhood, which was one of the poorest in the city), it provided her with the means by which she placed herself on the right side of the tracks. Lake Street, in broad terms, represented to her the dividing line between the haves and the have-nots. It was also one of the racial demarcation lines that separated the whites from the blacks.

My father, however, was somehow misplaced. It wasn't that he didn't want to live in Minneapolis. He had, after all, chosen it over moving back to Neshoba County. It was that something inside him was reaching for more, something shapeless and without definition that would therefore have eluded him no matter where he put down roots. He had chosen a wife whose core values were the same as those of his mother and sisters: love of home, family, tradition, and religion. And so his wanderlust went unsatisfied, his geographical move merely a shift away from the South and the farm, rather than a dramatic change in lifestyle. He was unanchored and restless, searching the periphery of his life for a center that had disappeared decades before.

It was not that my father lacked a complete sense of direction. It was more that he moved in circles. On his days off, he wanted to go to the barbershop, play cards, or drive around the city, his destinations little diners and import shops, or filling stations with garages where he could stand with the grease monkeys and shoot the breeze while his brakes were being fixed. He wanted to watch college basketball and take a nap in front of the television set. Instead, he drove my mother to the doctor and to the grocery store. When the Lind Girls put their mother in a nursing home fifty miles west of Minneapolis, my father spent his days off there, napping in a reclining chair while my mother and Grandma Lind watched *As the World Turns*, ate chicken noodle soup in the cafeteria, and attended mass and communion.

Perhaps Aunt Louise had invited them for dinner, in her big home on Lake Minnetonka, or Aunt Billy was giving a luncheon at the Interlachen Country Club. Maybe Grandma Lind had finished our mending. Maybe my brother needed to buy a special wrench at the hardware store. Ann might have had a field trip to the Minneapolis Planetarium, and Linda was probably getting ready for a dance at the KC hall. Whatever it was, somebody needed a ride.

So he took care of his personal business in the evenings. In time, we would find out about his various hangouts around the city. We'd learn that Uncle Frank had used my father's gambling as the basis for reneging on his promise of a small business start-up loan. We would begin to suspect that for painful personal reasons my mother's refusal to learn to drive was in no small part a way to keep him close to the nest. But for now my father was the family chauffeur, and I know that he never told my mother that he had his own errands to run in his free time, as certainly as I know that he spent most of his adult life complaining to his kids about it behind her back.

I RAN AWAY from home for the first time when I was eleven years old. I wrapped a doughnut in a napkin, tucked a couple of library books under my arm, and slipped out the side door. I headed south, down the alley, walking two blocks to where Minnehaha Creek cut an S-shaped ribbon through our south Minneapolis neighborhood. From the lowest branch of a giant cottonwood hung a thick rope, knotted at the end, over where the creek widened into a deep swimming hole. My brother and his friends would take the rope in their hands, climb back up the hill as high as they could, and with a running start swing out over the opposite bank and back to the middle of the water, where they let go and jumped, the water splashing on impact into a thousand exploding prisms.

But today the swing hung limp, the grassy banks were empty, and the narrow path through the elm and sugar maple woods just beyond waited for me familiarly. My sister Ann and I often had picnics there, taking with us egg salad sandwiches wrapped in waxed paper and a thermos of Kool-Aid, walking in as far as the daylight would allow.

Which was what I meant to do now. Walk as far as I could. I thought I couldn't take it anymore. I sat on the narrow retaining wall beside the creek and racked up grievances as if it were my job to send everyone in the neighborhood to confession, where the priest would send them all straight to purgatory to atone for all the things they'd done to make my life miserable.

I was glad the boys weren't at the swing. I'd had it with boys. The victim of one of my mother's home permanents, I knew what they'd say about my hair, and I wasn't up for the humiliation. She'd sat me down on a high stool in the kitchen and covered my shoulders with an old sheet. She squeezed the wicked-smelling solution—a cross between paint thinner and the sewer gas that rose from the round grate in the basement floor—onto my scalp and with her fingers rubbed the chemicals over every strand of my black, baby-fine hair. The smell made the inside of my nose burn, and I turned my head from side to side to try to get away from it, which movement only made her grab my jaw with an ammonia-smeared glove and straighten my face dead center. As a result, my skin had broken out into a flaming case of impetigo, with pizzalike burns in the shape of her fingers over the left side of my face.

Instead of curling my hair, the permanent had kinked it up so that I looked like a witch with a bad case of acne. So my mother took the kitchen shears and cut my hair close to the scalp so that each strand, now two inches long from every chemical-seared root, resembled the short curly hairs I'd find in the tub after my father had finished bathing. In short, I was a mess.

Luckily for me, it was summer vacation, and I didn't have to go to school the next day. The abuse from the neighborhood kids was bad enough; facing a classroom full of perfect hair and creamy white complexions would have been torture. My brother and his friends had taken a hiatus from their normal routine—telling me that I looked like I came from another planet—to build a go-kart in a friend's garage. So I'd been safe for a brief, forty-eight-hour period post-permanent. But I'd made the tactical error of passing by the garage earlier in the day, and they'd fallen all over themselves finding suitable insults for the way I looked.

"Boys will be boys," my mother said. She leaned her head over the teakettle, steaming thimble-size curls into her dark, wavy hair, and I wondered what she meant. She was on her way downtown, and I followed her into the bathroom to watch her get ready. She opened the medicine cabinet and took from the shelf a small bottle of Revlon Touch 'n Glo foundation, shook it, and dabbed dots of it all over her face. "I heard that you should wear foundation when you're gardening," she said, smoothing the creamy tan liquid over her cheeks. I picked up the bottle from the sink and looked at the label.

"It protects your skin from the sun," she went on and closed her lips so that they disappeared while she rubbed the makeup with her fingers over her chin and under her nose. Then she took a black crayon and filled in her eyebrows, twisted her gold-tone lipstick tube and applied red to her lips. "Hand me a piece of toilet paper," she said. I turned around and unrolled two squares from the roller on the wall behind me and handed it to her. She folded it in half, put it up to her mouth, and pressed her lips together. When she tossed it into the wastebasket there was a red kiss mark on it.

I sat on her bed while she pulled a pair of immaculate white cotton gloves from her top dresser drawer, checked to make sure her slip wasn't showing, and put on her kidney-shaped black hat that sat tightly on her head so that her hair curled up around it. She made sure she had tokens for the bus, clicked her purse shut, and kissed me good-bye. She never went downtown without a hat and white gloves, and as I watched her walk down our street and disappear around the corner, it seemed to me that nobody could ever criticize her for not looking good enough.

I was exotic-looking, people said when I entered a room. At holidays, when Aunt Jane's living room was full to bursting with blonde-haired, blue-eyed cousins, I stuck out as freakish, too small for my age, black hair that usually brought to mind Moe from the Three Stooges and a look on my face that desperately wanted to apologize. My cousin Missy said that I looked like an Indian. My brother said that I was butt-ugly. So I'd station myself in the bathroom until dinner, cursing God in front of the mirror for making what I figured was his biggest mistake since allowing Eve to be sweet-talked by a snake into biting the cursed apple. If it was true, as the nuns said it was, that God was the Supreme Being, responsible for everything, then I laid this at his door.

I was convinced that God knew what he was doing and could do anything, but I wasn't convinced that he was good. Good was too unfairly distributed. It was for the cousins who sat pink-ribboned at the dining room table with the grown-ups, and for some cosmic reason the big steaming bowl of it had passed me by completely.

My mother was always trying to improve my appearance. "My heavenly days, put a smile on your face," she'd say when I came down for breakfast in the morning. "Nobody likes a moper."

We were the relations on the Lind side of the family that everyone felt sorry for, what with their lake homes and country club memberships and ski trips to Aspen. They'd bag up last year's clothes and send them to my mother, and she'd pull out blue-smocked dresses and white blouses with Peter Pan collars, holding them up to me, trying to talk me into liking them. "This will be perfect for church," she said as I stood beside her bed in my spanky pants and undershirt, trying on a plaid jumper that brought to mind those perky tartan coats and tams you sometimes see on hairless little Chihuahuas.

My sister Linda worked on me too. At sixteen, she'd begun to leave the house in the morning with her hair teased up into a bubble that resembled the tangled nests my mother pulled out of the family hairbrushes every couple of weeks before soaking them in ammonia water. Linda covered her skin with an orangy pancake makeup that she applied to her face with a damp sponge. She used Maybelline eyeliner, the kind that came in a little red compact with its own brush that you ran under water and swirled over the black cake inside, drawing lines around the eyes like the rings of Saturn. Though I was only eleven, she tried a few of these so-called improvements on me, thinking it would help. "Just run the brush backward through the crown for a little height," she said, with all the confidence of a regular reader of *Seventeen* magazine, succeeding only in breaking off much of what was left of my burned, brittle hair. "And a little concealer over those welts," she went on, holding my chin in her hand and dabbing at the impetigo with a salmon-toned stick of waxy makeup in a plastic lipstick tube.

The effect was stunning. The pizza marks looked like we'd added another layer of mozzarella, and the hair—well, a black Labrador stricken with mange would have elicited more sympathy than the newly formed bald spots that appeared at the top of my head.

I was a disgrace to the Lind Girl legacy, a failure at hiding my scalp and scars. And the ill-fitting castoffs, bad haircut, and layers of cheap makeup only succeeded in making my misery ludicrous. It was no use. I was a wrinkle down the front of a blouse that just wouldn't iron smooth: a Lind Girl public relations nightmare. "Well, maybe you'll outgrow it," my exasperated mother finally said, throwing up her hands in despair. "In the meantime, just offer it up."

This was often her last attempt at consolation—offering it up. On her dresser, draped in an ancient rosary, stood a plaster statue of Saint Jude, patron saint of lost causes. In later years, when Vatican II was downsizing and stripped many patron saints of their duties, Saint Jude's lost-cause status had survived. I'd always liked the fact that there was an actual saint for little girls like me. I'd made the short pilgrimage to my mother's dresser-top shrine on several occasions, on the off chance that here was someone who might advocate for me. If God had let me slip through the cracks, at least he'd made certain allowances for it. I'd given him that much, which didn't go very far, given that despite everyone's efforts to conceal it, I stayed exotic-looking for the next several years.

So I headed for the creek. My best friend at the time was Laura Ingalls Wilder. Here was a family worth knowing. Pioneer stock. A schoolteacher mother who taught her daughters to read by the light of a kerosene lamp. A father who stayed home at night and played the fiddle for his little girls. I could lean back into the cool grass and pretend that this was my family, forgetting for a few hours that I'd have to go home eventually. For this gift of temporary oblivion, Saint Jude made a certain kind of sense.

And so the circularity of our lives persisted, any notion of breaking free made impossible by its very absence from our consciousness. When you have to spend a good part of your day praying to cope with a family whose size you didn't choose; when a pope whose name you can't remember has commanded you to do so, regardless of the stability of your marriage, the adequacy of your income, or the stamina of your body; and when whatever is left of you gets divided between color-coordinating your towels, raising five kids, and caring for an errant husband, what gets missed?

I ran away the summer of 1964. I was eleven years old.

For all of the telephone conversations my father had with his family in Philadelphia that summer, he never talked to us about the disappearance of the three civil rights workers. In fact, he never sat with us as we watched the events unfold throughout the summer on television. So we heard about it each evening from Walter Cronkite, who brought us the latest news from what he called "bloody Neshoba."

While my father sat outside on the front stoop smoking cigarettes and drinking beer with the neighbors, my mother stood at the stove making the gravy for the pot roast. Ann and I were in our living room watching film footage of our first glimpses of the little town of Philadelphia. We saw the charred foundation of a rural church that had been firebombed by the Ku Klux Klan. We watched newsreels of hooded men and burning crosses. The Reverend Martin Luther King Jr. spoke from the steps of the county courthouse while police holding billy clubs waited at the edge of the mostly black crowd.

My father's silence on the subject signaled to us that we were to be silent too. He talked to us about the snakes in Grandma Ora's henhouse but never said a word to us about the Klan's infiltration of local government in Neshoba County.

Night after night, we saw the FBI poster of the three missing young men. Dick Gregory arrived to help with the search for the bodies. Reserve officers in coast guard vessels dragged the Pearl River. The burned skeleton of a station wagon was pulled from a swamp. Still, my father said nothing. For all the attachment we felt to the news reports, we might as well have been watching *Gunsmoke*.

The search continued for six weeks with no major developments, and hope flagged that the three young men would be found alive. During these slow news days, the coverage of the incident included more and more clips of the white population of Philadelphia, to show how they were coping.

If something terrible had taken place, nobody would ever know it. The place was the picture of calm. Old men sat in rocking chairs on sweeping front porches that were shaded with flowering magnolia. A group of men stood laughing with a uniformed officer in a cowboy hat, who put his foot up on the hood of a squad car, slapped his leg, and spat tobacco into the street. Women in dresses, high heels, and hats walked out of the Mars Brothers Department Store. They carried shopping bags and waved to a neighbor in a passing car.

From a thousand miles to the north, we participated in their avoidance, joining countless others whose desire for normalcy looked suspiciously like indifference. I heard my father use the word *hoax* on the telephone. But that was all I heard. He went to work in the morning and came home at night as if nothing unusual in his hometown had happened at all. Mississippi Congressman Arthur Winstead, another of my father's cousins, about whom my father spoke with respect, repeated his belief that it had to be a hoax. If not, he said, it was certainly an isolated incident.

In August, there was the shaky aerial footage from a helicopter of a dam being excavated with a bulldozer. The county coroner spoke to reporters that the bodies of the three young men had been found. James Chaney's parents, faces stricken, followed behind his flower-covered coffin, holding the hands of a little boy who cried for his brother. Andrew Goodman's mother collapsed into her husband's arms when her son's coffin was lowered from the plane at Newark International Airport. A slim young woman in sunglasses, Mickey Schwerner's widow, Rita, walked out of church after her husband's funeral.

There were stories to tell, but my father wasn't telling them.

Again he belonged to neither place and tried to balance the two forces that pulled at him, but the life that had formed him constrained him to silence. Years later, when we finally discussed what had happened, my father's memory—normally so clear—couldn't bring it back with certainty. Perhaps nobody from home talked with him about it. Perhaps he didn't ask. Perhaps he didn't read the newspaper stories. This he did remember: he believed, as many did, that if he didn't talk about it, the crisis would simply blow over in time. Perhaps somewhere there were families who talked about these things at the dinner table, but that steaming plate of goodness had apparently passed us by.

PART TWO

Kin

CHAPTER 8

The Soft Glow of Our Ignorance

EVERY YEAR, a morning would come in early May when my mother took down her sheer white priscillas from the living room windows and laundered them for spring housecleaning. This afternoon both of us worked in the dining room. She stood there ironing.

Earlier, she'd put the curtains through the wringer, fresh from rinse water that was tinted with bluing, then rolled them up and placed them in the freezer. When they were frozen, she removed them one by one and spread them crisp and slightly stiffened over the ironing board. Then she put her index finger in her mouth and touched it to the bottom of the iron for a split second. If it was hot enough to hiss, she'd place the iron facedown and nose its tip into each ruffle, smoothing the wrinkles with the crackle and pop of a ship's bow breaking through a thin layer of ice.

Behind her, the windows she'd polished with pieces of newspaper stood naked. Without the curtains they normally hid behind, the

sun shone too brightly through the unfiltered glass, and it seemed
to me that they let too much of the world in.

The room had that twice-a-year smell: slightly of vinegar, slightly
of ammonia. Each spring and fall my mother tore the house apart
and cleaned each cupboard, washed down all the walls, polished
every bit of tarnished silver, and laundered dust ruffles, slipcovers,
and every curtain in the house. For my mother, it was important
to prepare for and recover from winter: as if the season were a kind
of affliction the calendar presented to her on a regular basis. Something predictable but beyond her control, over which she could only
exert the power to scrub and disinfect. Since cleanliness was her
solution to just about anything, it was thus the means by which my
mother ordered the world, a comfort that got her through her af-
flictions, especially those she never talked about.

But this day was different. The house was breezy from doors and
windows open to air the rooms at the end of a long, dreary winter.
It was 1966; May was my birthday month, and in two weeks I would
be thirteen. My mother must have decided that this would be the
right time to speak to me. She stood behind the ironing board,
shoulders stooped over her silver and black Proctor-Silex, her upper
arm stiff above a bent elbow that worked back and forth, pushing
with her forearm the weight of her whole body, smoothing out a
frosty white field of curtain.

I sat at the dining room table. The felt-lined box that held her
silver service—a long-ago wedding gift from Grandma and Papa
Lind—was open before me. I took from it cake servers, teaspoons,
and butter knives, and wiped them down with an old pair of my
father's cotton briefs that my mother had transformed into a rag by
cutting away the elastic waistband. I wrapped the rag around my
hand and dipped it into the open jar of silver polish, careful not to
let my fingers touch the opening in the front of the brief that once
had been the fly.

"I suppose you're at the age now when you'll want to have this on hand," she said into the ironing board. I looked up from my work. She set the iron upright, anchoring down a corner of the curtain to keep it from slipping entirely to the floor. The rest cascaded down in front like a floor-length skirt and fell into sheer white folds at her feet. The soft, cool breeze from the open windows rippled across the folds, as if unseen fingers were lifting them slightly. If it hadn't been for the red-and-white-checked apron she wore for housecleaning—the one that covered her whole front—my mother would have looked like a bride, with the fullness of a white gown billowing out before her.

She reached into the pocket of her apron. From it she pulled out a small pink box, with the words KOTEX JUNIOR STARTER KIT printed on the top.

I took the box and opened it. Inside was a rectangular cotton pad covered with white gauze that extended out a few inches on each end, and a white elastic belt shaped like two Vs sewn together, a silver garter attached to the point of each.

I was so embarrassed, I didn't know what to say. Had she noticed that I'd stuffed wads of toilet paper between my legs last week? In the middle of *Bonanza*, I'd doubled over with cramps, jumped up from the vinyl ottoman, and once safely locked in the bathroom, found a red stain on the cotton panel of my Days of the Week underpants.

If she did, she didn't say so. "The instructions are in the box," she said, and I pulled out a small booklet with drawings of faceless, hairless, breastless figures fastening the elastic belt around their hips and slipping the gauze ends of the pad through the garters.

Months later, I would lock myself in the bathroom and squat over a hand mirror I'd placed on the cold linoleum beneath me. An instruction sheet in one hand, a slim tampon in a white cardboard tube in the other, I fumbled to insert the tube into just the right place in all those unfamiliar folds, horrified at what I saw in the mirror and frightened at the prospect of pain. What if I put it in the wrong opening? How would I know? The diagram showed a drawing that looked like a flower, with three holes: top, middle, and bottom. I was aiming for the middle.

Against the teaching of Sister St. Edmund, who told us in our marriage and family life class that the church forbade unmarried girls to use tampons, I dug with my fingers between the petals of my perineum, then took a deep breath and inserted the white tube.

It wasn't a tidy job. I'd failed to read the part of the instructions that said that the tube was to be discarded. So for two hours I waddled around the house with a sharp pain in my vagina that oddly reminded me of the way my throat felt when a nurse had forced me to swallow a horse-size aspirin with only a tiny sip of water after I'd had my tonsils out.

But for now, the box with the pad and the elastic belt were just enough. I got up from the table, went into my bedroom, and put the box behind the white cotton slips and flat, cupless bras with the tiniest of bows at the straps that my mother had folded neatly into snowy piles in my underwear drawer. We said nothing more to each other when I came back into the dining room. She was doubly bent over her ironing, as if there wasn't muscle enough in her whole body to remove the wrinkles from the immaculate white curtain. I sat back down at the table and resumed my work. With one hand, I picked up a silver pickle fork from the felted wooden box, and with the other hand the white cotton rag, making sure, as I always did, that my fingers wouldn't touch the opening in the front where once upon a time the fly used to be.

IN JUNE OF 1966, when he was forty-six years old, my father bought his first new car. It was a four-door Dodge Coronet sedan in a kind of no-frills dull bronze that lacked chrome trim, whitewall tires, and a radio. Worse, it had no air-conditioning, and vinyl seats that got so hot that when you opened the doors the interior belched out the aroma of burning tennis shoes. But it was reliable, and in it he and my mother could take us on our first family exodus from Minnesota—destination: Mississippi.

We left in July, and the entire week beforehand woke to summer mornings so hot and humid that the cotton shorts and tops we pulled from our dresser drawers went limp before we put them on.

Linda had graduated from high school in June. She had a summer job behind the cosmetics counter at the System Drug, and stayed behind to work. So we numbered six. Once my mother had crammed Gene, Ann, and me shoulder to shoulder into the backseat, she wedged the cargo she thought we needed onto the floor in front of us. The result was that our feet rested on suitcases, boxes of gifts, coolers of food, and thermoses of Kool-Aid, our legs bent at the knees and our thighs pushed up against our chests. Blocking the rear window were blankets and pillows that she'd stacked up behind us, just in case we wanted to sleep along the way.

For three sultry twelve-hour days we drove south along two-lane highways that followed the twists and turns of the Mississippi River. With my father at the helm, we passed through a suffocating heat wave. It was like Moses parting the Red Sea: the deeper south we drove, the more heavily the heat and humidity rose up on either side of us.

The sun beat down upon our small car until I was sure that the paint on the hood would bubble. Flies and moths melted when they hit the windshield, and the asphalt shimmered up ahead. In the car's close, steamy interior, our bare shoulders burned when they brushed against the metal trim around the windows. The blankets and pillows stacked on the window ledge behind us baked in the sun like bread in an oven. They even smelled yeasty.

Ann and I gasped for air. Thinking we could crack open the window for a breath or a breeze, we used our shirttails to protect our fingers when we grabbed the red-hot window handles. But our efforts were rewarded only with a rush of fire-breathing wind that soldered damp hair to sticky foreheads and offered no relief.

My brother felt superior for being fifteen and having his learner's permit, and from time to time my father would pull over and let him drive the car. But most of the time he rolled up his window and calmly turned the pages of *Mad* magazine, cool and detached. When I rolled my window open, the wind ripped apart the pages of his magazine and he leaned across Ann to whack me in the gut with it.

"Mom, make Gene stop it," Ann complained, her head back against the seat.

"Can't we stop soon?" My stomach was starting to seize up.

My mother, for fear of becoming carsick herself, sat sphinxlike in the front seat across from my father, fanning herself with the folded-up road map. She kept her movements to a minimum and looked straight out the window at the road ahead. "You kids shut up and behave back there," she said without turning around. The impact of her words hit the windshield and lost all their force by the time they reached us in the backseat.

The shoulders of her white blouse had grown dark with perspiration. She reached down into the striped canvas bag at her feet and pulled out a powder puff she'd made with one of my father's white cotton handkerchiefs.

Before we left, she'd poured a cupful of cornstarch into the middle of the handkerchief and tied the four corners together into a knot. Holding the knot in her hand, she dabbed at her arms and neck with the homemade powder puff, leaving a sheer film of white cornstarch over her skin, making it look paler and even more ghostly, since she was already gray from feeling queasy.

She went back to fanning herself with the road map, an AAA TripTik that showed the route my father was taking from Minneapolis to Meridian. Gene smiled. "Hey Mom, let me take a look at the map," he said.

She turned around and handed over her fan with a sigh.

He took the map and hit me on the arm with it.

I was fishing in my pocket for one of the foil-wrapped towelettes I'd taken from the gas station bathroom at our last stop. Rubbing my arm with one hand, I tore the package open with my teeth, unfolded the spongy wet paper, and wiped my face with it. It smelled like a combination of rubbing alcohol and Jergens lotion, and for a moment, I forgot about the heat.

By the afternoon the vinyl upholstery grew slippery with sweat, so my mother spread our pink Barbie and Ken beach towels over the backseat for us to sit on. Soon drenched with perspiration, however, Barbie and Ken slid back and forth across the wet vinyl, bunching up between our legs, behind the smalls of our backs, and into the infinitesimal space between each of our bodies.

We suffered for lack of air-conditioning, and we really missed the radio. My father, who loved to whistle when he drove, blew his heart into his entire repertoire, which totaled about six songs. Lips puckered, cheeks puffed out like Dizzy Gillespie, he whistled from Minneapolis to Davenport, from Davenport to Cairo, and from Cairo to Memphis. From "All I Want for Christmas Is My Two Front Teeth" to "I'm an Old Cowhand from the Rio Grande," to "Zip-a-dee-doo-dah," over and over and over again.

"Get your elbows out of my side," Ann yelled at Gene, who liked to tickle us until it hurt.

Then she began to whine. "Mom, my leg aches."

No response.

Ann whined again, this time ratcheting up her voice a notch. I knew she wanted to move into the front seat, displacing Liz, who sat between my mother and my father.

Liz kicked the seat and let out a wail.

Just then, for the fourth time in half an hour, my father began to whistle "I Found My Thrill on Blueberry Hill."

My mother broke. "Windy, stop it," she shouted and pressed her hands against her temples. "You people are driving me crazy."

The car went silent. She held her lips pressed together in a straight line that made me wish she'd yell again, or tell my father to turn the car around and go home: anything to ease the tension. My father, who'd been driving with his left hand, his right arm resting across the top of the front seat, put both hands on the wheel. Liz shrank back into herself.

Ann and I glanced at each other sideways.

Gene was looking at the highway signs. After a few moments he began to read aloud, "Welcome to Hannibal, Missouri, Boyhood Home of Samuel Langhorne Clemens—the Famous Mark Twain."

"This is it," my father said. "We're stopping here."

We pulled off the highway and drove through Hannibal, past three-story white houses that were set back from the sidewalks, with wide, sweeping lawns, open front porches, and tall shade trees. My father was following signs that pointed in the direction of the Elks Club Picnic Area. He turned right, and the car passed under an archway of tree branches made to look like a pair of antlers. We stopped beside a small grassy picnic area. The river bordered one end of the park, and grain elevators rose up on the opposite bank.

I don't think we ate a single meal in a restaurant the entire three days we drove to Mississippi. Had we been stranded along some remote stretch of Tennessee highway for a week, my mother was prepared. She'd packed boxes with jars of peanut butter and loaves of Wonder Bread, hot dog buns, bags of raisins and tiny boxes of cereal that we could slit open down the front, eat from, and throw away afterward. There were containers of Carnation powdered milk that she mixed with water in a mason jar, shook, and poured (warm and lumpy) over the cereal, instant Tang that we drank from paper Dixie cups, a thermos and envelopes of presweetened Kool-Aid. She'd brought potato chips, Hydrox cookies, and Fig Newtons. There was a bag of navel oranges and a bunch of fragrant brown bananas.

In the cooler she'd packed frozen hot dogs, a ring of bologna, Miracle Whip, butter, ketchup, mustard, and a jar of Welch's grape jelly. She'd cut up carrot and celery sticks, little bite-sized radishes and pickle slices. There was a portable barbecue grill and a bag of charcoal, paper plates, cups, and napkins, and a box of plastic knives, forks, and spoons that we washed in gas station bathrooms and reused.

My father parked the car beside a stone table with attached benches. Gene lugged the picnic basket over, and my mother handed me a roll of paper towels, which I tore off one by one and placed in front of everyone. She took out peanut butter sandwiches wrapped in waxed paper and passed them out. Liz had to pee and was running around the table with her hand between her legs, her breath coming out in short puffs, her little forehead puckered with anxiety. My mother got up and took her behind a cluster of trees. Ann poured the Kool-Aid.

My father took his sandwich, folded it down the middle, and ate it in two gulps. He washed it down with a cupful of cherry Kool-Aid, grabbed a handful of radishes, and lay down on his back in the grass beside the table. With one arm, he shaded his eyes from the sun. With the other, he popped radishes, one by one, into his mouth.

"Y'know, this heat is nothin'," he began. "We picked cotton in heat worse'n this, day in and day out." He popped in another radish then sketched the scene for us. We'd heard about picking cotton before, especially when we dared complain about helping with dishes or making our beds. He'd had it worse than we did for his entire childhood. We didn't really understand it, though we would get a clearer picture of it very soon.

"Come end of August, we all harvested cotton, ever' one of us, no matter how small. We crawled down rows so long we couldn't see the end of 'em. Mama couldn't keep up with patchin' the holes we wore in the knees of our pants, so we didn't bother tellin' her when they wore out, though she could see it well enough."

Behind him, the Mississippi River flowed wide and calm. The breeze cooled as it passed eastward over the water, and when it reached us it carried the damp smells of mud and rotting fish. Here the river was so deep that it had turned black. Just beyond us, it disappeared around a bend.

"Wasn't nothin' she could do about the sunburn on our necks 'cept give us a hat that did nothin', really, but get in the way, and sometimes she'd rub a liniment of lard into the cuts on our hands at the end of the day."

An ant was carrying a bread crumb across the stone table. I poked at it with a shoestring potato. Across from me, my mother opened up the box of vanilla wafers and gave one to Liz. Then she sighed, got up, and crossed the grass to the car. Gene had finished his sandwich and was standing over the open hood, checking the oil with a paper towel. My mother sat down in the front seat, shaded now by a tree overhead, left the door open, laid her head back, and closed her eyes.

"At the end of each row Daddy Bob'd planted a watermelon," he went on. "So at the end of summer when we'd finished picking a row of cotton, he'd call over to us to set beside him. Then he'd break open one of the watermelons that he'd been watchin' all summer, and tell his stories. Wasn't any shade 'cept 'bout a sliver from the mule and plow. The flies was ever'where bitin' our legs and arms and we'd shoo 'em away with our hats, though our hands was so sticky that they come right back to eat the sweetness off 'em."

Gene went to a small pump by the river and filled a thermos that he carried back to the car. He unscrewed the radiator cap and poured in the water.

"Daddy Bob told us that Uncle Titus'd been caught with his hand in the school district's till two years before. Five thousand dollars gone."

Liz crawled into the car beside my mother. My mother didn't open her eyes, and my father didn't stop talking. Ann and I sat down on the grass, one on either side of him, passing the box of vanilla wafers back and forth across the field of Munsingwear blue that was my father's sport shirt.

"We knew that Daddy Bob'd mortgaged the farm to repay Titus's debt and that we had Titus to thank that we were livin' with Pappy and pickin' someone else's cotton in pants with no knees and no seat, though Daddy never said a bad word about Titus. He just helped 'im out and restored the family name."

In the car, my mother had fallen asleep with her mouth open, her head leaning against the back of the seat. Liz was also asleep, her head in my mother's lap. My father sat up and looked over at them. "You two be good girls now and clean this up for your mother," he said to Ann and me. He got up, put his hands in his pockets, and began to whistle. He walked across the grass to the curb, where my brother squatted beside the car, testing the air pressure on the tires.

Just south of Memphis, my father started looking for U.S. Highway 61. It would take us across the Tennessee line into Mississippi and south all the way to Vicksburg. "Here it is," he said when the sign appeared. "Vicksburg, two hundred and fifty-five miles."

The farther we drove from home, the more the state of Mississippi became The South. Stories filled the spaces between the mile markers and were illustrated by the changing landscape of the river, trees, farms, and cities. Beyond the changing colors of the waterway, the silvery shimmer of leaves, the hills bordered by snake-rail fences and the silhouettes of weathered farm buildings, history was not remembered but translated, and my father was its interpreter.

"Y'know, the Civil War wasn't about slavery," he said. "It was about states' rights."

States' rights. That spring, states' rights had been my undoing. In the Civil War unit of my American history class, two eighth grade teams had held a debate. The team from Sister Geralda's class had argued for the South, and my team, from Sister St. Edmund's class, had argued for the North. The North had come to the debate woefully unprepared. Certain of victory, we'd assumed that since the North had won the war, we would naturally win the debate. Our opponents, however, had done their homework. The South argued for the sovereignty of states. "Local control of government," Sharon O'Brien had argued. "The right of the people to make their own rules, without federal interference."

We had nothing to refute them with. We had concentrated wholly on slavery as immoral and therefore to be abolished. Period.

"Lincoln was interested in preserving the Union," Sharon shot back. "Slavery was not the first thing on his mind."

We were indignant. "What about the Emancipation Proclamation? Wasn't Lincoln an abolitionist martyr?"

Sharon pulled out a biography of Lincoln, opened it to a previously marked page, and began to read. "The Emancipation Proclamation freed no slaves. It only freed slaves in the South, where Lincoln had no jurisdiction." And on and on while we sat, silent and stupid.

Had we read Mississippi's Declaration of Secession, we would have known that Mississippi broke away from the Union precisely to preserve the institution of slavery:

> Our position is so thoroughly identified with the institution of slavery—the greatest material interest of the world. Its labor supplies the product which constitutes by far the largest and most important portions of commerce of the earth. These products are peculiar to the climate verging on the tropical regions, and by an imperious law of nature, none but the black race can bear exposure to the tropical sun. These products have become necessities of the world, and a blow at slavery is a blow at commerce and civilization.
>
> . . .
>
> It [the North] advocates Negro equality, socially and politically, and promotes insurrection and incendiarism in our midst.

Had we done our homework, we would have known that Lincoln had been constrained by the Constitution: legally, a slave was a man's property; under the Constitution, nobody could be deprived of his property without due process of law. We would have known that Lincoln was against slavery on moral grounds but that he had also spoken out about the inferiority of the black race. The abolition of slavery finally came about in no small measure to help Lincoln win the war: each side needed allies, but France and England would only come to the aid of whichever side would oppose slavery.

Yet the rhetoric on both sides of the argument had become so sanitized that the South was convinced that the war was about states' rights and the North believed that it had a mandate from President Lincoln to abolish slavery.

"How do you think the mills in the North sold their goods at low prices to good Yankee ladies if the South couldn't sell its cotton cheaply?" Sharon concluded.

Had the South been as well prepared for battle as our opponents, the Confederacy may well have won the war. As it was, we were not able to deal with the idea that the North had benefited from slavery too, and that Lincoln had used the issue shrewdly, as a tool to bring the Union back together.

But it would be many years before I studied these details carefully. On that hot summer day in 1966, all I knew was that ideologically, the South had won our class debate.

"That's right," my father said. "Don't let nobody tell you the North won cause it was better'n the South." He cleared his throat. "The North won because the South ran out of supplies and men. Then they won again because the carpetbaggers took everything we had and left us to fend for ourselves. There was nothin' left. Not for a long time. A hundred years."

As my father drove us to Mississippi, the patina of his ideal shone untarnished in the soft glow of our ignorance. His stories distracted us from our leg cramps, heat prostration, and bickering. From the way my father told it, you'd think the battle of Vicksburg was still being fought. The valor of the citizens under siege in the city, starving as they were in dugouts, rose up glorious in our minds. Confederate flags were hoisted up in our imaginations. Southern ladies were making bandages. Young men signed up willingly to fight.

"Did anybody in your family fight in the Civil War?" I asked from the backseat.

"Yep," he said. "Pappy had a brother who died. Uncle Henry.

Got shot in Vicksburg, sticking his hand out of a dugout to reach for an apple. Ruby'll know. She knows all that. Who died when and where and of what."

It turns out that Great Uncle Henry didn't even fight at Vicksburg. He was shot during a minor skirmish in northern Mississippi, died, and was buried before he got to the hospital. As an adult, I was given a newspaper clipping from 1864 that refuted the story.

My father was on his way home, and if there were painful events to remember, they weren't told outright. It was present, however, in his need to transform them into something beautiful. Somewhere beneath the surface he must have believed that the truth was a small sacrifice to make in order to preserve the monument of the South that rose up in his memory.

CHAPTER 9

Monuments and Ruins

WHEN WE CROSSED THE STATE LINE into Mississippi—
THE MAGNOLIA STATE WELCOMES YOU—we started to
count the number of small towns we passed along the
highway: Glover, Tunica, Dundee, Clarksdale, Hushkupena, Shelby,
Winstonville, and Mound Bayou. We had to count thirty before we
could stop to use a bathroom. My father saw a sign in the shape of
a shell on our left, pulled into a gas station somewhere past Mound
Bayou, and told the man in the blue coveralls to fill it up with
regular.

Just beside the gas station was a building whose white paint was
flaking off the siding like dry skin. The tin-colored sky above it
shimmered in the heat from the roof reflecting upward. A scoliotic
front porch stretched across the front of the building, where two
Negro men sat talking to each other on the steps. Their faces were
lined, their shoulders stooped, and each wore a white dress shirt and
a brown felt hat, the kind Perry Mason wore on television. They
got up when my father approached the steps. Suspenders held up

their trousers, and one of them hooked his thumbs behind them.

"Afternoon, boys," my father said, and went up to the porch, where there stood a red Coca-Cola vending machine. He fished a dime out of his pocket, put it into the slot in the machine, opened the little door, and out came a small, green bottle of Coke. He stuck the top of the bottle into the opener on the front of the machine and popped off the cap. Then he tilted his head back and drank the whole bottle at once, his Adam's apple bobbing with every swallow. The men at the bottom of the steps watched him too, smiling, and didn't sit back down until he'd passed them again at the bottom of the stairs. "Hot today, ain't it?" my father said.

"Yes, sir, it is," one of the men replied.

At thirteen, I'm sure it was the first time I'd ever seen a black person firsthand. My images of black people had come right out of central casting, scripted in Hollywood and bound by television and movie screens. I'd seen the contented slaves in *Gone With the Wind*, the deferential black housekeepers in *Miracle on 34th Street*, *It's a Wonderful Life*, and *Mr. Blandings Builds His Dream House*. I'd seen Sidney Poitier in *Lilies of the Field* and watched Martin Luther King Jr. on television. From time to time we'd laughed at Godfrey Cambridge or Dick Gregory on *The Ed Sullivan Show*.

I stared now at the scene that had unfolded before my eyes as though I were sitting in my living room at home.

CLARKSDALE. Mound Bayou. Blues lovers everywhere knew that in 1937, Bessie Smith had died needlessly after a car accident because the hospital in Clarksdale, Mississippi, had refused to treat a black woman. What they may not have known was that because of it, nearby Mound Bayou had later become the first black town in Mississippi to begin to organize for voting rights. Mound Bayou was different: its leadership had successfully created a separate but equal black community, whose citizens had been empowered to work in their own self-interest and that of their town. As a result, they conducted a fund-raising campaign to build a hospital for blacks, and were able to raise more than a hundred thousand dollars from local contributions. In 1942, the fifty-two-bed Taborian Hospital opened its doors. Never again would a black person die in the delta for lack of treatment.

But the construction of the hospital had larger implications. By necessity it drew black medical professionals to the area, and these highly educated and successful men and women used their influence to organize local citizens to begin the struggle for equal rights. In 1956, leaders from the community had made the decision to focus their efforts on the issue of voting rights. By 1963, they had worked with national civil rights organizations to plan Freedom Summer, and decided to recruit college kids from the North to participate.

One of those leaders was Clarksdale pharmacist Aaron Henry, who two years earlier, in 1964, had traveled to Queens College in New York City, where he stood before an audience of undergraduate students and described the situation for them in detail. Blacks were being intimidated and beaten for trying to register to vote. Blacks were required to pass, to the registrar's satisfaction, a prohibitively difficult examination in order to register, having to interpret the U.S. Constitution or a section of Mississippi's state constitution and answer ridiculous questions like, "How many bubbles in a bar of soap?"

Of course the loophole lay in the words "to the registrar's satisfaction." Voting records show that even blacks that had been able to interpret either constitution almost always failed the examination, while whites that left whole sections blank had had their applications approved. Often the white registrar hadn't even graduated from high school, while a black professional with a Ph.D. failed the test.

Dr. Henry's talk had taken place during Freedom Week, and he was one of several speakers who had come to convince this group of students that the time for action was now. One of his listeners was Andy Goodman.

———

MY MOTHER came out of the bathroom at the side of the gas station and handed the key to Ann and me. "It's filthy," she said. "Cover the seat with paper and don't touch anything."

I do not remember if there were signs that said COLORED or WHITES ONLY over the doors of the bathrooms. I did not cringe when my father called the men "boys." I wouldn't have known what lay behind the men's deferential behavior toward my father.

I did notice that the window in the bathroom was broken and had been patched with a piece of brown cardboard. I noticed that the toilet seat had dried blotches on it and that the water inside of the toilet was rusty red. I noticed that the man who pumped the gasoline and cleaned the bugs off the windshield had grease on his hands and under his fingernails. I noticed that he had a grizzly beard and brownish teeth.

I resented that my father got to drink a cold bottle of pop while in the backseat my mother was pouring lukewarm Kool-Aid for the rest of us. I didn't want the lukewarm Kool-Aid. When I asked my dad if I could have a dime to buy a bottle of pop, he said okay. He gave me a dime, but when I started for the steps where the old men sat, he told me to give him the dime. Then he went to the steps and the men got up again and he brought the cold bottle of pop to the car. We shared it, us four kids, each one taking a swig, wiping off the top with a paper towel and passing it around. When Ann wanted to take the empty bottle back to the porch to put it in the empties case, my father took it from her and carried it back himself. Once again, the men stood up when he went up the steps and didn't sit back down until he got to the car.

When we arrived in Vicksburg, my father stopped to look at the map. We were going to stay with Uncle Arby, Aunt Emily, and our cousin Darla, but he didn't know where they lived. He and Gene unfolded the map across the hood of the car and bent over it, talking. My mother moved into the backseat and Gene took her place in front, the map folded in his hand so that he could help my father find his way.

When we pulled up in front of the house, Uncle Arby pushed open the front door, having been on the lookout for us. He walked across the lawn, taking long-legged strides to greet us, a smile on his face and a hand waving hello. He opened the door to help my mother from the car.

The most remarkable resemblance between my father and his brother was the way they laughed, which happened simultaneously when my father emerged from behind the wheel. Like a pair of Precious Pups from the cartoons, their necks almost disappeared between hunched-up shoulders that shook up and down in tandem. Their eyes crinkled shut to a slit, and each one put his tongue between his teeth so that the air hissed on the exhale.

It would be many years before the children of the northern relations could fully appreciate the southern relations. We weren't friendly children, and it must have been as difficult for family on my father's side to get to know us as it was for us to feel comfortable with them. Let's face it: we'd never traveled out of our home state and had rarely ventured forth from our little Catholic enclave. Plus, we'd had hardly more than our father's stories to prepare us for the differences.

Aunt Emily was a wonderful cook, but from the looks of our plates at the end of a meal, you'd think she'd given us rattlesnake meat. In fact, she'd prepared fried okra with a crunchy cornmeal crust, and black-eyed peas, and butter beans cooked with pork. These delicacies were staples in the kitchens of southern cooks, but to my northern palate, they were inedible. The okra tasted bitter, the butter beans mushy and tasteless, and the black-eyed peas so unappetizing to look at that I couldn't put one in my mouth. The corn bread was white, dry, and unsweetened, the iced tea full of sugar, and the fried chicken greasy. Ann and I picked at our food, moving it around the plate with our forks to make it look like we'd eaten something.

After dinner we went outside with Darla, who was five years younger than I was and whose drawl made her difficult to understand. It took her twice as long to say something, as simple words like *meat* and *milk* became polysyllabic.

I was also unable to see Darla for who she was: the much-beloved and long-awaited only child of parents who, in middle age, had had a daughter born on her daddy's birthday. Instead, I was envious. Darla was pretty. Her hair fell down over her shoulders in thick blonde curls.

Darla was confident. Both her parents adored her, but it was very clear that her relationship with Uncle Arby was something special. It didn't matter what he was discussing, or with whom; if Darla came into the room, his attention turned toward her like a leaf toward a window, and she climbed into his lap comfortably, settling in while he went back to his conversation. It was wonderful to watch, but something inside of me twisted up with envy.

I wasn't good at making new friends and had spent a good deal of the past couple of years in my room, where the characters in the books I read had become better friends to me than any others I could imagine existed in the real world. So I naturally lacked the social skills that might have allowed me to become happily acquainted with my cousin Darla, and I showed it by turning resentful.

"What do y'all do in Minnenap'lis?" she asked Ann and me while she opened her pink Barbie case and started showing us a yellow strapless evening gown with an overskirt. I was too old for Barbies, and tried to look bored. Yet we were eyeing each other, scoping each other out. So I picked up a tiny black shoe from the drawer at the bottom of the Barbie case, just to see what she would do.

"Nothing," I said. It seemed true. What did we do at home? I couldn't come up with anything that would have sounded interesting. Darla had lived in California. There wasn't much to boast about, by comparison.

She took the shoe from me and slipped it over Barbie's foot. "I don't like people to touch my Barbie stuff," she said.

Virginia Winstead, 1940.
(AUTHOR'S FAMILY COLLECTION)

Wilbur Winstead, USMC, ca. 1941.
(AUTHOR'S FAMILY COLLECTION)

Winstead siblings, Christmas 1962. From left: Gene, Mary, Ann,
Linda and Liz (in Linda's lap). (AUTHOR'S FAMILY COLLECTION)

Grandma Ora, ca. 1916. (AUTHOR'S FAMILY COLLECTION)

Sharecroppers at Grandma Ora's funeral, 1943. (AUTHOR'S FAMILY COLLECTION)

Grandma and Papa Lind, 1952. (AUTHOR'S FAMILY COLLECTION)

Andrew Goodman, ten years old.
(FAMILY COLLECTION OF CAROLYN GOODMAN)

Andrew Goodman in off-Broadway play,
twenty years old.
(FAMILY COLLECTION OF CAROLYN GOODMAN)

*Wilbur Winstead and Knights of
Columbus basketball team, ca. 1965.*

(AUTHOR'S FAMILY COLLECTION)

MISSING
CALL FBI

THE FBI IS SEEKING INFORMATION CONCERNING THE DISAPPEARANCE AT
PHILADELPHIA, MISSISSIPPI, OF THESE THREE INDIVIDUALS ON JUNE 21, 1964. EXTENSIVE
INVESTIGATION IS BEING CONDUCTED TO LOCATE GOODMAN, CHANEY, AND SCHWERNER,
WHO ARE DESCRIBED AS FOLLOWS:

	ANDREW GOODMAN	JAMES EARL CHANEY	MICHAEL HENRY SCHWERNER
RACE:	White	Negro	White
SEX:	Male	Male	Male
DOB:	November 23, 1943	May 30, 1943	November 6, 1939
POB:	New York City	Meridian, Mississippi	New York City
AGE:	20 years	21 years	24 years
HEIGHT:	5'10"	5'7"	5'9" to 5'10"
WEIGHT:	150 pounds	135 to 140 pounds	170 to 180 pounds
HAIR:	Dark brown; wavy	Black	Brown
EYES:	Brown	Brown	Light blue
TEETH:	Good; none missing		
SCARS AND MARKS:		1 inch cut scar 2 inches above left ear	Pock mark center of forehead, slight scar on bridge of nose, appendectomy scar, broken leg scar.

**SHOULD YOU HAVE OR IN THE FUTURE RECEIVE ANY INFORMATION
CONCERNING THE WHEREABOUTS OF THESE INDIVIDUALS, YOU ARE
REQUESTED TO NOTIFY ME OR THE NEAREST OFFICE OF THE FBI.
TELEPHONE NUMBER IS LISTED BELOW.**

DIRECTOR
FEDERAL BUREAU OF INVESTIGATION
UNITED STATES DEPARTMENT OF JUSTICE
WASHINGTON, D. C. 20535
TELEPHONE, NATIONAL 8-7117

June 29, 1964

*FBI poster of Andrew Goodman,
Michael Schwerner and James Chaney.*

(CORBIS)

Robert and Carolyn Goodman at Newark Airport, August 7, 1964. (CORBIS)

Mothers of the three slain civil rights workers leaving memorial service for Andrew Goodman, August 9, 1964. From left: Fannie Lee Chaney, Carolyn Goodman and Anne Schwerner. (ASSOCIATED PRESS)

Deputy Sheriff Cecil Price and Sheriff Lawrence Rainey during their arraignment for conspiracy, December 1964. Behind them: Jimmy Lee Townsend, Travis M. Barnette, a spectator, and Herman Tucker. (BLACK STAR)

Carolyn Goodman greets Stanley Dearman, editor of the Neshoba Democrat *(1966–2001) at his retirement gathering in Philadelphia, Mississippi, February 2001.*

(NESHOBA *DEMOCRAT*)

"Then why did you bring it out?" I asked, getting up. I wanted to go in the house and watch television.

"Because Mama and Daddy told me to," she said.

"Y'know, you talk funny," I said.

Darla just looked at me. Then she closed up her Barbie case and took it inside, slamming the back door behind her. Ann and I looked at each other. When we got inside, my father was hanging up the phone, laughing.

"That was Ruby," he said to Aunt Emily. "She said, 'I want to see me some kin.'"

Uncle Arby came out of Darla's room. "Why don't y'all go in and watch television with Darla?" he asked. So in we went.

Am I dreaming or was her bedroom pink: pink walls, pink ruffled curtains, and a pink bedspread with tiny white polka dots? Was the lampshade like a pink skirt with a white crinoline skirt underneath?

I remember a collection of Madame Alexander dolls sitting on a shelf, their blue eyes looking out at me from white porcelain faces whose cheeks had been painted pink. One was dressed like a bride, one like a queen, and another like a Gibson girl. Their hair was done up in pompadours or held back by tiaras, or crowned with white silk roses and layers of netting.

I'd never seen anything like it. Without thinking, I walked over to a blonde-haired doll dressed in a cowgirl outfit. She wore a suede-fringed skirt and matching vest. Her nose was sprinkled with freckles, her hair braided into pigtails, and on her head she wore a black Stetson hat studded around the brim with little silver coins, the kind Dale Evans always wore.

Even though I'd given up dolls a few years ago, that cowgirl stirred up a longing in me that I could not suppress. If I could have, I would have put the doll in my suitcase. I turned, red-faced, away from the cowgirl and the childhood bounty that she represented. I wanted to go home. I wanted my mother's cooking, my own bed, and the yellow walls that closed it in, my private cocoon.

The next morning, Aunt Emily served us bowls of steaming grits.

While my father poured milk over his, loaded them with sugar, and melted a pat of butter in the middle, I tried to find ways to avoid eating mine. I wanted cornflakes, bacon—*normal* food. I was hungry but said I wasn't, and got up from the table to watch cartoons in the living room. Darla followed me.

"Why don't y'all like grits?" she asked.

"Because they taste awful," I said. "And you talk funny and you have stupid toys."

I had underestimated my cousin. She stood up, put her hands on her hips, and shook her blonde curls. "I didn't ask you to come, you know. And besides, this is MY home. If you don't like it you can just go home to Minnenap'lis."

But we didn't go home, and over the next three days, Darla came with us as we toured the cemetery at Vicksburg, drove under the Memorial Arch, and took a picture of Liz straddling a Civil War cannon on Confederate Avenue. We got out of the car and walked to the Minnesota memorial, where a bronze woman held a sword and a shield. "This is Peace," Arby read from a mimeographed leaflet. "She holds weapons from both sides." We then stood in front of the Mississippi monument, which was taller and grander, with another bronze lady who sat watching two sets of soldiers, frozen in midfight.

The fall of Vicksburg took place on July 4, 1863, when the Union army, under the leadership of General Ulysses S. Grant, marched into the city and took control of the Mississippi River. It was a humiliating loss for the South, and also the beginning of a series of marches throughout Tennessee, Mississippi, and Georgia by William Tecumseh Sherman, whose aim was to burn cities and railroads and farms, and to bring a defeated people to its knees.

Like the cemetery at Gettysburg, the battlefield at Vicksburg is the hallowed resting place of thousands of Union and Confederate dead. Perhaps the restless souls on both sides of the conflict had sounded the call here for their unresolved causes to be avenged. Certainly the call had been passed down from one generation to the next, and had echoed throughout the South since the end of the Civil War. Lincoln's hope for a new birth of freedom would not occur before solders of a different kind had squared off yet again in Mississippi a century later.

THE ENEMY that Sam Bowers had warned Klansmen about at his prayer meeting in May of 1964 was being trained in Oxford, Ohio, and would within a week cross over into Mississippi and begin to infiltrate its front lines: the polling places in county and municipal courthouses across the state. Only this time they weren't after territory and, unlike Sherman, would not arrive with an army that was ordered to burn and destroy. They were students from Princeton and Cornell, Harvard, Stanford, Berkeley, and the Universities of Chicago and Wisconsin. All had volunteered for Freedom Summer, and had come to Ohio for training in nonviolent activism that was sponsored by the National Council of Churches.

When Andy Goodman arrived in Oxford in mid-June, he joined hundreds of other young people in a kind of boot camp, where those who conducted the training taught the students to be prepared for arrests, beatings, and humiliation from citizens and law enforcement officers. Here Andy was trained by Mickey Schwerner, J. E. Chaney, and other seasoned civil rights workers, who taught him how to protect himself from billy clubs, kicks, and pistol-whipping at the hands of angry Klansmen. He practiced curling up into a fetal position on the floor, with his knees pulled up to protect his abdomen and groin, and his arms folded around his head to shield his skull and the back of his neck.

The students would, of course, be unarmed in Mississippi, and were being taught to respond to insults and verbal abuse with respect; to go peacefully with law enforcement officers if arrested, and never to answer violence with violence. The majority of them were scared. Most were young, idealistic, and had never even seen the inside of a jail. "I may be killed and you may be killed," warned

James Forman, executive director of the Student Non-violent Coordinating Committee (SNCC), one of the groups that fell under the Council of Federated Organizations (COFO) umbrella. "If you recognize that, the question of whether you are arrested becomes very, very minute."

A thousand miles to the south, at dusk on June 16, 1964, approximately seventy of Preacher Killen's new recruits into the Lauderdalc and Neshoba County klaverns of the White Knights of Mississippi were gathering in the abandoned gymnasium of the old Bloomo School, about four miles east of Philadelphia. Preacher Killen had no sooner begun to make a few announcements when former sheriff "Hop" Barnett interrupted him to say that he'd noticed that there was some kind of gathering in nearby Longdale, at the Mount Zion Methodist Church, an all-black congregation.

Mickey Schwerner, whose movements the Klan had closely watched since his arrival in Meridian in January, had spoken at Mount Zion two weeks previous, to ask the leaders if the building could be used as a freedom school. If the congregation agreed, the church would house voter registration drives.

Preacher Killen asked the Klansmen gathered before him if they wanted to do something about the meeting at Mount Zion. It was suggested that a civil rights meeting was under way at the church, and that "Goatee," or Schwerner, was possibly present. Hands went up, and the group agreed that only those who were armed would drive over to the church. Preacher Killen did not accompany them but stayed behind at the Bloomo School. This was to become his pattern: to recruit, plan, and incite others to violence, then to retreat into the shadows behind an alibi.

When the Klansmen arrived at Mount Zion, a meeting of church elders had just come to a close. The leaders were locking up when they noticed a convoy of cars full of white men pulling into the parking lot. The Klansmen blocked the driveway, cut their headlights, and piled out of their vehicles wielding guns and clubs. They pulled the church elders from their automobiles, threw them to the ground, and demanded to know where the civil rights workers were. Naturally, the civil rights workers weren't there. They were in Ohio, training the volunteers.

The church elders weren't aware of Mickey Schwerner's whereabouts, and their denials enraged the Klansmen who'd come looking for a fight. They didn't want to leave unsatisfied and lashed out. First, they took down Bud Cole, one of Mount Zion's deacons, beating him in the head with the butt of a pistol while his stunned wife, Beatrice, looked on.

"Lord have mercy. Don't let them kill my husband," Mrs. Cole cried, falling to her knees. Another of the Klansmen lunged at her with a club. He drew back to hit her as she kneeled before him, her arms outstretched. There was a policeman standing behind him.

The Klansman stood over Mrs. Cole, club poised to strike, when she asked the policeman behind him if she could pray.

"If you think it will do you any good, you'd better pray," the policeman said.

"It's too late to pray," said the Klansman with the club.

She lifted high her outstretched arms. "Father, I stretch out my hands to thee," she prayed aloud. "No other help I know. If thou withdrew thy help from me, whither shall I go?"

The policeman said to let her go. "He looked kind of sick about it," Mrs. Cole later testified.

The Klansmen left Bud Cole and a few other Mount Zion elders bleeding in the church parking lot and returned to the Bloomo gym forty-five minutes later. They arrived jubilant, reporting that they'd beaten all of the Negroes at Mount Zion. Wayne Roberts, a Klansman from Meridian, waved a bloody fist in the air to prove it.

Billy Birdsong, however, another Meridian Klansman, accused the Neshoba members of being sissies: they had allowed the Negroes on their side of the church to escape unharmed.

Billy Posey, a garage mechanic from Philadelphia, and a member of the Neshoba Klan, shot back that they hadn't been looking for niggers, and that Goatee hadn't been there anyway.

"Whipping them niggers tonight wasn't such a big deal," another member of the Neshoba klavern said. "Hell, we can whip niggers anytime we want to on the streets of Philadelphia."

But their prestige as warriors had been challenged. Later that night, wounded by the scorn of the Klansmen from Meridian, several of the Neshoba members got drunk and drove back to the Mount Zion Church, where they threw firebombs into the empty building and burned it to the ground.

For months afterward Preacher Killen and his Neshoba Klan buddies bragged that the church had been burned precisely to lure Goatee back into Neshoba County. Whether the trap had indeed been premeditated lent only disgrace to Preacher Killen's claims. Once Mickey learned of the fire at Mount Zion, he immediately headed back to Mississippi from Ohio with his friend J. E. and a new recruit, Andy Goodman.

Andy called his parents twice during the training. He called June 17, three days into the session, to let them know that he had decided to go to Canton, Mississippi, with Eric Weinberger, a civil rights worker who'd asked him to spend his summer helping there. Once Schwerner had received word that the Mount Zion church had been burned, however, Andy changed his mind. He then phoned his parents on June 19 to inform them of his change of plans. Instead of going to Canton with Weinberger, he was to drive all night to Meridian, then into Neshoba County with Schwerner and Chaney.

When they arrived in Mississippi, Andy stopped to write a postcard to send his parents, to reassure them that the trip south had been uneventful; they'd arrived in Meridian safely and the weather was fine. He dropped it in a mailbox just before they drove to Longdale to investigate the Mount Zion fire.

On their way back from Longdale they were arrested for speeding by Neshoba County Deputy Sheriff Cecil Price, who detained them in the county jail for several hours. During that time Price consulted with his boss, Sheriff Lawrence Rainey, and with Preacher Killen, in conversations that sealed the fate of the civil rights workers in his custody. Later that night, at about ten-thirty, the deputy sheriff released Andy, Mickey, and J. E. He got into his patrol car and followed their station wagon as far as the Philadelphia city limits. The three then drove off into the darkness where another car was waiting for them, and disappeared.

VICKSBURG NATIONAL BATTLEGROUND and Cemetery is situated on a bluff overlooking the Mississippi River. We drove over the battlefield along a long, narrow road that wound past hundreds and hundreds of white grave markers, all the same, row upon row, like teeth rising up out of a bite they had once taken in the soft brown earth. We drove past the U.S.S. *Cairo.* "A Yankee gunboat," Uncle Arby said. We then stopped to look at a column of breastworks where, during Civil War reenactments, Arby told us, men dressed up like Confederate soldiers played war games and shot off their cannons.

Uncle Arby then drove south for half an hour or so to Port Gibson. He stopped before an historic site, where dozens of tall pillars rose up from tall weeds and a sign read WINDSOR RUINS.

"Built by a wealthy planter between 1859 and 1861," Arby said, looking down at his pamphlet. "Name was Smith Coffee Daniel the Second," he went on. "The Confederates used it as an observation post. After the battle of Port Gibson, the Union used it as a hospital. It survived the war, but was burned when a guest threw a cigarette into a wastebasket in 1890. All that's left are these twenty-three Corinthian columns, each forty-five feet high."

We got out of the car and ran among the ruins, crossing an empty grassy area that was bordered by a row of tall columns, all that remained of the plantation's antebellum splendor. My mother called out for us to slow down, but the heart of where the house once stood became for us a playground, where we climbed up the low foundations of the tall, scrolled pillars, jumped into the grass, and ran the itchy feeling out of our legs.

Of course Smith Coffee Daniel the Second hadn't constructed the Windsor Plantation with his bare hands. Slaves had built it. But they were as invisible to us as the long-lost mansion, and nobody thought to ask whether the remains of those who built the plantation lay beneath the grassy area upon which we played.

We then drove home with Uncle Arby and Darla, to where Aunt Emily waited for us in the kitchen with a ham in the oven and a pot of butter beans boiling on the stove.

These first days of our visit in Mississippi reflected the best of my father's memories: stone monuments that spanned a continent and a century, and his family united in the dailiness of life with its intimacies and rituals: children playing, food on the table, and the reunion of past and present in the meeting of the generations.

CHAPTER 10

At the Reservoir

R ECENTLY MY FATHER RECEIVED a snapshot from Darla, who now lives in Meridian with her husband and has taken a leave from work to care for Aunt Emily, who is dying of cancer. The photograph was taken in 1966, and the color is fading, but the mood is unmistakable, and Darla herself remarks on it in her written comment on the back, *What a Crew.*

The photograph is crammed full of people, half of whom are smiling, half of whom look miserable. Smiling are the Mississippi relatives: Aunt Lumiere and Uncle Ed, Arby and Emily and Darla. Frowning are my parents, Gene, my sisters Ann and Liz, and me. We stand in front of Lumiere and Ed's house in Meridian, in the driveway under the carport.

I look like I am thirteen years old, but inside I feel like a child. It wasn't so much that I wanted to remain a child; it was that I wanted to go back and do it over. In this new setting, I felt my deficiencies magnified somehow, so that not only were my outer flaws visible, but also everything on the inside that I hoped I could hide. Now that I had reached adolescence, I felt more completely alone than I had before. It was as though I was betraying my child-hood by growing out of it, as though the very fact of my growing up was an abandonment of the little girl I'd left behind in Min-nesota. There were no second chances now. The past was past, and hope was stored in a little box with my smocked dresses and my Barbie doll and my rosary, all of it wrapped in pink tissue and put away.

Why the others look miserable is anyone's guess: Liz's restless-ness, Ann's and Gene's boredom, my parents spending more time in each other's company than they had in years. Maybe it was a bad morning. Perhaps nobody had slept well the night before. It was August in Mississippi, and hot; it may have been that the heat had drained us of energy and ambition.

When we first arrived in Meridian after several days in Vicks-burg, Ann and I ran to the backyard, where the grown-ups were sitting at a picnic table on a cement patio beside a small shed. Everything had recently been given a fresh coat of white paint to match the house. They sat under a sloped canopy in the shade.

"Run along and look inside," Uncle Ed told us. Ed was tall and thin, and his reddish hair was slightly gray. He smiled easily and held an unfiltered cigarette between fingertips that were stained a faint shade of ocher.

We ran into the shed. Stacked up against the back walls were cases of pop: Coca-Cola, Orange Crush, and grape Fanta bottles in wooden boxes. We never bought soda at home. Never. We squealed and backed out of the shed. "Did you see that?" I asked my father, who was laughing with Ed and Lumiere. It didn't occur to me that we could actually *have* some of it, so I didn't think to ask. Ann and I just stood there with our mouths open.

"Go ahead," Ed said. "Take some."

Because of this I was slightly in awe of Uncle Ed, who had thought to stockpile the soda in the shed so that his nieces and nephew could have as much as we wanted. After this, Uncle Ed stood very tall in my esteem.

Aunt Lumiere and Uncle Ed lived in a small house whose interior was dark and cool, with windows shaded by awnings, blinds, and heavy drapes. The front rooms were quiet as a museum, the walls covered with shelves and breakfronts that held Auntie Lu's collections of dishes and glassware.

Lumiere and Ed worked during the week, and on the weekends they loved to fish. They owned a mobile home on a small patch of wooded property in Lauderdale County just outside of Meridian on the shore of a man-made lake. Here they escaped the heat of the city and cooled off in the shade of tall pines and the breeze that came off the lake. We spent an afternoon at the reservoir, bringing our bathing suits and changing in the trailer. Gene, Ann, and I swam out to a wooden dock in the middle, through warm, amber water that got its color from the clay that the runoff seeped through. The water level was low but deep enough that we couldn't touch bottom, so we couldn't really gauge the depth.

I was afraid of swimming in unfamiliar lakes when I didn't know how deep the water was. When we reached the dock, we climbed the wooden ladder to the top, which rose about ten feet from the surface. My brother did a running cannonball, making a splash that sprang up around him like a cyclone. I leaned over the side, bent my body at the waist, and dived in. But my fear caused me to leap too far out, not wanting to go straight down, and so I did a belly flop, and slammed into the water facedown. Stunned, I grabbed for one of the slimy wooden supports that anchored the dock to the bottom of the lake. Ann and Gene were swimming on the other side. I didn't want to jump in again.

"I'm going back," I called over to them, and swam on my back toward the shore. My hands finned in and out at my sides, my ankles working up and down to propel me through the water. My face was turned to the bright and cloudless sky, but my thoughts did not fly upward. I knew that the lake had been a quarry that now, filled with water, sank down from steep sides to a bottom far below me. My breath came from high in my chest, and from time to time I turned over onto my stomach to see how far I was from land. People in miniature moved from doll-size cars to small trailers, and everything went liquid through my wet, gritty eyes. I flipped again onto my back and swallowed. I wasn't afraid of the fish that I knew swam all around me. It was the opacity of the yellow water and its depths as I moved slowly across its surface.

THOUGH MANY CLUES in the investigation of the disappearance pointed in the direction of foul play, most people in Philadelphia believed that the whole thing was a hoax that COFO had dreamed up to publicize the Mississippi Summer Project. The following article appeared in the *Meridian Star* on June 25, three days after the charred remains of the station wagon belonging to Goodman, Schwerner, and Chaney had been discovered in the Bogue Chitto swamp, in Neshoba County, just outside Philadelphia. Congressman Winstead gave his speech on the floor of the House of Representatives in Washington, both to combat the idea of sending federal marshals into Mississippi to conduct the search, and to soothe the jittery nerves of his constituency, who did not want to believe that the three had been murdered. Another of my father's cousins, the congressman was double kin: related on both sides and thus caught in the same web of family ties that connected Preacher Killen to him and to us.

May Be Publicity Hoax, Winstead Tells House

WASHINGTON (UPI) Rep. Arthur Winstead suggested today that the disappearance of three civil rights workers near his home-town of Philadelphia, Miss., may be a hoax.

He told the House there is no evidence that the trio has been harmed. "Some people" think the disappearance was a hoax arranged for publicity purposes, Winstead said.

He made his remark after Rep. Leonard Farbstein, D-NY, called for the use of federal marshals in Mississippi to protect the several hundred young people from other states who are moving into Mississippi for a summer civil rights drive.

Winstead said he had been in touch with the mayor, the sheriff and other responsible citizens in the area, and that they are making every effort to find out what happened in the case.

The trio dropped from sight Sunday night after being held briefly on a traffic charge.

"Nobody knows whether there has been any violence in this case," said Winstead, protesting demands of Farbstein and others for federal action. "Some people think it's a hoax to get the kind of publicity this case has got. I hope it is."

Winstead said earlier that the situation created by the influx of integrationists is "beyond comprehension."

"No one knows yet what has happened. These trouble-makers moving in from the outside only serve to confuse the issue, and it would not be surprising if more trouble occurs because of their presence at the scene. They really are there for the purpose of making trouble and getting publicity.

"It is foolish for them to ask for protection by the federal government. President Kennedy was well protected by the Secret Service and others in Dallas, yet he was assassinated in President Johnson's home state. This should prove that anything can happen to anyone, anywhere these days," said Winstead.

Winstead called the "disappearance" an "isolated incident" and said that too much pressure was being put on Mississippi, "pressure intended to put our state in a bad light."

In 1964, Mississippi led the nation in the number of documented lynchings: from 1882 until the death of Emmett Till in 1955, more than five hundred African Americans were *known* to have been murdered. After 1955, countless other lynchings would take place in counties throughout the state, most of which were never recorded. And as much as we wanted it to be different, the county my father came from was no exception to the rule.

During the search for Goodman, Schwerner, and Chaney, a fisherman in Tallulah, Louisiana, found the lower half of a human torso snagged up against a log in the Old River. The ankles had been tied together with a cord. On the chance that the fisherman had found a Klan burial place, navy frogmen dragged the muddy bottom of the river and found the lower half of another human body. At first they thought it might be two of the three missing civil rights workers, but forensic evidence showed that they were the remains of two young black men, Charlie Eddie Moore and Henry Hezekiah Dee, both of Meadville, Mississippi, who had disappeared in early May of 1964.

Four months after the disappearance of Dee and Moore, the FBI and local police officers arrested James Ford Seale, a twenty-nine-year-old truck driver, and Charles Marcus Edwards, a thirty-one-year-old paper mill worker. The state of Mississippi charged them with murder, but authorities later reported that they could not develop sufficient evidence to take the case before a grand jury, and the charges were dropped.

Perhaps the outcome of the infamous Emmett Till murder trial nine years earlier was the most emboldening for the murderers of Goodman, Schwerner, and Chaney.

In August of 1955, Mamie Till Bradley, a Mississippi native who'd moved to Chicago in the early 1940s, put her fourteen-year-old son Emmett on the Illinois Central to Mississippi to spend part of his summer vacation with his cousins in Tallahatchie County.

What happened the night that Till disappeared has been the subject of much disagreement: According to the teens who were with him, Till had begun bragging about his white Chicago girlfriend when a couple of his companions dared him to go inside a store and talk to the white woman behind the counter.

In other accounts, Till wolf-whistled at her.

In any case, on the following Saturday, Roy Bryant, the woman's husband, and his half-brother J. W. Milam woke the Wright household at 2:30 A.M., demanding that Moses Wright, Till's uncle, deliver the boy to them. Wright let them know that he had severely admonished his nephew, pleading with them not to take him.

"You niggers get back to sleep," Milam said as Till got dressed and was marched outside. At the car, someone asked if this was the right boy, and from inside came the answer yes. He was then told to lie down on the bed of Milam's pickup truck. It was the last time anyone in Emmett Till's family saw the teenager alive.

Milam and Bryant were picked up later that day and admitted that they'd abducted "a little nigger boy," but didn't confess to the murder they'd committed just hours earlier.

Three days later his hideously battered and decomposed body was found by a youth who was fishing in the river. Police called to the scene reported that the beating the body had received was the worst they'd ever seen. On one finger was a ring inscribed with the initials *L. T.*

The body was so badly mangled and decomposed that Moses Wright could only identify it by the initialed ring.

The sheriff had asked for an immediate burial, but Till's mother intervened and demanded that the corpse of her son be shipped home. Though the sheriff had ordered that the casket remain sealed, Mrs. Bradley insisted on having his casket open during his funeral so that others could see what had been done to her son. *Jet* magazine published a photograph of Till's mutilated body, a rare instance in which the lynching of a black person was propelled into the national spotlight.

Other national publications covered the murder. *Commonweal* magazine was unwilling to point the finger solely at Mississippi and indicted the North *and* the South: "It is the same disease that created the northern ghetto in which he lived, [and] the Southern shack from which he was taken to his death."

But national publicity was not enough to sway local juries, and the two men were tried and acquitted. Months later, a reporter paid both men to tell their story. Both confessed to beating Till, shooting him in the head, and tying a heavy fan around his neck so that his body would sink to the bottom of the Tallahatchie River.

Lynching, according to some sociologists, is not an act of vengeance against a single individual, but a means by which to enforce social conformity. The fact that locals retaliated against outsiders, however, lends a certain irony to both the Till and civil rights workers' cases. The increased publicity did bring the status quo into the unflattering light of national scrutiny. The broader visibility in the Till case did not bring about immediate changes in the state of racial affairs, however, and the bedrock of community norms, though shaken, would not begin to erode for another decade.

The publicity in the Till case had also presented Washington, D.C., with political challenges. After the acquittal of Till's murderers, the Eisenhower administration's policy of silence on matters of civil rights for blacks became increasingly strained. Because of states' rights laws that had been on the books since Reconstruction, apparently no federal law had been violated. And Eisenhower was loath to alienate the recent GOP converts from the Dixiecrat party, while at the same time trying to placate swing voters among northern blacks, who probably shared the disgust of Roy Wilkins with a president who "said nothing and did nothing." Eisenhower did not even respond to a telegram from Till's mother, urging him to intervene in the kind of violence against blacks that had taken her son's life. Vice President Nixon completely derailed the prospect of any action toward civil rights justice during a meeting in December of 1955, when he suggested that to avoid revealing the passivity of a Republican president, the matter be turned over to Congress. He argued that any legislation that might get out of committee would then face a southern Democratic filibuster, and would reveal the disarray within the Democratic Party on the subject of civil rights.

The lynching of black people in Mississippi declined after 1955, but it did not stop. The roster includes the 1955 lynchings of Clinton Melton, a gas station attendant in Glendora; and of Gus Courts and George Lee, both of Belzoni. Mack Charles Parker, a young army veteran from Poplarville, was killed in 1959; and voting rights activist and father of nine George Herbert Lee was lynched in Amite County in 1961, as was one of his witnesses, Lewis Allen. Lamar Smith from Brookhaven was killed in 1963 while trying to register to vote.

That same year, NAACP leader Medgar Evers was murdered in his driveway in Jackson as his wife and children looked on from inside the house. His killer wasn't tried for murder until 1994, when he was found guilty and sentenced to life in prison. In 1965, George Metcalf, president of the Natchez Chapter of the NAACP, was critically injured when a bomb went off in his car. Two years later, Wharlest Jackson, former treasurer of the Natchez chapter, was murdered by yet another car bomb. The man who killed Ben Chester White in Natchez in 1966 was acquitted the following year. Thirty-two years after the 1966 murder of Vernon Dahmer in Hattiesburg, Sam Bowers, imperial wizard of the White Knights of the Ku Klux Klan, was convicted of murder. And as of April 1, 2002, the killers of Andrew Goodman, Michael Schwerner, and James Chaney in Neshoba County in 1964 have yet to be tried for murder.

THERE WAS NO BEACH along the shore, only a ladder I climbed on the side of a pontoon that was anchored at the water's edge. As I walked across the small patch of lawn that led to the trailer, I felt my teeth unclench, my stomach muscles relax, my fists open at my sides. After a few blinks, my eyelashes shed the drops of water that had made a halo appear at the periphery of my vision, and the world I now entered became clearer and more distinct.

Lumiere sat at a picnic table that stood under a tall tree to the left of the trailer. There, she cleaned a mess of fresh-caught crappies, using the side of her knife to slide them across a wooden board where they fell into a rubber dishpan that sat in front of her on the picnic bench. It was half full of pink flesh wrapped in silvery black scales. The sun that streaked through the leaves overhead left finger-size rainbows across the luminous sides of the headless, tailless fish.

My father stood beside them, talking. My mother was in the trailer, her head down, her face half-hidden and framed by the small window beside the door. I spread out my Barbie beach towel on the picnic bench and sat down to listen. I drew my legs up and hugged them to my chest.

Lumiere took a fish the size of her hand and sliced off its head right below the gills. The board was bright with blood as she pushed the head with the knife's blade onto a piece of newspaper that lay beneath the cutting board.

She looked at me and smiled her beautiful smile. "Have a good swim?" On her head was a wide-brimmed straw hat that protected her face. Her smile was like sun breaking through the shade, and it warmed me as I had never been warmed by another person before.

"The water's warm," I said. I could smell the fish.

Ed sat back and lit a cigarette. "Ever' spring they load the lake with fish: crappies, bluegills, bass. All kinds. We come up here almost ever' weekend. Don't we, hon?"

"That's so," Lumiere replied. Her knife had a narrow, curved blade, about six inches long. She cut off the tail fin of a decapitated fish and pushed it onto the newspaper.

My father was laughing. "But Lumiere, you don't eat fish."

"Now, Chub," she went on. "I don't have to eat 'em to like catching 'em." Auntie Lu's eyes had little lights in them when she laughed. Her hands worked quickly, opening up a medium-size bass with a quick slice and filleting it in one swift motion, lifting up the delicate spine and tiny bones protruding slantwise from it. My father watched her intently, a broad smile on his face. She made it look so easy.

"Tomorrow you'll carry everybody out to Ruby's," she said to my father. "She's waitin' on y'all."

"She called us at Arby's," he replied.

The look on his face as he watched his sister was like nothing I'd ever seen before. He looked relaxed. He leaned against a tree and smoked a cigarette. Ed was opening the silver ice chest, pulling out shiny wet bottles of Coca-Cola. He opened one and passed it to my father, who tipped the bottle back and took a long drink.

"Y'know, it seems to me I remember Ruby drivin' those eighteen-wheelers fulla cotton herself," my father said, as much in my direction as anyone else's. "And pullin' 'em up to be weighed." There was admiration in his voice. "Not too many women back in those days'd haul cotton like she did."

Unlike the generation of aunts I grew up with in the North, wage earning in my father's family was not bound by gender. My father's sisters and sisters-in-law had worked outside the home ever since they were old enough to be useful. When they were children, nobody was dispensable when it came to the family's economic survival.

In the photographs of Grandma Ora from the 1930s, she stands tall and appears to be in robust health, but her face begins to show the harsh effects of the work she had no choice but to do for the sake of her family. She does not smile. The skin over her high cheekbones is taut as canvas stretched over a frame. Her hands are those of a worker: rough, knuckly, and strong, as though used to being in hot water and lye soap and countless numbers of cotton bolls whose sharp edges bit into her hands like weevils. Her daughters grew up expecting to work, and throughout their adult lives shouldered the role of breadwinner alongside their husbands.

Lumiere picked up another fish and removed the head, pushing it aside onto the ever-growing pile of fish heads, fins, and bones on the newspaper beside her. "That's true," she replied. "Ruby knows all about a hard day's work."

There was a pause before my father spoke again. "Arby'n me had some good talks the other night. Y'know, nobody knew how hard we worked when it was just him'n me at home. And I used to get pretty riled at Daddy back then."

"Now, Chub," Auntie Lu said. "Don't you go talkin' ugly. Daddy was good and kind, and you know it."

"No, I mean it," he went on. "Lemme explain. You weren't there like I was. Arby loved a good time. When he was old enough to go out, sometimes he went all weekend and I stayed home and worked with Daddy. Sun to sun. The work didn't stop just cause Arby wasn't there."

"Lawds," Lumiere said, and shook her head at my father's complaints.

"Come on now, Lu."

For the first time in my life, I noticed in my father's voice a wheedling quality that must have worked for him when he was little, seeing as he was the youngest child in the family. "You were gone by then, but Daddy'd say he was gonna whoop Arby when he got home. The next thing I knew, the two of 'em was comin' up the road arm in arm and Arby had a carton of cigarettes for Dad."

Lumiere made a little clucking sound, like she was laughing on the inside in spite of herself.

"It's true," he said. "I'd be madder'n hell. That Arby knew how to charm people. No doubt about it."

"Workin' hard didn't hurt you none, Chub, and you know it," Lumiere said.

The reality of hard work was tied to the progress of the region, both in economics and technology, and my grandmother, dying young as she did, didn't live to enjoy the benefits of either. Electricity did not come into Neshoba County until after my father left to join the marines in 1940. Until then the milk was kept cool in the well, the house was lit with kerosene lamps, and the boys sawed logs and kept the woodpile stacked so that Great-grandma Donie and Grandma Ora could heat the house and cook.

"She'd hide food from us," my father said. "If she didn't, Arby and I would eat anything that was in sight. We'd drink a gallon of milk after school and finish off an entire pie, if it was sitting out. We'd look for the food too. But she was too sharp for us and we never found it. Lucky thing too. Because she made the best dinners. And sometimes out of nothin'. And I mean nothin'."

Lumiere looked up. "Mama was a good cook," she said. *"Good."*

The sky peeked clear and blue through the tops of the tall pines. A slight breeze blew in cool from the reservoir. Still in my wet bathing suit, I shivered slightly. Goose bumps rose up on my arms.

"You get in and put on somethin' dry, darlin'," Lumiere said. I walked in my bare feet over a layer of prickly pine straw to the car to find my white sweater.

I opened the car door and sat in the backseat, out of the wind. I dug in my mother's picnic basket for a package of saltines and put one after another into my mouth, then washed them down with a swallow of warm and syrupy Kool-Aid from the bottom of the thermos. A little sob closed up my throat.

I didn't know how to respond to Auntie Lu's kindness. I wanted to be close to her, but I didn't know what to do. I'd always taken care of these incongruous feelings by shutting myself off with a book, but I'd already finished those I'd brought with me. I thought about my yellow room at the back of the house on the second floor where I could lie on my bed in the middle of the afternoon. Books took me away, which was what I wanted now. I took a blanket from the rear window, spread it over the warm hood of the car, and sat down. I could see Ann and Gene in the lake, tiny dots still splashing and jumping from the dock in the middle. The sound of their voices laughing and shouting to each other carried across the water so that I could hear them. Liz was asleep in the trailer. I lay back and closed my eyes.

I had been protected all my life from anything that was different from me. It was as though I'd been raised in a small town, and now, a thousand miles away, I wanted only to go back. It was not so much that I missed the dozen or so streets and houses that made up my landscape and asked nothing of me except that I walk them familiarly. For the first time I became aware that without the safety of my room and the distraction of books I lacked my most tangible means of escape. I would begin high school in less than a month, and each day that brought me closer to that first day brought with it increasing measures of fear. I carried with me that constant feeling of apprehension, and reading was my way of getting away from it, if only for a time.

I'd had this feeling before. Over the past year, boys my age had begun to talk to me after class and at parties, and my wallet was full of school pictures that boys had autographed on the back. *To Mary, Love Mike* or *Jerry* or *Mark*, they'd written. We were naturally outgrowing those childhood cruelties that had given us the power to label one another, but it took me longer than it did the other girls to believe that a boy's interest might be sincere. I didn't trust them, just as I didn't trust the kindness I was experiencing now.

Here I was, surrounded by familial strangers whose love contradicted the fears that were more real than the actuality of where I was and the way I was being treated. I was safely sleeping in strange beds, eating food whose tastes were growing on me every day, and yet not able to relax and trust it. Instead of being reassured by the love that surrounded me, I felt homesick for that hiding place that was as comfortable and familiar to me as my own first name.

I must have looked like I was sleeping. The grown-ups were still talking. "Seems to me nothin' happens out there without Ruby's say-so," my father said with a laugh.

Lumiere laughed with him. "She does speak her mind," she said. "But she's good to everybody. Gives her tenants credit on her account. Makes sure people have food. Clothes too. Colored and whites alike."

"You need somethin', you get it from Ruby," my father replied. "It's a way of life."

I must have slipped into sleep for a few minutes. When I woke up, the sun was shining more warmly through the trees and my bathing suit had dried. My father and Lumiere were still talking.

Lumiere worked in an office in Meridian, and had several women reporting to her. Many of them were colored, she told my father.

"I don't think they's any reason to be ugly about it," she said. "I'll hire colored, and I'll pay 'em too. If they've got pride and do a good job.

"Now Ruby, she'll tell you that the colored out there don't want their kids to go to school with the white children. That's her opinion, and she's got her reasons for it. But it seems to me that times is changin' and you can't do nothin' to stop it."

"Ruby's run that county for twenty years," my father said.

"She's good to everybody," Lumiere said. "Lafe, too. They'll give you the shirt off their back, Chub, and you know it. Don't forget that, now."

I sat up, rubbed my eyes, and was rewarded with the sight of my father smiling at my mother as she stepped out of the trailer with a bowl of potato salad in her hands.

"Ginny makes a great potato salad, Lu," he said. My mother sniffed the air and wrinkled her nose. "Ooh, that fish smell. It's a good thing we didn't bring Susie, or she'd be rolling in all that dead fish." Susie, our black mutt at home, was part cocker spaniel, part dachshund, and loved to roll around in things that smelled bad.

"I'm not much for a dog," Auntie Lu said. " 'Cept Ed's dog that he's just crazy about. A cat neither. 'Cept maybe one of those big ol' cats t'roam aroun' the yard an' catch rats." She lifted her hat and pushed a lock of hair away from her sweaty forehead with the back of her hand. "If they never do nobody no harm or git in the way," she went on, picking up her knife. "But keep them ol' dogs and cats out'n my face."

Uncle Ed pressed his lips together and looked like he wanted to laugh, but he shook his head instead, smiling at Auntie Lu as if he could eat her up. Then he lifted up the dishpan full of fish. "We'll fry these up in cornmeal and have us a treat," he said.

CHAPTER 11

On the Farm

M Y AUNT RUBY and Uncle Lafe were the richest farmers in Neshoba County. But to look at them, you'd never know it.

Ruby's front yard, in fact the whole of the farm, was at first glimpse a cemetery for rusting machinery. Ancient tractors, plows, and cultivators were sinking into the topsoil at various points. It wasn't messy, exactly. It struck me that it was very convenient. It made me think that when something was broken, the thing to do was to let it lie where it fell and try to get around it if you could.

Ruby was my father's oldest sister, the matriarch of the family, and prided herself in never having left the state of Mississippi for the whole of her life. My first image of her was in the front yard of their one-story house, where half-drawn shades made the windows look sleepy behind a porch whose white wrought-iron supports rose in a flowery pattern to the sloping roof. A black-and-white Border collie napped at the bottom of the cement stoop. Redheaded chickens ran in all directions over the lawn.

She sat in a straight-backed kitchen chair, beneath the pecan trees that bordered the yard, shelling snap peas into an enamel dishpan that lay at her feet. She was huge—big-boned, my father said—the mass of her body falling into folds beneath her layers of clothing: a pale blue sweater over an ill-fitting print housedress that gaped at the buttons, white ankle socks, and dusty yellow tennis shoes with no laces. She brought to mind an overflowing basket of unsorted laundry. Her face was fleshy and broad beneath a wide-brimmed straw hat. The sound of the car pulling up into the circular drive had caused her to pause for a moment and turn toward us.

She didn't get up to meet us but waited for us to come to her. She had lost her teeth but wasn't wearing dentures, and her whole mouth collapsed around her gums prunelike, her words eaten away halfway through an utterance.

"Lawda mussy if ya'll don't favor Chub," she said. She reached out her arms to my father and said, "You look like you could use some sugar. Lemme love your neck."

He leaned down and embraced his sister while the rest of us stood in the yard, waiting to be introduced. "Come and meet your kin," she called, and we shook hands with Uncle Lafe, a man in blue overalls who didn't say much but whose eyes smiled beneath his cap, and all the cousins and their growing brood of shy, sun-burned children who barely lifted their eyes from the grass to say hey.

To be kin, even though we lived a thousand miles to the north, was to be loved through to the bone, and from that moment forward my sister Liz, not quite five years old, was toted around so that her feet almost never touched the ground.

Ruby took a deep breath and hoisted the whole burden of herself out of the chair after a series of rocking movements that gave her the momentum she needed to rise and go forward. Reaching into her mouth with her finger, she dislodged a plug of brown tobacco and flung it into the grass. She turned her head and spat. "Y'all must be hungry," she said, ambling across the lawn toward the house. I looked over at my mother, whose jaw had dropped so far it looked like her face was melting into her neck and would soon begin to puddle. I doubted that she was hungry.

While the rest of the family followed Ruby, my father put his hand on my shoulder and we went around back with Uncle Lafe, who wanted to show him something in the barn. "C'mon, Spook. You'll want to see this." Lafe looked over at us but said nothing until we got past the weathered doors that leaned sideways from their hinges—like wings on either side of the opening. We'd picked our way past milk cans and big wooden buckets that now were planted with red and white petunias. A sleepy yellow cat blinked at us from a spot of sun beside a building that seemed ready to rain shingles on whoever dared stand inside.

I'd hoped to see animals, but instead, the barn was full of freezers that lined the walls and were nestled into the sawdust on the floor. Stuffed into the rafters were rocking chairs, wagon wheels, and boxes covered with a choking layer of dust. A small window let in a square of dim sunlight, so Lafe flipped a switch, and a couple of bare bulbs hanging from wires strung across the ceiling made it easier to see. He opened the lid of the first freezer chest and began to speak, giving us the inventory of its contents. "We eat good," he said. "Ham, pork, butter beans. Corn, beef, English peas." As he spoke, he pulled from the center a whole frozen leg of a hog. My father looked down at me, and Lafe laughed.

"She's never seen a hog butchered, I 'spect," Uncle Lafe said. He was right. I'd never set foot on a farm before. I blushed, and with the sole of one immaculate white tennis shoe tried to rub some of the dirt from the barn's floor onto the toe of the other.

To the west of the barn had been planted a sprawling kitchen garden, where tomatoes the size of Christmas balls hung ripe and heavy from waist-high vines that were tied with twine to slanting sticks of white pine. Two Negro women bent over from their waists like open clothespins, picking greens. The sun was about an hour away from the horizon, and Lafe stopped for a moment to watch.

The women wore faded mail-order dresses, and the wind blew the skirts around as if they were still drying on the line. "Tha's Lil and her girl Lillie," he said. "They help Ruby in the kitchen." Lil picked with one hand, the other pushed against the small of her back, her elbow bent to create an open triangle that pointed slant-ways toward the house. Lillie pulled greens quickly with one hand. Her free arm hugged a round basket to her waist that was full of tomatoes, husks of corn, and bunches of dark green leaves.

"Y'all'd think them niggers'd know enough to save they backs and pick from they knees," Lafe said, looking at my father.

I felt as though I was watching an historical tableau, a faded mural painted against the wall of yellowing sky, but the word *nigger* woke me from the dream. Back home we didn't use that word, except for my father when he sat in our front yard and told his stories. To hear it now—describing people who were working, talking to each other, reaching down to pull something green from the furrows of reddish brown dirt—kept the women at a distance. Almost as far away from us in this backyard as in the front yard at home.

My father put his hand back on my shoulder and we walked to the house together. In the kitchen, my mother's discomfort was palpable. Back home, she cooked meat loaf and baked potatoes. She spent as little time in the kitchen as possible, and she cleaned up as she went. In Ruby's kitchen, the women prepared food in a joyous mess of cornmeal, flour, and buttermilk that kneaded themselves between Ruby's fingers into biscuits so light that my father described them this way: "To say that they melt in your mouth is to insult them." They moved their well-fed bodies easily from table to stove to countertop, joking and laughing, Auntie Lu washing collard greens to fry up with bits of bacon, my cousin Susie Lee heating the cast iron skillet to crust up the edges of the corn bread. My mother stood awkward at the door, watching them.

She sat at the table with her hair coiffed like a poodle, wearing a skirt, blouse, and cinnamon-colored hose, picking at her food and unsure of what to put in her mouth. My father sat at the other end, stuffing biscuit with the other men, huge men who wrapped their fists around their forks: Uncles Lafe and Ed and Cousins Jimmy, Tommy and Susie Lee's husband, Frank. I'd never noticed before how small and uncomfortable my mother was. Maybe it was because I had grown, or maybe it was the first time I'd ever seen how difficult it was for her to converse with anyone who wasn't a Lind girl.

Lil was in the kitchen. She'd piled food into serving bowls and onto oval-shaped platters, which she and Lillie carried to us now in the dining room. The table stood in the middle of a long, narrow room papered in yellow, the color of cooked squash. Large portraits of Miss Effie and Mr. Matthew, Lafe's parents, long dead (college educated, my father said), hung from triangles of wire from the cornice along the ceiling to the corners of the frames.

Lillie's dark skin was pink in the creases of her hands, and her hands trembled as she passed blue china dishes of steaming sweet potatoes and mashed turnips. Her wrists were thin as slats of pine and transparent, revealing veins the same color as Ruby's meat platter. The shaking was slight—small tremors, really—as though someone had tied too heavy a weight to a plumb line that was about ready to break.

She didn't speak, and her silence seemed customary, serving the family at table. Her slim body moved easily between the chairs, and she kept her eyes focused on the food. When she went back into the kitchen, I dug my spoon into the small mountain of sweet potatoes before me. Ruby had flavored them with butter and brown sugar; they tasted like Christmas. My father downed a glass of buttermilk in one swallow, and the white clots stuck to the edges of his mouth until he stuffed another biscuit in, this time full of grape jelly. "You do like this, Spook," he demonstrated, spooning the jelly into a hole he'd dug into the middle of a biscuit with his thumb. We used to call it a jug." I picked up a biscuit from the platter to try it for myself.

The conversation stopped for a moment until Lillie came back into the dining room, this time carrying a platter full of meat. She handed it to Lafe, then took the half-empty bowl of butter beans to refill in the kitchen. Uncle Lafe stuck the meat fork into the center of the roast, took the carving knife, and with a sawing motion sliced off thick slabs of pork that everyone lifted their plates to receive. Tommy pushed his chair back and Lillie caught her foot behind the leg, lost her balance, and put her hand out to the wall to steady herself. But not before spilling the butter beans onto the floor.

"It's all right now," Ruby said, her voice calm and unconcerned. Lil came out from the kitchen to help clean up the mess. When the mother and daughter had wiped up the floor, Lafe leaned over his plate and looked at my father.

"We've always been good to our colored," he said, as though in answer to an unasked question. Then he looked at Lil. "Haven't we?"

"Yes, sir," Lil said, nodding with a smile. Then she wiped her hands on her apron and walked with her daughter back into the kitchen. The door closed behind them.

"How come you call your kids Spook, Chub?" someone asked. "Isn't that a word y'all use for colored?" I put my spoon beside my plate and listened anew to the conversation. While my father had always sprinkled his anecdotes with racial epithets, I'd never heard this one before. Or perhaps, when listening to him, I'd chosen never to hear it. Until now, his words sketched the characters in his stories and the sounds of the way people spoke. It wasn't as though he was talking about real people.

But now it was about real people, and it included me. A word I'd heard so often that it had taken on a warm, intimate sound, as comfortable and familiar as a well-worn piece of furniture, stood out now in shabby relief against the unconsciousness of everyday speech.

And it was inspired by a girl—not much bigger than I was, whose hands passed me a warm dish and whose voice did not speak to me when she served.

It was a small incident, and it was our first night there, but sometimes something small can change how everything looks afterward. I stopped eating and my chest heated up into a fire that made my throat burn. I wanted to get away, but couldn't move. Where would I go anyway? I looked down into my lap. I opened my hands and saw that I had forgotten to wash them before dinner.

My father pulled slightly away from me and said, "Now don't get all upset, Spook. It's none of your doin'." I knew that it wasn't something I had done. My pet name was suddenly something disgraceful. It was part of who I was.

"May I use the bathroom?" I asked. I wanted to wash my hands.

My mother sat across from me, holding her fork suspended in midair. "She's always been too sensitive," she explained, as if to apologize. Then the dinner conversation resumed, and the moment got eaten up with the greens from the garden and the roast pork that, cold now on my plate, had lost all its flavor.

WE ARRIVED TOO LATE for the Neshoba County Fair, which was featured years later in *National Geographic* magazine as "Mississippi's Giant House Party." Families came from all across the state, and often stayed the duration of the fair in cabins on the fairgrounds that they owned or rented. Everyone talked about the fair. There was an exhibition hall where people displayed farm products: animals, cotton, grain, and produce. In the old days, farmers had competed in good fun for the tallest stalk of corn, the cotton stem with the most bolls, the biggest watermelon, and best bunch of peanuts. Prizes were awarded for sewing and handcrafts, knitting and needlepoint. Baking and cooking competitions were divided into categories that included pies, cakes, and fresh or canned fruits and vegetables. Since the early days of the fair, it had provided people in the area with the opportunity to gather, to show off a little, take a break from the rigors of farm life, and enjoy the company of friends and relations. My father remembered it from when he was a kid. He remembered blocks of ice being kept frozen under sawdust so the kids could have cold lemonade and ice cream.

There was a midway and concert pavilion, a grandstand for races, arcades, and games. Politicians came to shake hands and give speeches. It was a party that lasted all week, and few who knew and loved the fair would miss it. We, however, had arrived too late and had lost our chance to participate in a community event that brought people together for the best of reasons.

The ugliness of the Klan's attempts to spoil previous fairs, exploiting them as they had in order to spread propaganda, had abated somewhat, and people had felt more at ease than they had two years before.

In August of 1964, six days after the bodies of the missing men were discovered, the White Knights of Mississippi had hired a low-flying plane that dropped leaflets welcoming visitors to the Neshoba County Fair. What follows are some of the questions and answers that appeared on the Klan's welcome flyer. It's hard to believe that anyone in the crowd could have taken the information seriously, and residents who wrote about it or described it later would report that most people stepped over them or threw them away. The leaflets contained the rant of insane rabble-rousers, agitators who didn't come from the outside, but from within:

Q. What is your explanation of why there have been so many National Police Agents involved in the case of the "Missing civil rights workers?" (*sic*)

A. First, I must correct you on your terms. Schwerner, Chaney and Goodman were not civil-rights workers. They were Communist Revolutionaries, actively working to undermine and destroy Christian Civilization.

Q. What persons would have a motive for killing them?

A. There are two groups which could have done it. (1) American patriots who are determined to resist Communism by every available means, and (2) the Communists themselves, who will always sacrifice their own members in order to achieve a propaganda victory.

Q. Isn't it unlikely that the Communists would do that in this case? Schwerner was a valuable man.

A. Not at all. The Communists never hesitate to murder one of their own if it will benefit the Party. Communism is pure, refined, scientific Cannibalism in action. A case in point is the murdered Kennedy. Certainly, no President could have been a more willing tool to the Communists than the late and unlamented "Red Jack". . . .

Q. Why is Mississippi always being attacked by Communists?

A. Mississippi is a Sovereign State in a Federal Union, and insists upon being so regarded. Communists are mongrelizers. They despise Sovereignty and Individuality. They despise local self-government, and local solution of political problems, the political factors which have made America great.

And so on.

The presence of the auxiliary police that year, citizens who'd been deputized to keep order, lent a bizarre sense of unreality to the 1964 county fair. In high boots, blue uniforms, and helmets, with guns and ammunition, they made their unofficial and Nazi-like head-quarters under a tree where they met with fellow Klansmen and together watched the crowds. I wonder now whether Preacher Killen was in their midst, or if, as usual, he was lying low, protecting himself from the scrutiny of the FBI.

This year, however, the tensions had abated somewhat. The fair had returned to its old self, much as something that is ailing finally takes a turn for the better; only we had missed it.

One sticky afternoon, just after lunch, when we'd run out of things to do, Uncle Lafe took all the kids for a ride in the back of his pickup truck. Badly in need of new shocks, the truck bounced us up and down and into one another in the straw-covered flatbed, over roads that twisted into turns so sharp we moved as a body in a centrifugal push against the waist-high sides. After each jolt Lafe checked on us through the rearview window, laughing at the sight of our arms and legs sticking up in all directions from the pile of yellow straw. When he pulled off the paved roads to drive into the pasture, the jolts became sharper, and we held tight to each other, screaming as we bounced up into the air. Again and again we cleared the straw by a jolt the size of a deep rut in the road and landed with a thud onto our sore backsides.

My father had told us all about the ruts on Neshoba County back roads. The major streets weren't paved until the 1940s, and some highways remained dirt roads for decades afterward. But what made Neshoba County back roads infamous was the red clay, and what made them impassable was what happened to the clay when it rained. "It made a thick muck that nobody could get through," my father told us the morning we'd driven into the country. Local lore had it that the muck could claim the shoes off a man's feet. My father remembered a few enterprising farmers who'd station a team of oxen at a low point in the road after a heavy rain and spend the day pulling wagons out of the mud for a nickel a pull.

When Lafe stopped the truck beside a scrub pine windbreak and opened the tailgate, we tumbled down onto the yellow grass, picking out straw from our tangled hair, our dusty faces tear-streaked.

Back home, being thirteen meant putting on ice blue eye shadow even if I wasn't going anywhere, and wearing stockings held up by a garter belt so that I had to be careful about how I crossed my legs when I sat down. Here I slowly shed the makeup, and without nylons I could sit however I pleased. It didn't take long to get comfortable being seen unvarnished.

It wasn't that my teenage cousins on the farm were unsophisticated, however. When Jimmy introduced us to his girlfriend on their way to the movies, her hair was puffed into the same bubble and her eyes made up with the heavy eyeliner that the models wore in *Seventeen*. It was something else. Here, I could be a kid, the kind of kid I didn't know about when I sat in front of my bedroom mirror applying frosted pink lipstick. Here I wasn't ugly. I blended in and was accepted. I felt safe and protected.

It was good to be one of the kids, a reclamation that I hadn't expected. I jumped from the truck and ran the soreness out of my legs. I chased my sister up and down the hills, past fat striped bees that buried themselves lazily into the sweetness of pink clover, sunny goldenrod, and honeysuckle. I jumped over fresh cow pies stuck through with hay. I felt the sting of hungry horseflies on my bare legs. Something had happened in the week I'd been in Mississippi. I was the person I always was, but I'd become more relaxed.

Hot and thirsty, we ran back to the truck, leaned against its warm metal side, and sank down into its hump-backed sliver of shade. Lafe had taken a pitchfork from the side of the truck and with slow, sweeping movements was throwing hay into the back. Just down the hill a dozen sleepy cows watched him, patiently swatting flies with their tails in the cool spot they had found in the shade of the tall pines.

The tenant farmers who worked for Uncle Lafe and Aunt Ruby lived in cabins on their property, some that sat back into the woods and some that stood close to the road. Their dirt yards were swept clean and separated from the road with a row of big stones or a windbreak of young trees or a wire fence. Across the front of each cabin, an open porch stretched its entire width.

Roofs sloped from a high point in the center and the boarded siding had weathered to the color of smoke. The small windows were paned with glass, and those that had broken were covered with newspaper, plywood, or cardboard. Many porches were stacked with boxes, picture frames, garden hoses, and furniture in various stages of repair, and some were empty except for a pair of rocking chairs.

Negro men in blue overalls sat in the rocking chairs, and in the swept yards barefoot children played in the dirt with sticks. Dogs barked at us, running the length of the yard as we passed in the car.

Everyone in the truck was talking except for me. I'd never before seen a neighborhood where people lived like this. I felt as though time had stopped, and that the truck was the only thing that was moving forward.

MUCH LIKE ANYPLACE that is undergoing major change, 1966 was a year of contradictions for Neshoba County. The summer before in Washington, President Johnson had signed the Voting Rights Act, which banished the poll taxes, literacy requirements, and examinations that had prohibited blacks from voting in the South since the time of Reconstruction. The attorney general had sent federal examiners to register blacks in any area where threats, intimidation, and other patterns of violence had kept people from the polls. Since the law had gone into effect, approximately 720 Neshoba County blacks had registered to vote without incident at the post office and at the courthouse. Mail service was begun in Independence Quarters and other black areas, and public works were initiated so that residents now enjoyed such basics as sewer, water, and electricity. In January of 1966, the signs in the courthouse and other public places that had segregated the washrooms, drinking fountains, and courtroom seating were removed.

On the other hand, just a few weeks before we visited our Neshoba County kin, Dr. Martin Luther King Jr. had led a march there to commemorate the two-year anniversary of the disappearance of Goodman, Schwerner, and Chaney. And the reaction by angry whites revealed the lingering tensions that would exist in the community as part of a process of change that would continue for the next several years.

On June 21, 1966, Reverend King had marched with twenty

others into Philadelphia, where approximately 150 black citizens who lived throughout Neshoba County joined them.

The march had gone from Independence Quarters to the county courthouse, and had been peaceful until the marchers reached the bottom of Depot Hill, half a mile from Courthouse Square. There they were met by a line of cars and trucks that were aimed at the marchers and were full of angry white people. Along the route to the courthouse, the hostile crowd shouted insults and cusswords and shook their fists while city police stood idly by.

Preacher Killen probably was in the crowd along with his friends, protected, as they were, by the sheer number of people as well as the apathy of law enforcement. Perhaps they felt publicly embold-ened by prior acquittals. Over the past two years, Mississippi judge after Mississippi judge had dismissed the charges the FBI had re-lentlessly tried to file against them.

When Dr. King reached the courthouse, having stopped to pray at the site of the jail where Goodman, Schwerner, and Chaney had been incarcerated two years before, Deputy Sheriff Price blocked him from stepping onto the stairs, where he had planned to stop and deliver his remarks. "You can't come up these steps," Price told King.

"Oh, yes," King replied. "You are the one who had Schwerner and the other fellows in jail."

"Yes, sir," Price replied.

Barred from the courthouse steps, King addressed the crowd from the curb, raising his voice in order to be heard above the jeering of the whites who'd gathered to watch and harass him. "In this county, Andrew Goodman, James Chaney, and Mickey Schwer-ner were brutally murdered," King began. "I believe the murderers are somewhere around me this moment."

"You damn right," King heard Price say, "they're right behind you."

"They ought to search their hearts," King continued. "I want them to know that we are not afraid. If they kill three of us, they will have to kill us all. I am not afraid of any man, whether he is in Mississippi or Michigan or Birmingham or Boston. I am not afraid. . . ."

"Hey Luther," someone from the crowd of whites shouted out—was it Preacher Killen? He was crazy enough to do it, especially in the safety of the crowd of whites that surrounded him. He did, after all, never get his hands really dirty. "Thought you wasn't scared of anybody. Come up here alone and prove it."

King would later remember the afternoon in Philadelphia as one of the most frightening moments of his life. He later told a reporter, "This is a terrible town, the worst I've seen. There is a complete reign of terror here."

Preacher Killen and his Klan buddies would make sure that things stayed that way for another year. Then the arrests would at long last result in a trial and a few key convictions, though some who deserved to be sentenced would go free.

ON OUR WAY HOME, Lafe turned off the main highway and backed up the truck in front of the general store that was owned by Cliff Winstead, another of my father's cousins on Daddy Bob's side. A narrow porch lined with wooden kitchen chairs stretched across the front of the clapboard building. When we'd passed the store earlier, the chairs stood empty on the porch, lined up in the noonday heat under a Royal Crown Cola sign. Now the sun had moved behind the building, the porch was shaded, and those chairs had filled up with white men in overalls, whose lower cheeks bulged with chewing tobacco and whose eyes were hidden beneath the shade of their hats. They watched us as we climbed down from the back of the truck. "These Chub's kids," Lafe said by way of introduction, nodding at Ann, Gene, Liz, and me as we went up the steps and walked over to the wooden screen door. The men nodded their greetings and went back to their conversations with one another.

It was dark inside the store, the light coming from the big picture window that was partially covered with hand-lettered signs that advertised Palmolive liquid for 39¢ and Sunshine bread for a dime. A small fan with wide blades whirled overhead to move the warm air around. Cliff stood beside an ornate cash register, behind a wooden counter. Behind him rose shelves full of merchandise: boxes of Duncan Hines cake mix, round tins of Brown's Mule and Red Man tobacco, cans of cling peaches and Bartlett pears, boxes of Ivory Snow and bars of Lifebuoy soap. Behind us was the candy rack where Cliff stocked Hershey bars, Bazooka bubble gum and Tootsie Roll pops. Uncle Lafe walked over to the red Coca-Cola cooler and looked inside. "Ya'll get yourself a cold drink," he said to us, and we picked out bottles of grape Fanta, 7UP, and root beer, wet from the ice melting in the cooler. Cliff brought over a rag, wiped off the bottles, and removed the caps using an opener in the cooler's side. "Just put this on my tab, Cliff," Uncle Lafe said.

Cliff nodded and turned to us, kneeling down so he was eye level with Liz, who held on to Ann's shirttail with one hand and clutched a bottle of root beer to her chest with the other. "How'd y'all like Mizippi?" he asked. Liz opened her eyes wide and said nothing. She put her head down and wrapped her mouth around the open end of the bottle.

Here again, we must not have impressed our southern relations with our friendliness. We had only begun to approach unfamiliar people and surroundings with curiosity or a sense of adventure. Even Gene looked as though he wished he were someplace else. Cliff laughed and stood up.

"Tell Chub that we're waitin' on 'im," he said to Uncle Lafe.

Outside the store, we sat in the truck bed, dangling our legs off the back and drinking our cold sodas while Lafe stood on the porch and talked with the men.

IN THE TWO YEARS that had passed since the bodies of Goodman, Schwerner, and Chaney had been found in Neshoba County, still no trial had taken place. Murder, unless it was committed on federal property, was not a federal offense, and the alternative was a highly unpromising state prosecution for murder. As the governor had earlier pointed out to the FBI, the state circuit judge was a strict white supremacist and was distantly related to many of the defendants.

Several of the indictments had been thrown out in a Mississippi court the year before. But in March of 1966, the United States Supreme Court had overturned that local decision and removed the last obstacle to the federal government's prosecution of the case. Another year would pass before the trial would take place, and though the FBI was still a visible presence in Neshoba County that summer, I do not remember that any of the adults in my family spoke of it. Perhaps the men on the porch of Cliff's store talked about it that summer day, but I didn't notice, nor did I think to notice. It wasn't something we discussed.

I doubt that it even came up.

CHAPTER 12

At the Cemetery

LATE IN THE AFTERNOON, Arby, Emily, and Darla arrived from Vicksburg. While we waited for them, Lafe and the other men blocked off the backyard. He and Uncle Ed unrolled lengths of wire fence from the corner of the house to the corner of the big barn, then did the same on the other side, from the house to the chicken yard. Once they were finished, the backyard was completely protected, and the only way to get there was through the house and out the kitchen door. They opened the barn's doors, and from the dark interior rolled out two cast-iron vats. Then they went to the woodpile beside the barn and carried armfuls of firewood to the spot in the yard where each vat stood on stumpy little legs. They brought kindling and newspapers and made pyramids of the logs, stuffing the smaller pieces of wood and shreds of newspaper inside.

My sister Ann and I watched them from the driveway on the other side of the fence, one eye on the men in the back, the other on the road. When Uncle Arby's car pulled in, the screen door opened and Aunt Ruby appeared on the front porch. She descended the front steps slowly and took her time crossing the lawn to meet them. "Lemme love your neck," she said to her brother when finally she reached the car. "And Darla, come give your Aunt Ruby some sugar."

Darla got out of the backseat and walked around the front of the car. When she rounded the driver's side, she went familiarly into Ruby's arms. After several days on the farm, I was glad to see my city-bred cousin. Only last week she'd seemed strange and new, but now she felt like kin. She seemed to sense the difference. She ran over to where we stood at the fence.

Suddenly we heard Ruby's voice from the front yard. "I do b'lieve I've gotta take me a pee," she called out. We turned around just in time to see her lift her skirt slightly, squat, and do her business in the grass.

Uncle Arby shook his head and patted his sister on the shoulder. "Ruby," he said. "You do beat all." Laughing, the grown-ups went into the house.

From our place behind the fence, we watched the backyard drama unfold. "Bring out the lard," Lafe shouted. The back door opened and several women filed out, lugging a gallon bucket of lard in each hand. Lumiere, Susie Lee, and Lil went first, followed by my mother and Ruby. They handed over the buckets to the men, who scooped it out and scraped it into the vats. Then Uncle Lafe lit the fires beneath them and shooed the little kids into the house.

We ran inside to see what the women were up to. In the kitchen, they were preparing dinner in an elegant assembly line that was wonderful to watch: a kind of visual overture to the culinary symphony that is southern fried chicken. Ruby stood at the sink, a mountain of pink chicken breasts, each the size of a catcher's mitt, piled on the drainboard beside her. One by one, she ran them under cold water from the tap, patted them with a paper towel, and placed them in an enamel dishpan. Beside her, Lumiere speared each breast—twice the size of one of her hands—with a bone-handled meat fork, and dipped it into a pie pan, where she'd mixed egg and milk together with salt and pepper. Next, Emily took up the chicken with a pair of long-handled tongs, each piece dripping with egg. Then she breaded it with a coating of flour, cornmeal, and crushed bread crumbs that Lil had been stirring together in the big silver mixing bowl at the table in the center of the room. Soon, two big roasters and a dishpan were stacked with breaded chicken breasts.

"They're ready," Lumiere called through the screen to Uncle Ed, who stood with the other men outside in back. Finished with one task, the women began wiping down the sink, table, and countertops to begin washing the greens.

Lafe and Ed came into the kitchen. "It's boilin'," Lafe said to Ruby, and waved to Uncle Arby and my father, who waited outside the screen door. Each man took a pan full of breaded chicken and brought it outside. I followed them out, and at my heels was my little sister Liz, who'd ducked under my mother's arm to see what was going on. Uncle Lafe turned around quickly, the only time I ever saw him move that fast, and called to my father to watch her.

"Keep ever'one away now, Chub," he said. "Specially that little one."

AUNT RUBY and Uncle Lafe had lost their son Brady when he was five years old.

At the cemetery the day before, Ruby had taken us to see his grave. "He didn't favor Tommy or Jimmy or Sue Lee," she said. "Brady was a tiny thing."

"Slender and blond," Auntie Lu added softly.

We heard the sound of a car pulling up onto the cemetery's gravel parking lot just behind us. A door opened and we turned around. A man got out and Ruby walked to the gate to greet him. "It's Uncle Claudie," she said.

Brady hadn't been quite old enough to go to school, and was playing by himself at home. Ruby and Lafe had gone to Meridian to be near Jimmy. "He was in the hospital havin' his tonsils out, or somethin'," Auntie Lu went on.

"Miss Effie had come down from the big house to stay with Brady, and one of the Killen girls was there," Auntie Lu told us. "Brady was a live wire," she said. "Full of mischief."

The women had been busy elsewhere in the house. Brady had pushed a chair over to the mantel in the living room and took down the box of matches.

He carried the matches to the barn, where Lafe kept cans of gasoline. "All of a sudden, BOOM, there was a big explosion," Lumiere said. "A black ball of fire, they told us."

"Now after that they advised everybody not to see him. They put Ruby and Lafe in a room. I didn't see him, but Miss Hattie did," Lumiere went on.

"Did they see him?" I asked.

"No. But you could hear him talkin'." Lumiere turned away from the headstone and opened her purse, fumbling inside until she found a Kleenex. "Jimmy was in the hospital and he'd gotten lots of toys. Of course Brady knew it, so he wanted him some of those toys. He was delirious, talkin' about those toys. And he died that night." Auntie Lu's voice broke, and she wiped her eyes with her tissue. My father put his arm around her shoulder.

"Lafe is tenderhearted, you know, and he rode down in the ambulance with him," she went on.

"When I came down after the funeral, Lafe just broke down the first time he saw me," my father said. "It must have brought it all back."

"Chub," Ruby called from the gate. "Come and say hey to Uncle Claudie." We walked back to the car, heavy with memories. Ruby didn't know what we'd been talking about.

"We don't bring it up too much with Ruby and we never, ever with Lafe," Auntie Lu said. "It was horrible, it really was. I wouldn't hurt them for the world."

———

IT HAD HAPPENED FIFTEEN YEARS AGO. "Keep all them younguns away now," Lafe said, and my mother gathered Liz up and brought her back inside. From the stoop, I could see that the lard was boiling inside the black vats, bubbling furiously like a witch's cauldron, and the men were dipping each chicken breast into the boiling fat with a long-handled fork. When they let it go, it floated to the top, bouncing rib side up from the pressure of the bubbles. When it was done it flipped over, the breading on its back having turned golden brown. Each one cooked for a short time before it was pulled out of the boiling fat.

When the pans were finally filled with crispy brown chicken breasts, the men brought them piled high into the kitchen. Ruby was pulling a cast-iron skillet of hot corn bread from the oven, Emily had a steaming bowl of butter beans in her hands, and Auntie Lu carried two glass pitchers of sweetened ice tea to the table in the dining room. My mother brought in the serving dish of creamed corn, and the table was set with butter, salt and pepper, two jars of strawberry preserves, and a jar of honey. "Bring in the salad, Mary," Ruby called to me, and I grabbed the bowl of greens that Lil had brought in fresh from the kitchen garden in the back, washed, and sprinkled with sliced red radishes.

We stood back and looked at the dining room. It was beautiful. The meal extended the whole length of the table that Ruby had first covered with white lace. Around the perimeter we'd set the table for fifteen with Grandma Ora's pink Depression glass plates and matching cut glass tumblers. Down the middle, the food spread out in a cacophony of color. The large wooden salad bowl held deep green lettuce tossed with little circles of white radishes rimmed in red. Steam rose from a cake of yellow cornbread, browned at the edges and slightly cracked across the top. The mounds of crispy fried chicken were stacked on blue china platters at either end, and the sun sparkled through the glass pitchers of honey-colored iced tea.

Corn, butter beans, and plenty of Ruby's hot, fluffy biscuits were piled into bowls and napkin-lined baskets near a cut-glass dish holding my father's favorite grape jelly. Uncle Lafe and Aunt Ruby looked around the room to make sure that no little ones were missing, since the lard was still hot in the vats out back. When the two of them sat down, we all followed.

Heads bowed while Ruby prayed. At the far end of the table, her pink scalp showed through the side part in her fine white hair. At the other end of the table, Lafe's hair, the color of steel, was brushed forward from the back. Around the table, my cousins had curly dark hair with a rich auburn luster, except for Darla, whose hair was the soft yellow color of wax beans. Across from me, my parents' bowed heads were streaked with gray.

After the Amen, the only sound in the room was the passing of dishes and the click of meat forks and serving spoons against Ruby's blue china platters and bowls. I piled my plate with chicken, corn bread, butter beans, and salad. "Don't let the children go without my creamed corn, Chub," Auntie Lu called across the table to my father, who put a spoonful of it on my plate. "Now, Ginny, don't be shy," she said to my mother, who sat beside her with small helpings of everything.

Then came the sighs of satisfaction as people began to eat. My knife broke through the crust on my piece of chicken and I sliced off a small bite, expecting it to be heavy with grease. But instead, the breading was light and crisp and the white meat inside moist and sweet without the slightest hint of fat. "It cooks too fast to be greazy," my father said. Ruby laughed from across the table. "She'll eat good tonight," she said, nodding over at me. I took bigger and bigger bites. I never knew chicken could taste so good.

It took a long time for us to eat, and when we were finished, there was no food left on the table. The women got up from their chairs and went into the kitchen, where Lil stood at the sink washing the pots and pans. The men went outside to put out the fires.

I walked toward the living room with my sister Ann. It was lined with big, comfortable reclining chairs. Beside each chair, either resting on the arm or sitting on an end table, was an empty can and a clean piece of paper towel. "For spittin' tobacco," my father said. After dinner, the grown-ups sat in these reclining chairs or in the chairs out front.

This evening was warm and the light still soft against the sky, as if the sun wasn't ready to give up on the day. Ann and I sat on the front steps while the grown-ups gathered on the porch. Ann had a may pop in her hand. Gene and Jimmy played catch in the yard. Darla pushed Liz in a rope swing that hung from one of the trees that bordered the lawn.

From time to time a truck would pass, hands waving to Ruby and Lafe from the open windows and a small cloud of red dust rising up from behind the back tires.

"Is there anybody around here you don't know?" my father asked Ruby with a laugh.

"Mostly they's kin, so we know 'em," she replied.

For a long time nobody spoke, and a silence filled the yard with the darkness that fell across it. Then small sounds rose up to where we sat on the porch. The muffled plop of the baseball caught in Jimmy's leather mitt. The swish and squeak of the rope swing and Liz's little squeals. A cricket chirped, then another and another, and then came muffled animal sounds from the buildings behind the house. It was quiet enough on this patch of earth under the rising moon so that we could hear the hens cackle, the crunch of hay underfoot as a cow shifted in its pen, and a soft lowing punctuated by an occasional snort. Frogs croaked in the creek bed.

Above us, the stars appeared one by one, and from the west came a breeze that rustled the leaves of the pecan trees and cooled our bare arms and legs. My father sighed.

"This is what I miss about Mississippi," he said.

"What, kin?" Ruby asked.

"That's what I'm talkin' about, Ruby," he said. "A night like this with everyone around you."

"So why don't y'all move back?" she asked.

"Now don't get started on that again, Ruby," my father said, but his voice wasn't angry. I didn't see anyone get angry here. I saw sadness and heard laughter and knew the satisfaction of eating home-cooked food that had in the span of eight days become delicious. Just across the field atop a low hill, the lights in Susie Lee's house went dark as she put her baby to bed. I felt the happiness of belonging.

This kind of fullness rarely happened to me, and any discomfort I might have had about my name, or the shacks people lived in, or the way Negroes were spoken about, vanished for a moment. There was a long, silent moment, during which you could almost hear the gears clicking in everybody's mind as we tried to put into words our different versions of the assumptions that we carried around with us but rarely said aloud.

"I know y'all think we's racist here," Ruby then said to nobody in particular. Obviously the conversation begun previously was about to be continued. "But y'all haven't had it the same way we have. Ain't that right, Chub?"

My father didn't say anything. He took a pack of Pall Malls from the front pocket of his shirt, shook out a cigarette, and lit it. He shook out the match and threw it into the grass.

"Well, okay, so they's none in your neighborhood," Ruby said when my father didn't answer.

That morning, at breakfast, my parents and Aunt Ruby had been talking about integration in the schools. "It's not just the white folks who don't want it, it's the niggers too," she'd said.

"How do you know that, Ruby?" my mother asked.

"Lil," Ruby called out.

Lil came out of the kitchen wearing an apron. In one hand was the skillet, just washed, in which she'd fried the eggs we'd had for breakfast. She was drying it with a striped dishtowel.

"Do you want your kids to go to school with the white folks' kids?" Ruby asked.

"No, Miss Ruby, I don't," Lil replied, and went back into the kitchen.

Ruby nodded her head and turned to my mother. "You have any colored where your kids go to school?"

"No, not really," my mother replied. She shifted uncomfortably in her seat and took a sip of coffee. "They go to a Catholic school, and there aren't any Negroes in our neighborhood."

Ruby got up and put her hands on the table. She shook her head.

"Then how can you have an opinion?" she asked.

My mother, obviously flummoxed, conceded the point. "I don't know, Ruby," she said. "I just don't know."

And now evening was upon us, and we'd gone through another full day on the farm. We'd eaten our dinner and were comfortably full. From the kitchen came the sounds of running water, of dishes being stacked and cupboards being closed.

Ruby finished her thought. "But what would you do if your son brought home a l'il nigger gal?"

"Ruby," Auntie Lu said. "Now you just stop that. Lawdamussy." She clicked her tongue.

I looked up at my father to see what he would say. He shook his head. "He wouldn't do it," he said. "It wouldn't happen. Gene's too all-around."

Silence. Another car drove by. From its open windows, we heard the radio playing.

Uncle Arby coughed and changed the subject. "Chub," he began, taking hold of a memory the way you might take hold of someone's hand to keep them from leaving just yet. "Remember when we'd take us half a watermelon, hewed out, and bury it empty side up under Pappy's back wagon wheels?" It was worth the entire trip just to watch the two brothers laugh in tandem.

"We waited till Pappy got in the wagon and watched the wheels spin and spin till the old man got off the seat, went to the back of the wagon, threw his hat to the ground, and started cussin'," my father continued.

"What'd he used to say? Oh, yeah. 'Them drotted boys.' " All the grown-ups were laughing aloud. "We hightailed it outta there but good," Arby said. "Pappy like to have killed us, that time."

"Ruby," Arby began again. "Do you remember when Lafe'd come over and we'd listen to the Grand Ole Opry?"

"Mama charged that ol' radio battery in a warm oven," Ruby recalled.

"I can still recite the closing poem," my father said.

"Naw," Arby said with a laugh.

"Really. Listen," my father replied, his voice earnest. Then he began to recite:

"It's time for the tall pines to pine,
and the bumblebees to bumble all around,
While the grasshopper hops,
and the eavesdropper drops,
And the old cow, she gently walks away."

Everyone laughed. "Remember?" my father asked. "It was Sunday night and we'd listen and roast peanuts."

With that, the grown-ups got up, and it was time for bed.

After a long day like today, I could see how they needed a rest.

CHAPTER 13

Lallapalooza

B Y THE TIME we returned home from Mississippi the follow-ing week, my moodiness had taken on several focal points: fear of going to a new school, fear of boys, and fear that I would be ridiculed. My greatest fears continued to be, however, that my parents were desperately unhappy with each other and would one day lower the boom and announce that they were getting a divorce.

The long drive home from Mississippi had been uneventful, which for me portended disaster. The silence between them for hours at a stretch worried me, and one of its casualties was my already tenuous peace of mind. I knew that my parents tried to shelter me from the grown-up troubles they experienced: the per-petual struggle to make ends meet, the time my father spent away from home, my mother's paralyzing fear of driving a car. Our trip to Mississippi had, however, cemented in my mind the kind of watchfulness that had been born years earlier, of trying to make sense of contradictions.

I'd seen my father as comfortable and relaxed as he'd ever been, though his years in the North had separated him from his kinfolks and had created in him differences in perspective that he wouldn't have developed had he stayed in Mississippi. And I saw in my mother similarities that should have allied her with my father. She shared many of the same values as her sisters-in-law: love of home and family, deep religious faith, and a strong connection to place. She was also protective of the northern, urban sensibility that she and my father shared, and yet this set *her* apart, made *her* seem more worldly, and caused the southern kin to shy away from talking with her more openly about their everyday lives. I wouldn't have known to call it defensiveness, and yet there were assumptions underneath the surface of what people said that created uneasy distances that nobody knew quite how to bridge.

I resumed my watchfulness over my parents like a cat in a window. I relied on a kind of animal sense that would give me an indication; some kind of advance warning that the ground beneath me was about to give way and it was time to run for cover.

THERE CAME A POINT in my adolescence when my father's life, November through April, revolved around basketball. He was less and less with us in the evenings, and when he was home, he was on the telephone. From the first tip-off of the college season through the last buzzer of the Final Four, the phone sat on his lap at mealtimes, during a Big Ten game on television, or while he listened to Villanova play Ball State on the radio. Sometimes all three at once.

They weren't real conversations, just numbers. When the phone rang during basketball, he never had to say hello. Hunched over my homework at the dining room table, I looked up from my blue spiral-bound notebook of algebra equations.

"Yeah," he said. "Duke. Seventy-nine to seventy-four. Purdue. Eighty-seven to eighty-three." He took a yellow sheet of paper, wrote the numbers into boxes on a grid and put the names beside the numbers: *Indiana. 66/58. Notre Dame. 56/53.* And so on.

I didn't know who he was talking to. To me they weren't real friends, but voices on the other end of the receiver. They didn't stop by our shuttered white house, where my mother had planted red geraniums into clay pots on either side of the front door. They didn't greet me by name when I said hello into the mouthpiece of the telephone. But I knew that they were important, because when the games were over for the day and he'd finished reading the names and numbers into the phone, my father folded the yellow paper into quarters, slipped it into the breast pocket of his brown sport coat, thrust his long arms into the sleeves, and walked out the door.

Basketball. A six-foot-three-inch center, my father had been captain of the House, Mississippi, high school team and led his teammates to the state championship in 1939. In a sepia-toned photograph, the team stands on the uneven wooden steps of a country school. My father is third from the end in the front row, the winning basketball under one arm. He tilts his head slightly to one side and looks small-town shy, a little like Andy Griffith.

Behind him the white paint peels in opaque layers from the shiplap. Above him a roll of black tar paper is nailed down over the roof but curls up at the edges in the heat. Someone has stenciled the word HOUSE onto a sign that hangs over the patched-up screen door. He stands half a head taller than the tallest of his teammates and wears a dark sleeveless jersey, number 17. His gap-toothed grin angles slightly beneath eyes that grin too, wrinkled at the corners. And above everything a shock of wavy black hair. My Uncle Arby is beside him, and except that he is an inch or two shorter than my father, the resemblance between the two of them is remarkable. "Coach used to have us switch jerseys," my father told me. "If I fouled out in the first half, I'd put on my brother's uniform at halftime and play the whole game. We looked so much alike, the refs never knew the difference."

His impossibly skinny legs rise from a pair of high-top brown leather athletic shoes that bring to mind the rotogravure pictures of the famous athletes of the day, like Lou Gehrig and Joe Lewis. He and Arby shared the shoes too. "Daddy Bob used to say it was the most expensive pair of shoes he'd bought in his life," he said.

He played on the Marine Corps team during boot camp in San Diego, then in Washington, D.C., toward the end of the war. He'd been sent back to the States from New Zealand to recover from pernicious malaria he'd contracted in the jungles of Guadalcanal. Just when he'd grown strong enough to play again, he ran full speed into the lip of a low stage at the end of the gymnasium, shattering his left ankle.

"We were three minutes into the second period of a close game against Navy," he said. "Already up twenty-six to nineteen. I was drivin' the ball down center court with a six-foot-two Swabby bearin' down on me hard. I never saw that stage. One minute I was jumpin' toward the hoop, the next minute I was on the ground with the coach's face next to mine. A first lieutenant. Looked like a bull-dog. I never knew what hit me."

What with the war and the military hospitals full of soldiers with combat injuries, his shattered ankle was neither given top priority nor properly set. The doctors manipulated the bones without surgery and wrapped a cast around his leg up to his thigh.

"Hurt? I nearly jumped off that table when they started workin' on my ankle. Like a hot knife runnin' up and down my leg. They gave me ether, but nothin' could stop that burnin'. Nothin'. They never calculated how bad the ankle'd swole up, either. I coulda lost my leg. Idiots. Every last one of 'em."

It was wartime, and a Marine on crutches received deferential treatment on buses and in restaurants. "People were suckers for an injured solder," he said. "Once, a couple saw me and a buddy eatin' a doughnut in a D.C. diner. We tole the waitress it was my birthday and she stuck it fulla candles. That couple came right over, right up next to my cast, stuck way out in the aisle. Invited us to dinner.

Tears in their eyes. 'We have a boy about your age,' the woman said. 'He's in the Solomon Islands. I can't bear to think of him having his birthday alone.' "

But he never disclosed just how he was injured. "To be wounded in combat meant home-cooked meals in strangers' homes and women fallin' all over you," he said. "Woulda broke their hearts to tell 'em the truth. It's how I met your mother, see. She couldn't keep her hands off me. I milked that thing for a couple of months before I let on what really happened."

On an ankle so poorly treated that it caused him to limp for the rest of his life, he never played again. So he coached a Knights of Columbus league for Catholic boys in Minneapolis. I remember our living room full of them: long-legged and acne ridden, my mother serving them plates and plates of spaghetti after games. I'd never known that boys could eat so much. They ate until my mother was scraping the last drops of sauce from the bottom of the pan and still they asked for more. So my mother handed me a five-dollar bill and my sister Ann and I rode our bikes to the Food Lane on the corner of Fiftieth and Xerxes, just two blocks away. We bought green boxes of spaghetti noodles, jars of red sauce, and long loaves of bread, and stuck them into the baskets on our handlebars for the short ride home.

By the time we carried the bags of food through the front door, my father had brought up from the basement the big green easel-back chalkboard we'd used for playing school. He stood in front of my mother's sheer white priscilla curtains and conducted the post-mortem on the last game.

"Now, Bevins, you got to work on your pivot. Pivot first. Then pass. You got that?" He drew Xs and Os while he spoke, and con-nected them with long, curvy lines.

"See," he said as the boys sat mopping up red sauce with hunks of garlic bread. "You got this guard with arms like meat hooks tryin' to force you to give up the ball." He tapped one of the Xs with the chalk a couple of times for emphasis.

"Don't let 'im scare you. He's just doin' his job. It's your job to think. Talk to each other. If you're playin' zones like this here, your man'll be where you want him." He overlapped the curvy lines of the diagram on the board until it began to resemble the third helpings of spaghetti my mother was bringing from the kitchen.

"Go low," he said, crouching down and bouncing from his knees. "Dribble. Find your man and pass off the ball. He'll shoot and you'll run in for the rebound. You got that?"

I was never sure whether they got it, because they didn't win very many games. Halfway through one desperate season, the team down one for six, my father had everyone turn in their jerseys. "Rip off all the numbers," he told my mother. And she sat down at the sewing machine and replaced the Arabic numbers with Roman numerals, my father's brainchild. "At least we'll scramble up the refs."

And they did. The rest of the season, the referees blew their whistles after a foul and paused for a minute to decipher the Roman numerals. "Traveling. Christ the King," the refs shouted toward the sidelines. "Um ... Ex ... And I guess it's ... Vee ... Eye Eye." They got so frustrated during a close game against Holy Name that they forgot to blow their whistles and the clock ran down three seconds postfoul. Though Dolan had obviously charged into the guard with the meat hook arms, he was able to dribble past him for a successful layup. Holy Name's coach jumped up and screamed.

"Foul, Ref. No score. What the hell's the matter with you?" He was a short, stumpy redhead who wore his tie loosened at the neck and his shirt with the sleeves rolled up to the elbows. His beefy forearms were peppered with freckles. He and my father squared off center court, nose to nose, fists tight at the ends of arms held stiff at their sides, each calling the other an idiot through clenched teeth until the ref made the call: no basket.

Dejected, my father sat back down on his folding chair in the midst of his losing team, folded his arms across his chest and shook his head, muttering something under his breath about thinnin' out the herd.

Frustrated with the boys, my father turned to the girls. When she was in seventh and eighth grades, my sister Linda played first-string forward on his team. The girls didn't understand his complicated chalkboard strategies any better, however, sitting in a circle on our living room floor, brushing one another's hair into ponytails after a losing game.

But I remember how proud he was of Linda. She inherited his long legs and dribbled a basketball so fast down the sidelines that nobody could catch up with her. She was an expert at free throws too, and her concentration was wonderful to watch. She bent over at the waist, bounced the ball twice, then held it up against her chest like she was praying, which she was. She chewed gum when she played. "Helps her rhythm," my father told the refs. And blowing a pink bubble almost as big as her bubble hairdo, she lifted her arms like the priest at the consecration of the Blessed Sacrament, tipped back her wrists, and shot. The ball sailed through the air in a perfect arc toward the basket. Nine times out of ten, it slipped through the net without grazing the rim.

Hands in his pants pockets, my father rocked back on his heels. "With a shot like that, you don't even need a backboard," he said.

My brother was too small for basketball, I was too awkward, and by the time my younger sisters Ann and Liz were old enough, my father was too tired to coach. So when Linda traded in her green satin jersey for cigarettes and boys, he turned to gambling on college games.

This was when I learned to hate basketball. Because in my mind, it's when my father went away.

"Don't interrupt your father," my mother would say when I'd sidle up beside him with my algebra homework. But his head for figures was engaged elsewhere. He'd wave me away with his free hand, the other furiously writing numbers into the boxes on the yellow paper. He cradled the telephone between his ear and his shoulder, and fixed his eyes on the Michigan playoff game against Marquette. By the time the games were over and the grid was full,

I'd finished my equations and gone to bed, and he'd driven off to deliver the numbers to his bookie.

One Saturday afternoon, when I was thirteen, he took me with him. I met Rocky, whose head seemed attached directly to his body so that he didn't need a neck, and whose perpetual frown made it look like one bushy brow had knit itself long enough to extend over both eyes. Rocky held court in a booth at the Butler Drug with a newspaper, a thermos of coffee, and a battered metal ashtray full of cigarette butts piled high into a foul-smelling pyramid.

"Look at this," Rocky said, pointing to a picture of Bobby Knight. "Army beat Navy again."

"How many chairs did he throw?" my father said, and they both laughed.

They finished their business and we left the smoky drugstore, stood on the corner until the light changed and crossed the street to the car. That's when he drove me over to High Times.

High Times was a head shop near the campus of the University of Minnesota. Behind the counter on high stools sat Pit and Jaju, a turbaned pair of brothers from Pakistan, who disappeared into the back room with my father.

I'd never been to High Times before, where pellets of jasmine incense smoldered in tiny metal pots. I liked watching ponytailed boys in tattered bell-bottoms and tie-dyed T-shirts buy thin blue packets of Zig-Zag rolling papers. Girls in halter tops fingered the filigreed hash pipes and admired the copper bong that sat on the counter by the cash register. Ropes and ropes of multicolored bead necklaces hung from hooks on the wall, beside the tooled leather belts and silver dangly earrings. The shelves were stocked with macramé bags the color of tea and batik bedspreads in purples and reds, and I remember thinking that when I grew up I was going to be a hippie.

My father was happy when he emerged from the back room, pushing aside the bead curtain that substituted for a door. He took me to Bridgeman's in Dinkytown after finishing up his business. "Get a Lallapalooza, Spook," he said. "I feel like celebrating."

But I didn't order the Lallapalooza. With its six scoops of ice cream, avalanche of hot fudge, sliced bananas, chopped walnuts, whipped cream, and a cherry on top, just looking at the photograph of it on the wall behind the cash register made me sick. So we split a root beer float, with two spoons and two straws, and drank it down to the sucking sound when we drained the glass. "I thought you said you weren't hungry." He laughed, taking from his pocket a wad of folding money and putting a dollar bill on the counter.

He only took me with him once before things got messy; I didn't really know how messy, and I still don't know. Except that High Times closed down, Rocky disappeared, and the phone sat on my father's lap during football season now. He began to speak in a gambler's jargon: *The Boy and the Girl for three,* and *The President and the General for four*: bookie talk for William and Mary and Washington and Lee.

In a couple of years when my friends started to drive, we cruised around the neighborhood near the alternative high school where I'd spend my junior year. Often we found his station wagon parked in front of the Butler Drug, the McDonald's on Twenty-fourth and Nicollet, or the Chef Cafe on Franklin and Bloomington. I liked knowing where he spent his evenings. Being in the same neighborhood brought me closer to him. But I didn't go into those places. There was an unspoken code against asking where he was, going in to see what he was doing, or knowing that I questioned his whereabouts.

None of this was about basketball anymore, of that I felt certain. It was about my father being gone. Sometimes I'd get up early in the morning, just to see him, the way I had when I was little. He'd sit at the dining room table in his red and white cotton bathrobe, the yellow sheets of paper stacked up all around him. We didn't talk. We just sat there across the table from each other. He filled up his grids with names and numbers, and I filled up my notebook with isosceles triangles and trapezoids. Then each of us got up from the table, stuffed our papers into our bags, and separated. He headed for the shower and I headed for the door, where my friends picked me up for school in a blue Ford Falcon.

I wouldn't see him again until the next morning, and only then if I got up early enough to watch him do the numbers.

But I missed him. Especially at night. I wanted him home. I wanted him whistling in the doorway. I wanted him asleep on the sofa, telling stories to the neighbors, in his bathrobe fixing bacon and eggs.

Instead, there was a hole where he used to be. I lay awake in bed each night, listening for the sound of his key in the door. Waiting in the dark, I wished that I'd been different. Really special. *Pretty like Linda*, I thought. *Or smart like Gene. Good like Ann. Or funny like Liz.* But I was none of these things. I was just quiet, and I missed him so much it made my chest feel hollow. And I wished I could fill it up again with basketball.

Maybe if I'd been born with long legs, I thought. *Or a head for figures. If only I'd ordered that Lallapalooza.*

CHAPTER 14

The Vietcong

I N THE FALL OF 1966, I would begin the ninth grade.

Earlier that summer my father had complained about going to Linda's high school graduation ceremony. "It's about as interesting as watching a Puerto Rican grocer unload melons off a truck," he said. Had I thought about his remark more carefully, I may have spared myself a great deal of self-inflicted misery. As it was, I dealt with my fears by trying to be just like everybody else. I had so convinced myself of an innate unattractiveness that my tendency to shy away from people, which had found momentary, if not completely successful, respite in Mississippi, had become a full-blown case of avoidance.

My older sister had set the bar for me by being pretty, athletic, and popular in high school. I'd watched my mother fuss over her and talk about her proudly with her sisters. She hated to sew but made an orange silk prom dress for Linda. She didn't drive, but she'd walk with us to the high school to watch Linda play basketball. Then, during halftime at the boys' varsity games, Linda danced in the girls' kick line. She'd march out to center court with nine other long-legged girls in matching leotards, hot pink short-shorts, fishnet stockings, and silver tap shoes. Over the PA system we'd hear a needle hit a scratchy record, and on cue, the girls began kicking in unison like the Rockettes.

So I borrowed my sister's clothes, plastered my face with pancake makeup, and had my hair cut to resemble hers.

My brother's reputation for doing well in chemistry, physics, and trigonometry had preceded me. My parents discussed his going to college to become an engineer. I, however, had developed into an inconsistent scholar. While I'd always done well in English, I'd earned Cs and Ds in math. So for me, going to high school was entering a larger arena in which my many shortcomings would be noticed in bold contrast to the successes of my older siblings, only this time on a grander scale.

Nevertheless, I signed up for algebra and geometry.

I tried out for the dance line and the girls' chorus, like Linda had, though my legs were short and my voice shaky and thin. In an autobiographical essay for health class the first week of high school, I'd written with all the earnestness I possessed that I knew that I wasn't pretty, but that if I was well groomed and involved in the right activities, people wouldn't be as likely to make fun of me.

ANDY GOODMAN was fourteen when he and one of his buddies from the Walden School decided to participate in their first civil rights demonstration. It was early autumn, and the two looked forward to the bus ride from New York to Washington, D.C., where they would meet up with thousands of others, black and white, in what was to be the CORE-sponsored Youth March for Integrated Schools. It didn't promise to be too much of an adventure, however, since half the student body was planning to attend, accompanied by faculty and several of the Walden parents.

So Andy and Ralph decided to take a separate bus, away from

the constraints of the crowd and the chaperones. Andy sat beside a black man for the five-hour trip, during which the two discussed racism and what the future held for black Americans. Not to be discouraged, Andy's youth and optimism showed in his reaction to the conversation once he and Ralph stepped off the bus in Washington. "Boy, is that guy a cynic," he said.

With their Walden friends, Andy and Ralph linked arms, alternating black and white, and marched that day with eight thousand others. The march didn't receive much publicity, being one of the earlier demonstrations, but it must have felt exhilarating to protest on the streets of the nation's capital.

Because Andy and Ralph didn't ride home with the others, they missed an incident that illustrated the need for the march in the first place. The bus carrying the rest of the Walden students stopped for dinner at a restaurant on U.S. Highway 40 in Maryland. After piling out of the bus, tired and hungry, the students, a mixed-race group, were refused service, after a day of protesting against discrimination, no less. The white students felt guilty for the privilege of eating in the restaurant and the black students resented their friends' naïveté. It wasn't a happy moment for any of the Walden kids, and discussions took place for weeks afterward in school, as teachers and students tried to come to terms with the jumble of feelings that the incident had aroused.

Discussions like these formed the foundation of the Walden School, as when Andy was eleven and his bike had been stolen when he and his friends were playing in Central Park. Carolyn Goodman explained to Andy that the person who stole the bike must have been poor and lacked the means to buy a bike of his own. At school, the teachers led classroom discussions about poverty and its root causes.

J. E. Chaney had his first experience with the civil rights movement in 1959 at age sixteen. He attended Harris Junior College, a combination high school and junior college for black students in Meridian. His best friends were the sons of C. R. Darden, the president of the Mississippi NAACP. The local chapter had announced a recruitment meeting at a black hotel. The Meridian chapter, like many others, did little more than collect names on its membership roster, though membership meant a certain level of prestige. J. E. and his sisters got dressed up and attended the recruitment meeting, but they didn't join. The two-dollar membership fee for each of them was more than the family could afford.

J. E. was undaunted, however, and he and the Darden brothers decided to take action themselves. With the approval of Mr. Darden, the three boys wore homemade NAACP buttons to school, where the idea caught on and other students began to make and wear buttons.

Though the school was black, the principal called the three boys into his office and ordered them to remove the buttons or be suspended. He was known for being strict, but his ultimatum surprised the students. They refused to take off the homemade NAACP buttons, and were suspended for a week. Despite his mother's pleas for J. E. to be readmitted, the principal stood firm and suspended him, on the condition that J. E. could only return if he agreed to leave the buttons at home.

He returned quietly to school the following week. The next year, when he was a junior, J. E. and the principal had a second clash. There had been a fight in the gym and the coach had singled J. E. and another boy out of the crowd, accusing them of starting the scuffle. Their denials were fruitless, as the principal had already branded them as troublemakers, and they were again suspended, this time for six weeks. As the two boys left the principal's office, he told them that they'd never amount to anything. At this, one of the boys grabbed an umbrella that was leaning against the door and hit the principal over the head with it. That was it. J. E. and his friend were expelled.

In contrast to the principal's feelings, J. E. wanted very much to make something of himself, especially to help his mother, who had been recently separated from his father and needed additional income to support the family. He tried to enlist in the army and passed the written test, but because of his asthma was classified 4-F. He tried other jobs, even hauling hay for a summer, but wanted something more for his life than day laboring and languishing in his spare time in the black neighborhoods of Meridian.

Learning his father's trade promised a way out of his doldrums. J. E. did well at plastering and helped his mother financially. But when he met a classmate from high school who'd become involved in local civil rights activities, he decided to volunteer, and found in the movement the sense of purpose that had eluded him for the past four years.

Mickey Schwerner had been the kid in his New York City neighborhood who loved animals and took care of everyone else's injured pets. In high school, he'd always said he wanted to be a vet. After a year at Michigan State University, Mickey transferred to Cornell to attend its School of Veterinary Medicine, but after a year changed his mind and chose conservation. Dissatisfied with that, he finally decided to major in sociology and felt that he had found a home.

Mickey had been taught to believe in people. His grandparents were European Jews, and his parents, both born in the United States, had moved philosophically from Judaism to humanism, and their son had followed their example. At thirteen, he chose not to go through his bar mitzvah. He was not a Jew, he explained. He was only a man.

Mickey was known to be a young person of high principle and unusual self-reflection, who told others that rather than original sin, he believed in original innocence. He didn't believe in an afterlife, which created in him a set of personal ethical standards for what he believed he should accomplish in this life. He was respectful toward those who disagreed with him, and felt a sense of obligation to help others and to make a positive mark on the world he inhabited for the time he inhabited it. After graduate school, he worked at the Hamilton-Madison Settlement House with children who lived in the nearby housing projects. He visited their families at home, provided after-school activities, and advocated for them when they got into trouble. When he learned of the upcoming March on Washington, he raised the funds to pay the transportation costs for ninety young black people from the Hamilton-Madison House to travel with him to Washington and participate.

Like his father, Mickey had become an avowed pacifist. At eighteen, he'd been willing to serve in the army if drafted, but he'd received two deferments: one as a student and one for being married. He soon decided that if he were drafted, he'd apply for conscientious objector status. Because of his personal convictions, however, Mickey wanted to be a part of the civil rights movement in the South. Not as a do-gooder, as a colleague would later say, or as some kind of savior, but because he believed that he had a responsibility, for the sake of his own integrity, to help where help was needed most.

WHILE MY PARENTS TOOK a special pride in Linda's looks and popularity, she also had a wild side that they despaired of. Despite the successes she achieved on the dance line (they were called Indianettes, after the Indian, our school mascot) and girls' chorus, she paid little attention to her studies and hid her report cards from my parents at the end of each trimester. And though she received attention from boys who were athletes and members of the student council, she preferred to hang out with a group of self-styled hoodlums that my father had nicknamed the Vietcong.

I didn't talk to my parents about boys. Boys had liked me in the past, but I'd been afraid of them. I didn't know what to say around them. Even if Jim Senestadt had asked me to dance at the eighth grade graduation party, and Mike Carroll had put his arm around me in Gabby Henley's basement, I didn't trust boys. No matter what they said or did, I felt certain that they secretly disliked me.

My parents didn't really welcome the boys who called me or came to the house. Maybe my father hadn't quite recovered from his experiences of Linda and the Vietcong. Maybe my mother needed for at least one of her daughters to imitate her own dating history. "Y'know, I had an inferiority complex in high school," she often told me. "And you're just like me." Maybe my parents weren't quite ready for their second daughter to come of age. In any case, of the many ways that my parents might have chosen to handle that small flame that began to light up in their middle child, they teased me. I became so tense that I walked with my shoulders hunched and my chest squished down. I tried to avoid boys altogether.

But the inevitable happened. Just before school began, I fell in love with a boy who—while completely different from the Vietcong—was in their eyes, even more unsuitable.

He was Cuban. His family had immigrated to the United States when Castro came to power. I met him in early September, weeks after my family returned from Mississippi, at the Fall Festival Dance at Holy Angels High School. We were introduced by Mary Jane Casey, a classmate of mine from Christ the King who had transferred to another school.

His name was Justas Diego. Justas was the perfect height for me (slightly taller than five three). He had deep brown eyes, black hair, and a brilliant smile. And he wasn't afraid to show me that he liked me, right away. He asked me to dance. Again and again, we slow-danced to the Beach Boys and the Beatles in the way kids did at the time: hanging over each other's shoulders like a deadweight while our feet shuffled somewhere down below.

He invited me to a party that Mary Jane was giving the following night. All day long I thought about him: a freshman at St. Thomas Academy (I was already thinking about the dress I'd wear to their Academy Ball), the hint of an accent when he said my name, the way he held my hand to and from the dance floor. For the first time in my life, the mirror before which I stood did not reflect back a girl whose nose was too big, whose skin was too sallow, and whose hair flew out from the sides in an unmanageable mess of tangles and waves and cowlicks. And if it did, it didn't make any difference.

I didn't tell my parents about him. It was too soon. When my father dropped me off at Mary Jane's house that night, I told him that I was getting a ride home from somebody else's parents. I wanted to stay a little later, and I didn't want to be made fun of.

Justas seemed different. He was kind, and didn't have that junior high edge of insecurity that many boys had. He'd been waiting for me in Mary Jane's living room, and when I walked through the door, he came up and told me how glad he was to see me.

"She's got a really cool attic," he said, taking my hand. "It's on the third floor."

I said hi to Mary Jane and walked up the two flights of stairs with Justas.

He was right. It was a cool attic. There were big pillows on the floor and a record player and a low table with a bowl of popcorn in the center. Other kids were talking in little groups under the dormers or dancing in the middle of the room. Justas led me to a big pillow and invited me to sit down.

He sat down beside me and held my hand. "I'm really glad to see you," he said. He told me about his family. His father was a doctor and they had fled Havana in early 1960, when Justas was seven years old. "I remember crying when I said good-bye to my grandmother," he said. "I didn't think I'd ever see her again."

He had mostly vague memories of his childhood in Cuba. He remembered going to mass on Sundays and his First Holy Communion procession, where he wore a white shirt and pants and with the other children followed the priest who carried the Blessed Sacrament down the street while the people they passed knelt and blessed themselves.

We talked for a long time. It was dark when I noticed that the other kids had gotten quiet and were making out on the pillows, along the sides of the darkened room. I felt embarrassed. Were we going to do that too?

Yes. Justas reached over and kissed me. It was the first time I'd ever let a boy lie down beside me, and it felt warm and more daring than I'd ever allowed myself to be. We kissed until Mary Jane's mother, at the bottom of the attic steps, turned on the lights, and called, "It's almost eleven. Time to go home."

I didn't have a ride. I'd forgotten to ask anyone, so I called my father, who sounded sleepy and annoyed but came to pick me up anyway. Justas waited outside with me, but I didn't want him to meet my father.

"Why not?" he asked. I didn't know what to say. I only knew that I didn't want my father to say something that would make me feel embarrassed in front of Justas. So when his Dodge Coronet pulled up in front of the house, I flew down the steps. My father looked out at Justas, who stood at the door under the light.

"Who the hell is that?" he asked. "Some wetback?"

"Just someone I met at the party," I said. Inside I felt hot and chokey. "Let's just forget it, okay?"

We were silent the rest of the way home. The next day when Justas called, my father answered the phone. We had one telephone, in the dining room, so there was no way to talk in private. We spoke for a couple of minutes, but I couldn't concentrate because I knew that behind me, my father was listening to every word. I told Justas that I had to go.

"I'll call you later," he said. I hung up the phone and took a deep breath.

"So who's the spic?" my father asked before I even turned around.

Linda was in the living room. "What are you talking about? What's going on?"

"I met a boy at a dance on Friday night," I said. "He's from Cuba."

"Cuba?" my father shouted and leaned over with a red face. "Not some Castro Commie Cuban. Not in this house."

"What's his name?" Linda asked.

My head felt light. I felt a kind of pressure in my chest, the same feeling of being choked that I'd felt the night before in my father's car.

"Justas Diego," I whispered.

"What?" Linda yelled. "Hoostas Da-go? Hoostas Da-go, Hoostas Da-go," she sang out, laughing. I got up.

I hadn't even noticed that my mother was in the room. "Mary," she said, in a low voice. "You know you could never really like a boy who is so different from you. You'd never have anything in common with him. You come from such different backgrounds. The next time he calls, just tell him you don't want to see him again."

I didn't stand up for myself. I didn't stand up for Justas. I just walked out of the living room and up the stairs. I closed my door and sat on my bed in the dark. I couldn't think. "Hoostas Da-go, Hoostas Da-go" echoed in my head like a bad song I couldn't get rid of. The comforting, familiar walls of my bedroom closed in on me like a prison. Solitary confinement. The shouting back I should have done just rose up in my throat and died. No tears came, just a claustrophobic dizziness that felt like there was no way out.

That night when Justas called, I told him I didn't want to go out with him. My words came out evenly. I had scripted them carefully. "Justas, I've decided that you shouldn't call me anymore."

"Why?" he asked. He sounded a little breathless, a little shocked.

"I just don't think we'd get along," I said, and hung up the phone.

"You did the right thing, Mary," my mother said from the living room. "Someday you'll understand and you'll thank us for it."

School began the following week. Before it started I cut my hair, styled it into a bubble, and covered my face with a mask of heavy makeup. In a yellow blouse that I borrowed from my sister, I walked in three-inch platform-soled shoes through the doors of the public high school on my very first day, carrying an algebra book under my arm. I never heard from Justas again.

PART THREE

Back to Mississippi

CHAPTER 15

The Collector's Fair

I DID NOT RETURN to Mississippi until 1981.

In the intervening years, my mother had tried to keep the family in one place, but we had begun to scatter. Hers was a difficult loyalty to disappoint: having spent her adult life raising children, she faced a role reversal that made it painful to let go. Each of us in our own way would recognize our need to create an independent life; but in our desire not to leave our mother stranded, it would take some of us longer than the others to achieve it. Not surprisingly, I was the last one to make the break.

In March of 1981 my brother Gene rented a Winnebago motor home and drove to visit the Mississippi relatives with my father, my husband, and me and our two young sons. Sam and Joe were three years old and five months old. My mother stayed home in Minnesota.

The route we'd traveled in 1966 had all but vanished. With the construction of the interstate highway system, it was smarter now to take the expressways: from Minneapolis to Chicago, from Chicago to Memphis, and from Memphis to Meridian. We ate in fast-food restaurants during the day, and stopped in the parking lots of KOA campgrounds each night. Scenic, it was not.

My father was in his early sixties and just beginning to show the signs of emphysema, but he had yet to quit smoking. He and my mother still lived in our childhood home on York Avenue, though most of the neighbors we'd known as kids had moved away and the place was now peopled with families who had a new generation of young children to raise.

My memories of this trip to Mississippi are sketchy and few. I remember Aunt Ruby calling me into her bedroom, then pulling an enormous pair of underpants from her dresser drawer and showing them to me, laughing and asking if I'd ever seen a pair so big. I hadn't. I remember going to the cemetery with Auntie Lu to visit Uncle Ed's grave. He had died in 1975 of lung cancer, and she squeezed my hand when we stood before his headstone. Uncle Maurice, whom I hardly knew, was living with Lumiere now. He had retired and was in a wheelchair. One of his legs had been amputated because of diabetes.

I remember my sons riding go-karts on the farm with Susie Lee's kids, and visiting with Darla, who'd driven in from Jackson to see us. She'd graduated from college and was selling insurance. She was smart and pretty and fun. Jimmy and his wife had two little kids, and had built a house not far from Ruby's.

IN 1970, sixteen years after *Brown*, Neshoba County had finally integrated its public schools. The media had converged on the county much as they had six years before, when they had found shocking images of Klan violence and murder to broadcast across the nation and around the world. Only this time there was no violence to report. Integration took place without incident and the event passed by with little coverage. Nobody in the national media had seen news value in the remarkable changes that the community had undergone in the aftermath of Freedom Summer; changes that had made it possible for peaceful integration to occur.

Because no blood had been shed the first day of school, the media had dispersed, disappointed that the events they'd come to cover hadn't taken place. It took a full year before an item would appear in the *New York Times*, announcing, "Philadelphia has abolished segregation as thoroughly and with as little friction as any place of its size and racial makeup in the South."

WHAT I DO REMEMBER vividly is the Collector's Fair.

Uncle Ed, whose obsession with antique clocks did not flower until after he had retired, wasn't the only collector in the family. Uncle Arby also collected objects and had been amassing things since the early 1950s, when he and Aunt Emily moved west to find and sell rare stones in California.

Thirty years later, Uncle Arby's hobby filled an extra room that he and Aunt Emily had built onto the side of their small house in Meridian, and they had begun to host a Collector's Fair. One weekend a month, collectors converged on the Lauderdale County Fairgrounds to walk up and down rows of tables upon which Arby had displayed his most recent acquisitions and the consignment items of other collectors and dealers: brass spittoons, hand-painted porcelain, Depression glass, lemonade sets, and vintage cookbooks. The tables stood in the shade beneath an enormous canopy, under which I pushed my sleeping baby in a stroller past displays of cut glass goblets in ruby red and emerald green, and stacks of transparent pink dessert plates etched with a dainty pattern of flowering magnolia.

People were everywhere. One woman picked up a copper teakettle and examined the bottom for holes. Another called her daughter over to look at a baby doll dressed in ivory lace, with pink cheeks painted on its white china face and dimples in its tiny hands. Children had gathered in front of a dollhouse filled with tiny furniture. Aunt Emily stood guard over the exhibit, to keep small hands from touching the irresistibly tiny spinning wheel, the doll-size apple pie on the miniature sideboard, or the little petit point footstool. The entire house was furnished in miniature, from the yellow and white checked canopy bed in the child's bedroom to the postage stamp–size portraits of Jefferson Davis and Robert E. Lee that hung over the little marble mantelpiece.

The men congregated with Uncle Arby around the tools and farm implements. There were rusted pitchforks with weathered wooden handles, claw foot hammers, awls, and two-handled saws. There were shovels and rakes and wheelbarrows, and gadgets whose uses had become obsolete: a wooden device for corking root beer bottles, a wire carpet beater, a wooden yoke for a team of oxen, and a harness for a team of mules.

Seated on a tall stool behind the cash register, wearing his Mississippi Southern baseball cap, Maurice rang up purchases and made change. Auntie Lu sold sandwiches and soda from behind the picnic table where the cash register stood, keeping her money in a carpenter's apron full of pockets that she wore around her waist.

I was touched by the familiarity of the scene. Uncle Maurice and Auntie Lu chatted with the customers, and laughter rose up easily and often from their side of the tent. The fair drew a crowd of regular customers and antique collectors. Long lines formed wherever Arby or Emily stood, waiting to shake hands, hug, and ask questions. It was the kind of activity that attracted the attention of those who had a personal interest in preserving objects that they believed held value and told a story about their heritage. When someone made a purchase, it was as though the treasures at the Collector's Fair were being kept in the family.

BACK IN 1970, in that first class of integrated six-year-olds, there were two boys, one black and the other white, one of whom was destined to receive national attention twelve years later. His name was Marcus Dupree, and by the time he was a junior in high school, he had become the best running back in the history of Philadelphia High School, and was considered by NCAA scouts to be one of the best running backs in the country.

In 1981, during his junior year, the top colleges and universities in the nation were recruiting Dupree. Neshoba County's embrace of a young man of color was uniting its people with a sense of shared community pride in a way that they had never before experienced.

The other boy was Cecil Price Jr., son of the former deputy sheriff, who was Dupree's teammate. Price was a substitute who didn't play much, but he helped Marcus with his uniform, brought him water, and from time to time sat beside him on the bench, his arm around Marcus's shoulders for moral support. Marcus Dupree would win the accolades of the community, sports media, and NCAA coaches who came to watch him play. Cecil Price Jr. would watch him proudly from the sidelines.

In 1975, when the two boys were in the fifth grade, CBS aired a prime time documentary about Freedom Summer, the Klan, and the murders of Goodman, Schwerner, and Chaney. The following day, young Price was beaten up by a group of black students at school, and the black community spoke out quickly against any violence directed toward the deputy sheriff's son.

"You can't blame the kids for what the parents were involved in," Dupree's mother had said. "That happened a whole generation ago. The kids now don't pay attention to color. It's not a big thing. They go to class together. They play ball together.

"But what happened seventeen years ago has to be remembered," she added. "It should always be remembered."

Cecil and Marcus became friends and visited in each other's homes. "I like him and he likes me," Marcus said.

Twenty years after Dupree's graduation from Philadelphia High School, I will meet Stanley Dearman, a reporter in the early 1960s for the *Meridian Star* who bought the *Neshoba Democrat* in 1966 and was its editor for the next thirty-five years. Stan will tell me that he remembers a rally for Marcus Dupree in the early 1980s, where the wife of one of the most outspoken white supremacists in town ("her husband was in the Klan big time," he said) had walked up to Marcus, given him a big hug, and asked him to autograph her football.

"You've come a long way, Margaret," Stan reflected to himself.

THE NOTION of value is, of course, subjective: what one person proudly displays on the mantelpiece is another person's twenty-five-cent yard sale bargain. What I might store in the attic for safekeeping, my neighbor will simply throw away. At the Collector's Fair, I'd had my eye on a brass basket with a handle that I could picture in my living room at home, on the oak bookcase that was built into the wall beside the fireplace. It was a house my husband and I had stretched to buy two years before, and would lose to foreclosure soon afterward. But I told nobody of my financial worries, though I looked longingly at the brass basket, its warm burnish catching a bit of light when I picked it up.

"You like that?" Uncle Arby asked, putting his arm around my shoulder.

"It's pretty, isn't it?" I said, and put it down. I didn't want him to know that I couldn't afford it. I walked back toward my father at the checkout table.

My Mississippi family lived close to one another, exchanged recipes, spent weekends together, dropped by in the afternoon for a visit, and knew when somebody was sick. If they didn't live in the neighborhood where they grew up, they lived in close proximity. Many of them had married their high school sweethearts. They knew one another's favorite foods. They shelled pecans together, crocheted afghans together, and called one another several times a week just to say hey. My cousins on the farm lived within shouting distance of their parents. Darla lived in Jackson, which was two hours away from Uncle Arby and Aunt Emily, but she called her parents frequently, just to check in. Maurice had moved into Auntie Lu's spare bedroom after Uncle Ed died, and they gardened together, shopped together, and Lumiere had a ramp installed over the front steps for his wheelchair. She fed him, drove him to the doctor, and in his last months, tended him at his bedside until he died.

Over the next decade, my father's stories would have to do with family tending to the sick and dying. Aunt Ruby and Uncle Lafe had someone from the family looking after them at home during their last days. Susie and her husband and teenaged kids, Jimmy and his family, Lumiere and the others rallied around Ruby and Lafe so that they were never left unattended. "That's the way we do for our people," Auntie Lu said. Auntie Lu was at Uncle Ed's bedside every day and through the night until he died.

I tried to think of something from home that would have brought the Lind family together in such an intimate way. Unlike my father's siblings, the Lind Girls had moved away from the home turf: Aunt Jane to Atlanta, Aunt Louise to Palm Springs, and Sophie to New York City. I hardly knew my East and West Coast cousins and I hadn't seen my cousin Missy for almost twenty years. We gathered for weddings and showers and the occasional Christmas party, and we relied on the Lind Girl pipeline for news about our cousins, which usually consisted of who was getting married, having a baby, moving, or getting a divorce. The divorces had begun a decade before, and though I didn't know it that afternoon of the Collector's Fair, I was next in line.

Divorce didn't occur south of the Mason-Dixon Line, at least not in my family. To be honest, it occurred, but we didn't talk about it. Uncle Maurice had gotten a divorce, but that was decades before, and he'd been happily married to his second wife for many years until her death in the 1970s. Marriage was for life, and divorce wouldn't touch my father's relations again for two generations, and not until the end of the century. Even then, despite the reassurance of parents, siblings, aunts, and cousins, the feeling was that divorce would somehow let the family down.

But here was Uncle Maurice in his Mississippi Southern hat, sitting behind the cash register at the Collector's Fair with my father, wearing his Ole Miss Rebel T-shirt, their laughter punctuated by big bites from the ham salad sandwiches Auntie Lu had handed them from behind the picnic table.

While they talked, customers lined up with armfuls of quilts, kerosene lamps, and copper bed warmers, but nobody seemed to mind. In fact, they were waiting to talk to my father, the prodigal, the long-lost son who'd come back to see his kin. So making change meant making small talk, slapping my father on the back and trading stories about who was sick, who'd died, and who was about to die. They talked about the weather, their farms, their kids, and their grandkids. One woman holding a ceramic chamber pot came up to my father and took his hand. "Chub," she said. "Just yesterday Mama was askin' after y'all. She'll be so proud that we had a chance to visit."

"You tell her I'm doin' fine," my father said to her. He squeezed her hand.

"Who was that?" I asked him after the woman turned to leave.

"I have no idea," he replied.

Throughout the afternoon I checked to see if anyone had purchased the brass basket. Though I knew I couldn't buy it, I was reassured when I saw that it was still there.

My husband had stayed back at the farm with Sam and Gene. They'd ridden tractors and watched television that afternoon. Which was where we were headed when we said good-bye and turned away from the tent. Joe started to cry, and I picked him up. My father had purchased something and placed the brown paper bag into the empty seat of the stroller, pushing it through the dusty parking lot toward the car.

I nursed the baby on the way back to Ruby's, where a hot dinner was on the table and my husband and little boy waited for me. I was strangely tired, more than what I'd usually feel at the end of a warm day. I was pregnant again, as I would discover at home the following month.

After dinner, Ruby took the baby and rocked him on the front porch while Sam played catch with his dad on the front lawn. My father came to the screen door and called me in. He handed me a paper bag. I opened it, and inside was the brass basket. "Arby wanted to surprise you," my father said.

It was one of the few things I took with me when I finally left my husband in 1985. That and a collection of dishes from Grandma Lind, packed carefully and toted in boxes from place to place. The brass basket sits on an oak bookcase near the fireplace in the house where I live now.

I'm a person who hangs on to things. Sometimes they bring me great happiness; a connection to the past, to events and people that only exist now in memory. Sometimes they stay with me but are hidden, though only to myself, until something happens and I see that they've been visible all the time. I've been dusting them off and keeping them in good repair, though I haven't even been aware of it. More often than not, these collections are just as familiar to me as my grandmother's dishes, but connect me to a history I'd rather not address.

The following year, my father and I traveled to Mississippi with my daughter, Sarah.

In the seven years since I'd been married, I had become a third-generation Lind Girl. I lived in my mother's neighborhood, did not work outside the home, and was financially dependent upon my husband. I hadn't finished college. I'd had lots of kids young. My life was spent worrying about money and rearranging the knick-knacks on my coffee table; I sewed Halloween costumes for my children and cooked pot roast for supper once a week.

I did not own a car. I didn't think I needed one. I'd slipped so easily into this life that I hadn't noticed that once I'd outgrown the identity I'd borrowed from my older sister, I'd easily taken on my mother's. Not that being a Lind Girl was a bad thing: it wasn't wrong to cook and clean and stay home with my children. The bad thing was that once again I'd taken on somebody else's personality because I hadn't developed one of my own.

My husband was a storyteller with a wonderful sense of humor. Nice looking and popular, he made friends easily. He also moved from job to job after college, and he spent more evenings than I liked away from home. My husband was very fervent in his faith, and I'd hoped that his Christian zeal would be our salvation. It wasn't. Our marriage was falling apart, and getting away for a few days to Mississippi seemed like a good idea.

My father and I stayed with the baby at Auntie Lu's in Meridian for several days before driving out to the farm to see Ruby. Over the weekend, my husband called. It was Sunday afternoon. Lumiere was in the bedroom, changing Sarah's diaper, and my father was asleep on the sofa, in front of the television set. I answered the phone. From the tone of my husband's voice on the other end, I knew that something was wrong.

One of the clocks on the mantel struck.

"No, the boys are fine," he said. Two and four years old, they were staying with my mother.

That's when I knew. "I'm so sorry," he said into the phone. "I'm so sorry." I heard him, but the words just hovered over me. I held my breath, as though waiting for a prompt, a cue, the exact words to say.

"Say something," he said. I heard myself tell him that I forgave him. And when I did, his voice became light and animated.

"I knew I'd feel better if I told you as soon as possible," he said. "I can't carry this stuff all by myself. You know that. You shouldn't have gone. I told you it was a big mistake."

I looked out the family room window. Just beyond the camellias was the small patch of garden, now covered with yellow pine straw, where Uncle Maurice had told me he would plant tomatoes, corn, and pole beans in the spring. He sat there now, sunning himself in his wheelchair, a brown paper sack on his lap and another on the grass beside him. With one hand, Maurice took a pecan from the bag on his lap, placed it between the pincers of the nutcracker he held in the other hand, and cracked it open. The shell splintered into the bag, freeing the pecan, which, in halves, he put into the bag beside him on the short, amber-colored grass.

My ears began to buzz, the sound growing louder and louder until it drowned out the drone of my husband's chatter on the other end of the line. I could hear nothing else above the buzzing. We were in deep financial trouble and were losing our home.

The grandfather clock behind me chimed six times. "What time is it?" I asked my husband.

"A quarter to three," he said.

Maurice took another pecan and cracked its shell with the nut-cracker. Again and again, one at a time, he cracked open the nuts and placed them in the bag at his feet.

Maurice had a daughter from his first marriage.

"That's her right here," my father says, pulling out Grandma Ora's funeral photograph again and pointing at a dark-haired girl of about ten who looks like she's ready to run away from the open casket but for her father's hand on her shoulder. Uncle Maurice hasn't seen his daughter in more than twenty years, though nobody says why. She lives in Arkansas and has children that Maurice never laid eyes on.

Just before he died, Maurice told Lumiere that he didn't want his daughter at the funeral. "If she didn't want to see me while I was alive, I don't want her squallin' over me when I'm dead," he told her. I never got to talk to Maurice about how it feels to be divorced, separated from people you love, and heartsick. I wonder what he could have told me. It takes heartache to understand heart-ache.

Maurice turned and wheeled himself toward the side of the house, where Lumiere had had a ramp installed over the steps so he could come in and out more easily in his chair. He took off his hat and, red-faced, maneuvered his wheelchair through the kitchen door. He placed the sack of pecans on the table. "I got about a quart, today," he called to Lumiere in the other room. He looked at me. "Y'all can take these home to your mama," he said.

"Hey, you still there?" my husband asked. I was still holding the receiver but hadn't said anything.

I shouldn't have gone. The words filled me. They covered me up. My head buzzed. My fingers tingled. I hung up the phone and went over to the table. I took half a pecan from the bag and bit into it. Its brown-skinned surface tasted dry and slightly bitter, but became mellow and soft when my teeth bit through to its inner meaty heart.

The next afternoon, we drove out to Ruby's.

In the morning I tucked Sarah into a pack on my back for a hike across the farm. I wanted to watch the sun rise over the hills the way my father did, when he was a boy and led his grandfather's cows to pasture before breakfast. Sixty years separated our early morning walks.

It was before dawn. The sky was pale and milky, and the sun had yet to rise. My father was still sleeping. I didn't tell him why I wanted to walk; nor would I have taken the car.

I tramped up and down a wide ridge, hilly and peppered with stones, watching for the sky to change. The landscape was unplowed and untilled, the horizon unbroken from one end of the farm to the other. The shuttered brick houses that belonged to my aunts and cousins, the faded red barns, the chicken coops flying with feathers, and canning shed full of jars of preserves were tucked back behind scrub pines, pecan groves, and miles and miles of green hills cut through here and there by a ravine, and at the bottom of the ravine, a creek.

It was a leafless, birdless December morning, two weeks before Christmas. My shoes made no tracks on the hard, grassless ground. I walked for an hour while Sarah babbled, making gurgling noises from her place in the pack behind me. Then, just before seven, the horizon began to change. A red coverlet pulled itself over the silhouette of low trees, and I sat on a boulder to watch.

The aurora, backlit and blood colored, stained the white sky till overhead everything turned crimson. Sarah began to squirm, frustrated that we were no longer moving. In a moment she was crying. The sun rose then as if suddenly awakened, like a redheaded woman in a rosy pink nightgown, running long yellow fingers through her fiery, tangled hair.

Sarah's cries became insistent and her hands, slapping the back of my neck, grabbed a hank of my hair and pulled. Hard. I reached behind me and removed her, howling, red and hungry, from the pack. Placing her, squirming, on my lap, I unbuttoned my sweater. Familiar with our ritual, she pushed her face against me, leaned her cheek against my breast, and nursed. Her tense little body relaxed against mine. I stroked her cheek and she wrapped her fist around my finger.

Everything became still except for the rhythm of her sucking and swallowing. Looking up from her face—eyes closed, nose and mouth pressed against me—to the wide, auburn sky above us, I thought of the blue-gray sky of home. Sarah pulled away from my breast and grinned, her breath blowing transparent bubbles of milk from her parted lips. I buttoned my sweater and tucked her back into the pack, the sky burning in flames all around me.

I became aware of a wide and uninhabited space inside of me and knew that for a long time I had been lonely. My marriage was in pieces. I missed my two little boys at home in Minnesota. My father waited for me down the road at his sister's, and a hot breakfast would greet me when I walked through the kitchen door. But I felt hungry for more than Ruby's biscuits. I felt hungry for what had become only an image of home, a place where I was supposed to belong and be welcomed, where I would feel secure and loved. But home was vanishing into a whisper of smoke before my eyes. I was homesick for a place that no longer existed.

The sky faded into the ordinariness of the day, and the ground where I stood became unremarkable in its emptiness. I had walked far away from the house. I stood up and headed back to Ruby's, walking the hard-packed shoulder of the red clay road.

A blue pickup truck slowed to a stop beside us. I saw the sky through a translucent Confederate flag that covered the rearview window. A pair of brown mongrels with thick necks and square muzzles panted in the cab beside a middle-aged man in a filthy DeKalb seed cap, who leaned out the window and asked, between corncob teeth, "Y'all Chub's girl?"

He spat a load of brown tobacco juice at my feet.

I'd never seen this man before. "Yes," I said. "And this is his grandbaby."

"Awright then," he said, and took the steering wheel with a hand from which a couple of fingers were missing. He pulled his head back into the cab, looked ahead at the road, and with an unsmiling nod, pulled away. There was a rack of shotguns in the flatbed. His bumper sticker read IF YOU THINK MY MULE IS UGLY, YOU SHOULD SEE MY WIFE.

Back at the house, my father sat at the kitchen table in his red bathrobe. His steely hair stood up at funny angles, sleep-slanted and full of unruly cowlicks. At the stove, Ruby fried thick strips of bacon in her cast-iron skillet. Grits bubbled in a saucepan. With both chubby hands, Sarah grabbed a biscuit from a platter on the table and stuffed it into her mouth. Honey dripped from her chin. I asked my father if he knew this man. Before he could answer, Ruby turned from the stove, put her hands on her hips and laughed.

"Don't matter," she said. "You kin."

CHAPTER 16

Salvage

ANOTHER FIFTEEN YEARS will pass before I go back to Mississippi. During that time, I will watch my children grow up to become young adults. I will be single again; only this time I will finish college, with three growing kids and on a waitress's salary. I will build a career and buy a little house. I will go to graduate school. Little by little, I will shed much of the clothing I'd borrowed from my sister and my mother over the years, and try to live with what I can't discard. I will slowly watch myself emerge from under all that secondhand laundry, and I'll begin to write about it.

The last time I was in Mississippi, my father drove me to visit his siblings. To Ruby in her kitchen, frying chicken in a cast-iron skillet; Maurice shelling pecans in the backyard; Arby making change behind the cash register at the Collector's Fair; Auntie Lu in a straw hat fishing for crappies at the reservoir.

This time, he's in the passenger seat and I'm driving him to cemeteries. Ruby and Lafe lie side by side behind the Pine Grove

Church. Maurice and Arby are buried at Magnolia Cemetery in Meridian, about ten minutes from Lumiere's. She and my father are the only ones left.

Like my father, I'm homesick for the Deep South of his boyhood. Time is swallowing it up acre by acre, and with it all those people whose memories once kept it alive. A big chunk of Lafe and Ruby's farm is now covered with auto salvage. Frank keeps their property neat: the lawn is mowed and the porch swept, but the place is quiet and still with the absence of life. Frank himself is about to retire, and who, if anyone, will care for these abandoned buildings when he's no longer able? He and Susie Lee now have an empty nest: their kids went away to school and are building lives in bigger cities throughout the South.

Cliff's store is a shell, and working people now chat with one another on weekends from behind their shopping carts at Wal-Mart. Jimmy's grandkids are dressed in outfits from Baby Gap and collect the Happy Meal toys from McDonald's. Auntie Lu's breakfast biscuits come out of the refrigerated section in the grocery store, and when Aunt Emily brings fried chicken, it's in a red and white striped carryout box. My generation is too busy to sit and visit on the front porch after supper. When I ask Susie Lee questions about the past, she shakes her head and says that she wishes she'd paid more attention to the old folks.

It was time for somebody to put the world my father knew on paper so that it would not vanish completely into the silence of a culture built on sameness. I decided to write things down.

I reconstructed my father's stories and began to interview him, taking a small tape recorder with me whenever I visited. Once a month for three years, we talked in the tiny den of the senior high-rise apartment where he and my mother, both in their eighties, now reside. My father has chronic lung disease: asthma, emphysema, and a host of allergies that without warning can send him into purple fits of coughing.

As his lungs deteriorated, he became more prone to pulmonary infections, and so I brought the recorder with me to visit him in the hospital, where he'd talk to me despite the tubes in his nostrils, the machines that helped him breathe, and the pills he had to take every fifteen minutes. Before he became too ill to travel, we took a series of short trips back to Mississippi, to listen to relatives I'd met before, kinfolks I'd heard about and family members who came alive again in stories.

Auntie Lu can't sit still. Her hands are always busy, and she likes to talk while she works. She ran away from home at sixteen to marry Uncle Ed, a farmer who was also sixteen. It was 1930, the year after Daddy Bob lost the farm. The family was living in a boxcar then, and would soon move in with Pappy and Donie.

"Ed was young, but he was responsible even then," Lumiere says, wiping the front of the stove with a wet rag. "He milked, plowed, and took care of his mama and daddy. You grew up fast then," she says. "You had to."

I'm leafing through one of Lumiere's photo albums, and pause for a moment at a snapshot of her, young and pretty, smiling the same smile she gives me now as I turn the pages. "My mama cried for two weeks when she found out what I'd done."

My father and Auntie Lu sit together now on the sofa, watching the Gatlin Brothers on television. I look up from my book. The two of them are holding hands. She cares for him by fixing mountains of food: eggs scrambled in bacon grease and biscuits dripping with scuppernong jelly for breakfast. Ham, butter beans, and lemon meringue pie for dinner. "Would y'all like more congealed salad?" she asks, passing a mold of red Jell-O studded with canned pineapple chunks and crowned with Cool Whip.

"No, thanks, honey," he says. "I eat too much already."

He cares for her by worrying about her health. "I don't like the sound of that," he says when she breaks into a coughing fit.

"Don't y'all worry about me," she told my father earlier when I was out of earshot. "M' fever broke last night. I swear I woke up sweatin' worse'n a nigger preacher." My father looked at me and put a finger to his lips when he told me this, out of earshot of Auntie Lu.

I close the photograph album on her smiling picture.

There's a shout just outside, and I get up to look out the kitchen window. From the house across the street, a disheveled man stumbles down the side steps. He looks as if he has slept in his clothes. His tousled black hair sticks up at crazy angles from his head, and his bloodshot eyes dart wildly from side to side. He licks his lips and begins to pace the driveway, zigzagging up and down the asphalt, shoulders stooped, an open Bible in one hand. He stops at the curb and begins to shout, quoting from the page he holds up to the sky.

"Blessed are the meek, for they shall inherit the earth," he yells into the street. He pauses, staggers across the lawn, and leans against the fence. "Who is this man that even the wind and the waves obey him?" He holds the Bible in one hand and waves the other hand around and around over his head, pointing upward with one finger, as if he were trying to mark a circle in the air.

Against our side of the fence, Lumiere's waxy green camellia droops slightly with tight, full buds that look as though they're ready to burst into blossoms. "Don't let ol' Dutch bother y'all none," Lumiere says from the sofa. She gets up from her place beside my father and comes over to the window. "He's paranoid skiptofrenic, but he wouldn't harm a flea."

I wake to shouts in the middle of the night. I've been asleep in the front bedroom, in the high double bed covered in pale blue quilts that Maurice slept in when he lived with Auntie Lu before he died, back in the 1980s. I step onto the wooden floor, cold against my bare feet, and tiptoe across the living room to the kitchen window. Dutch stands alone in his driveway, bathed in light from a streetlamp just above him. He is dressed in a brown T-shirt and green surgical pants. He stands in his bare feet.

In a repeat of his earlier performance, he holds his Bible in one hand, but this time the other hand is clenched into a fist that he's shaking at the sky. He gets even crazier at night, and sprinkles the verses with cusswords in a thick, raspy voice that sputters with coughing. "And then I saw the mother fuckin' seven horsemen riding up the mother fuckin' hill."

He closes the Bible and bends over at the waist, coughing so hard that he spits a throatful of something horrible into the street.

Then he looks up, shakes his fist, and opens his Bible to read again. He repeats this over and over—the shouting, coughing, spitting, and shaking—trancelike, a kind of street performance that reminds me of the apocalyptic televangelists whose faces twitch with anger as they preach into the camera. I imagine the entire neighborhood watching him from inside their houses, peering at him in the middle of the night from behind their windows, like me, holding the curtain aside just so, to get a better look.

Lumiere appears noiselessly beside me in pink pajamas, her pageboy held back from her face with bobby pins. "I had that streetlamp put in," she whispers, and takes a glass from the cupboard beside the sink. "Mercy," she goes on, filling the glass with water from the tap. "I didn't want 'im sneakin' up on me and shoutin' in my yard. This way we all can see him, the whole neighborhood. Pearl, Nelson, ever'body."

She takes a drink of water and looks back out at Dutch, who is shouting and shaking his fist at the sky. "'Cept now I think he b'lieves he's got him a stage." She chuckles a little, pats me on the cheek with a "good night, darlin'," and we both go back to bed.

MY FATHER and I are sitting with our backs against a gum tree. The sap is running, and the bark is sticky, leaving a milky resin on our clothes. He wears a wool sweater that smells like wet fur. His unshaved face is grizzly beneath a fuzzy brown slouch hat. His arthritis acts up in humid weather, and he has ambled to this spot from the road below. He stopped once to catch his breath and when he reached the tree, lowered himself down slowly beside me.

We sit midpoint on a low hill. The ground is damp beneath us, the branches above us just beginning to bud. "In a month or so these buds'll leaf out real nice," he says. Below us a silver pond, round as a nickel, shines cold in the dim February sunlight.

When he was a boy, my father liked to take his dog Pup into these woods and watch him kill rattlesnakes.

"What kind of dog was it?" I ask.

"Just a hound, a coon dog, I guess," he says. "We'd go down to that pond. Pappy's house was just over yonder." He points to a spot only he can see, a two-room shack, shabby and overgrown, that in his childhood stood somewhere back behind a stand of tall pines, a grove of gum, and by the water a pair of weeping willows. The hills are covered with hard, thin soil that only a few seasons of planting cotton ravaged and left useless over a century ago. Pappy had actually seen the results: the fierce economic competition on this farm between poor whites and the blacks who were supposed to be free. My father, now seventy-seven, was just a boy when he heard the stories from his Pappy, tramping with him up and down these hills, hunting for snakes with his dog.

More and more he blends what he's seen with what was told him: armed men in sheets, blacks and whites shot; garage mechanics and farmers and deputy sheriffs fighting again and again the battle for Philadelphia, the seat of Neshoba County. At first he told me that Pappy was in the Klan. Now he says he never was. Then he tells me that his father was a member.

"But it was like a church group back then," he says.

"A church group?" I look at my father.

He is silent for a moment.

"A church group?" I repeat.

"Yeah. You know, they met and prayed," he says. He changes the subject and points down the hill. "When they couldn't farm this land anymore, they let the trees take over. And when I was little, these pastures was just loaded with snakes," he says.

"Snakes?" We sit on a winter's blanketing of wet leaves. I expect that from under twig and leaf and rotting compost at any moment we might see a diamondback slither out toward us.

My father laughs. "We're too high up. They like to stay low, down by the pond in the tall grass."

"Did you wear boots?" I ask, looking down at my loafers. All of a sudden the soles seem flimsy, the socks that cover my ankles too thin.

"Didn't own boots. I went barefoot all summer. By the time August rolled around, the soles of my feet were so tough I could strike a match off the calluses."

The breeze coming up the hill is too cool to be comfortable, and I shift a little, leaning closer in to my father. I look up at his face: jowly, ruddy, with tiny red veins showing beneath the thin skin of his nose.

"Didn't Pup get bit?" I ask.

"Pup'd been bit by rattlesnakes so many times he was full of antidote. He knew a rattlesnake better'n anyone. He'd see a snake sunnin' himself in the grass and he'd circle that snake, making him nervous.

"The snake'd begin to coil, but Pup just kept circlin', patient and slow. When the snake was coiled up tight as a bedspring, Pup'd set there on all fours and watch 'im. Seemed like forever. Two sets of eyes jus' starin' each other down. The snake shook and rattled and finally it STRUCK."

I jump, startled, and my father laughs again.

"That ol' dog knew just when and where the rattler would spring. And he was ready. He'd jump up quicker'n spit, grab the rattlesnake by the neck and shake 'im dead."

As he speaks, I look over at the pond and re-create the scene in my mind. In it, my father isn't my father anymore but a boy with his face shadowed, hiding in the crotch of a low-slung gum tree. The sap rises slowly from its roots, and from its branches he watches me. And I am running through the tall grass down the hill, circling the perimeter of the farm. I jump over small rises in the earth. I listen for the sound of footsteps and watch for the S-shaped slither of a snake.

I've walked away from my father, away from the tree. And as I disappear down the hill, he calls after me. "Be careful down there." But I can't hear him. I am a child again, and forty years will pass before I even enter the scene and play it out in this way.

ONCE I'D BEGUN to read about the murders of Andy Goodman, J. E. Chaney, and Mickey Schwerner, I wondered if there was anyone in the family I could talk to about them. Right away, my sister Liz suggested that I ask our cousin Jimmy, Ruby's son. "He's great," she'd said. "He gets it that we're interested. He's interested too."

My cousin Jimmy didn't have any problem talking to me about what it had been like back then. I saw in him a friend whom I could trust, and I was rewarded with his trust as well. I knew that he was a good person, and he knew that I knew it. So when I asked him to take me to the places where the three young men had spent the last day of their lives, he said sure, and invited his teenage son to come along for the ride.

What follows are the words of a federal grand jury indictment returned against eighteen men implicated in the 1964 murders in Neshoba County of Michael Schwerner, Andrew Goodman, and James Chaney:

"It was part of the plan and purpose of the conspiracy that Cecil Ray Price, while having Michael Henry Schwerner, James Earl Chaney, and Andrew Goodman in custody in the Neshoba County Jail located in Philadelphia, Mississippi, would release them from custody at such time that he, Cecil Ray Price, Jimmy Arledge, Horace Doyle Barnette, Travis Maryn Barnette, Alton Wayne Roberts, Jimmie Snowden, James E. Jordan, Billy Wayne Posey, Jerry McGrew Sharpe and Jimmy Lee Townsend could and would intercept Michael Henry Schwerner, James Earl Chaney and Andrew Goodman in the Neshoba County Jail, and threaten, assault, shoot and kill them . . ."

"I don't know anyone from around here who's in the Klan," Jimmy tells me, and I believe him.

It's Sunday afternoon. We've just finished dinner on the farm, and my father is settling down in Jimmy's recliner for a nap. "What the hell do you want to do that for?" he asks when we announce that Jimmy is going to take me and his son Will for a drive to trace the path that Andrew Goodman, Mickey Schwerner, and James Chaney took the last few hours of their lives. "It was just a bunch of goddamn outsiders did it. The Klan from Meridian. Nobody from around here. Besides, what were they doing here in the first place? Just came to stir up trouble." He is asleep by the time we leave the house.

We drive to Bogue Chitto first, a moccasin-infested swamp that borders one of the Choctaw reservations. Johnny pulls off the road. "Just over yonder." He points to a section of low water out of which rise black bare tree stumps, and beyond which lies an island covered with mossy gum trees. "That's where they burned the station wagon and tried to sink it under water. But the FBI found it right away," he said. "And Jill [Jimmy's wife] remembers them towing the car on the road right in front of her house."

We're en route to the Mount Zion Methodist Church.

"I just don't understand how something like this could've happened," he says. "When we were little, the black kids were our friends. We played with them every day." Later, as part of my research on the South, I read Jimmy Carter's memoir about growing up in rural Georgia. The childhood intimacy he shared with his black friends in the 1920s echoes the intimacy that my cousin recalls from the 1950s, and I become aware of the holes in my own segregated childhood.

The Mount Zion Church has been rebuilt of red brick, like so many of the structures we pass, made from the clay that rises on either side of the roads that are cut into the low red hills. Two monuments have been erected there to the memory of Goodman, Schwerner, and Chaney: one a county marker that we can see by the side of the road; the other a headstone of polished granite, engraved with their three names and the words, "Dedicated to the memory of their struggle to bring equality to all people." A bell hangs by the door. It's all that remains of the church that the Klan had firebombed and burned before the three visited, a fire that Preacher Killen later claimed they had set to lure Mickey Schwerner into the county.

Just before midnight on June 21, 1964, the three were released from the Neshoba County Jail in the center of Philadelphia, where they'd been held for several hours on a trumped-up speeding charge.

I'm surprised at how small the building is, just a lean-to really, converted now into a real estate office. Just around the corner is the First Philadelphia State Bank. My father told me that Aunt Ruby owned the bank for thirty years. It stands beside the county courthouse, facing Courthouse Square.

This was where Dr. Martin Luther King Jr. stood and addressed the hostile crowd that gathered to listen to him speak. Sheriff Rainey was watching the crowd from the sidelines with a walkie-talkie in his hands.

"I do know this," my father would tell me later. "Ruby was on the other end of that walkie-talkie, making sure that nothin' happened at the bank."

After Andy, Mickey, and J. E. were released, two cars overtook their station wagon just outside the city limits. One was a patrol car driven by Deputy Sheriff Cecil Price, who'd arrested the young men that afternoon on Highway 19 and detained them in the jail without access to the customary phone call. The other car was a Ford that belonged to Horace Doyle Barnette, a Klansman from Meridian. There were four men altogether in the cars, and they forced Schwerner, Goodman, and Chaney into the backseat of the deputy sheriff's car.

Jimmy turns his Ford Explorer onto the Rock Cut Road just south of Philadelphia. The road is just recently paved and loops around nooselike to and from Highway 19 for about five miles. Once winding through a remote and wooded area, the road now leads to a popular new seafood restaurant. Houses under construction rise skeletal from clearings every few hundred feet. A pine bough hangs upside down from the ridge beam of one. Two men carry Sheetrock up the gravel drive to another.

The vehicles, one the deputy sheriff's patrol car with the three young men in the backseat, and another full of Klansmen, headed in the direction of the Rock Cut Road. Two of them, Wayne Roberts and James Jordan, were volunteers from Meridian. They stopped at a place to the left of the road where the clay banks rise up on both sides. Roberts jumped out of Travis Barnette's Ford, opened the left rear door of the deputy sheriff's squad car, and pulled Mickey Schwerner out of the backseat.

"You the nigger lover?" he asked.

Roberts pushed the nose of a revolver into Mickey's chest.

"Sir, I know just how you feel," Mickey replied. A moment later Roberts shot him in the heart. Roberts had his hand on the young man's shoulder before pushing him backward into the ditch. He was twenty-four years old.

After watching Schwerner die, Roberts then pulled Andy Goodman from the car, put the revolver to his heart and pulled the trigger at point-blank range. Andy fell into the ditch on top of his companion. It was his second night in Mississippi, and he was twenty years old.

Jimmy slows the Explorer down and points to a rusty trailer on the left. It looks like a can of chewing tobacco left out in the rain. It sags atop crumbling cinder blocks; the screen door falls sideways from the hinges. The yard is littered with old tires and black garbage bags torn open, probably by animals foraging for food. Their contents are strewn across the lawn. A mangy dog with patches of yellow fur pokes his nose into one of the bags.

"You know who lives here, don't you?" He looks over at me. "The Preacher. Cousin Edgar Ray."

Cousin Edgar Ray. I've imagined Edgar Ray Killen sitting in a booth in the Longhorn Drive-in. It's after dinner, perhaps eight o'clock. It's early summer, so there's still plenty of time before the sun goes down. The deputy sheriff drives past and tips his hat. Cousin Edgar Ray nods and goes to the phone. He fishes in his pockets for dimes and a folded-up scrap of paper. He looks down at the paper and dials the numbers on the rotary phone. He mumbles the word "goatee" into the phone, hangs up, and dials again. The sheriff has a problem, he says.

I've never met Cousin Edgar Ray. But from everything I've read, I feel like I know him: a kleagle for the White Knights of Mississippi. Recruiting Klansmen into the Lauderdale and Neshoba County klaverns. On the lookout for a kid from New York. And then, on a June night in 1964, the night of his life, he's focused, careful, and busy. Buying rubber gloves and gassing up the cars. Gathering the guns and the ammunition. Making sure the burial site is ready. Finding someone to run the bulldozer. Handpicking just the right men.

I feel carsick.

Mickey and Andy lay dead in the ditch. "Save one for me," James Jordan said to Roberts. He got out of the deputy's car and pulled James Chaney from the backseat. J. E. was the only African American of the three and the only Mississippi native. J. E. backed up and stood on the bank on the other side of the ditch. Some reports suggest that he ran. Jordan stood in the middle of the road and shot him. "You didn't leave me anything but a nigger," he said. "But at least I killed me a nigger." J. E. was twenty-one.

The autopsy later showed that of the three who were murdered that night, only J. E. had been beaten before he was shot.

Edgar Ray Killen, along with Sheriff Rainey and Sam Bowers, Imperial Wizard of the White Knights of Mississippi, were indicted: "To injure, oppress, threaten, and intimidate Michael Henry

Schwerner, Andrew Goodman and James Earl Chaney, each a citizen of the United States, in the free exercise and enjoyment of the right and privilege secured to them by the 14th Amendment of the Constitution of the United States not to be deprived of life or liberty without due process of law."

"I thought you didn't know anybody in the Klan," I say.

"No more than you do," Jimmy says. He pauses for a moment before he speaks again.

"We don't claim him."

Earlier, in the library, I'd come across a newspaper editorial from the *Neshoba Democrat*, dated April 4, 1964, three months after Mickey Schwerner had arrived in Mississippi. Jack Long Tannehill, editor since 1954, had written it. "Outsiders who come in here and try to stir up trouble should be dealt with in a manner they won't forget," he wrote. Would it have changed anything if he had seen the flaw in his thinking? It's not the dead who remember, after all. It's those of us who remain behind.

IN 1964, Neshoba County covered twenty-four square miles of pine-woods and pastures. The twenty thousand people who lived there were made up of fifteen thousand whites, the remaining five thousand split evenly between African Americans and Choctaw. Most Choctaw lived on the Pearl River Reservation six miles south of Philadelphia. Most Philadelphia blacks lived in Independence Quarters and a neighborhood the whites called Shaky Ground.

Those who didn't live in Philadelphia resided in clusters of country neighborhoods off the main road with a little land and a handful of small churches.

Jimmy has helped me see a great deal. But for the most part, the information from my father's kin is the kind that would fill a family Bible: who married whom, whose uncle died when, the date of a baby's birth. When I ask about Mississippi politics, history, and culture, however, a wall goes up. What I want to know about my father's home state, county, and local community, I will have to discover in books. And once I begin, I find that my appetite for information grows. I order books over the Internet, haunt libraries, and sit in the corners of bookstores. I want to know about Mississippi's history, its politics and people.

And I want to know how, in a place where people have always shown me such warmth and affection, three young strangers could have been murdered, and the Klan so in control. I want to know how a family member could have been involved and I want to know if anyone I knew—especially those who had always been so good to me—were aware of what was going on. I want to know how this was possible. Could it have happened in any community? Could it have happened in my community? How could it have happened at all?

MIDWAY THROUGH my father's leather-bound copy of *The Attic*, House High School's annual for 1940, his senior year, a face looks out from the center of the page devoted to the freshman class. The kid looks shy, and something about the way his lips are slightly parted makes it appear as though he could use a little encouragement. With dark hair, dark eyes, and a heart-shaped face, he looks intense. Years later, I see his mug shot in a book, and his empty face with its hard features is almost Proustian: vacant and roomy as an untenanted house. "Did you know him, growing up?" I ask my father.

"No, not really. I knew that my aunt had married a Killen, but I don't remember much of Edgar Ray," he says. "I might have seen him at revivals. Maybe at holidays. He probably showed up at family reunions. That type a deal."

CHAPTER 17

Bogue Chitto

AT THE BOTTOM OF MY POCKET is a copper-colored stone that I worry over with my thumb. I feel its ridges, solid and unyielding, in moments of anxiety, which means that I reach for it often throughout the day. Its shape brings to mind a variety of images: the broken-off fragment of a toppled headstone or the head of a bear, its skin convoluted in pouches of deep red wrinkles. The porous stone warms when my hand closes over it, and I almost expect the ridges to become supple under the warmth, like scar tissue over a childhood wound.

I extracted the stone from the mouth of a cave, below the belly of Nanih Waiya, the grass-covered burial mound that rises from the edges of the Bogue Chitto swamp, just north of the Neshoba County line. I loosened it easily, like picking off a scab, and noticed that its contours resembled a face worn into folds that reminded me of Lincoln's: craggy like that.

From the cave's narrow opening I heard the sound of water dripping deep inside.

My father was anxious about the cave and waited for me in the car. Seventy years ago, he and Arby had crawled in on their stomachs, far into the darkness where all around them water snaked down the damp, dark walls and dripped with the sound of footsteps into shallow pools on the cool limestone floor. Arby took the lead with the lantern and my father followed him partway, but backed out screaming.

"I thought I heard voices in there," he says. "Saying, 'Stop. Stop. Stop.' I b'lieved that cave was haunted."

I believe that it's haunted too. I could tell when I loosened the stone. I felt that I wasn't alone, as if angels stood guard at either side of the opening. "The tomb is empty," they seemed to say, perhaps as a way to keep strangers out. Their voices do not really speak, but I trace their faces with my finger as I remove the stone and hold it in my hand.

The Choctaw Indians believe that Nanih Waiya is the center of the world, and that the mound holds the remains of some eighteen thousand Choctaw, whose history in the area goes back to the beginning of the Common Era, some two thousand years.

THE MONDAY MORNING after the three had disappeared, their COFO colleagues had driven to Philadelphia from Meridian along Highway 19, looking for any signs of what might have happened to their friends. The normally sleepy Courthouse Square seemed even more somnolent that summer morning. A man in overalls was washing the display windows of the Mars Brothers Department Store. Someone inside the First Philadelphia State Bank was unlocking the front door. A Sunshine Bakery truck pulled up in front of the Piggly Wiggly. The sheriff and his deputy were nowhere in sight.

Stan Dearman, reporter at the time for the *Meridian Star*, had also heard about the disappearance. When Andy, Mickey, and J. E. hadn't returned to the COFO headquarters in Meridian, the staff had begun calling police stations and newspaper reporters in the area. He, too, had driven to Philadelphia to find out what was going on. He parked on Courthouse Square, walked up the steps, and found Deputy Sheriff Price in his office. They exchanged greetings.

"What did he tell you?" I ask when we meet in the fall of 2001.

"Cecil Price gave me his alibi," Stan tells me. "He looked at me, and calm as you please, told me that he had held the three in jail for six hours until they could post bond and that it took him that long to find the justice of the peace."

Price went on to say that at 10:30 P.M. he had released them and followed their blue Ford station wagon along Main Street to Highway 19 and down to Hospital Road—the city limit—where he turned and drove back to the courthouse. That was the last he'd seen of them, he'd said.

"Was there anything that struck you as odd?" I ask.

"Well, it seemed to me that his answer was too pat, too rehearsed. He had all the details just right. I remember wondering that if nothing had happened, if this had been a routine arrest and detention, why would he have bothered to note all the particulars?"

Stan shakes his head. "Of course, we know now that he was lying."

On Tuesday morning, June 23, FBI agent John Proctor received a phone call from Lonnie Hardin, the superintendent of the Indian Agency on the Choctaw reservation. Reluctant to give any information on the phone, Hardin asked Proctor to meet him on the reservation. When Proctor arrived, the superintendent told him that the evening before, several Choctaw had found a car smoldering off Highway 21 in the Bogue Chitto swamp.

That afternoon, Proctor and two other field agents found the car about eighty feet off the highway on an old logging road that was overgrown with kudzu and blackberry brambles. The car was burned down to its skeleton. It had been a blue 1963 Ford Fairlane station wagon, and its Hinds County license plates, still intact, read H25 503. It was the car that the three civil rights workers had driven from Meridian the Sunday before.

A man's watch was found in the car, charred and stopped at 12:45. It was later identified as Mickey Schwerner's.

Proctor knew that the highway patrol used the same radio frequency as the FBI, so he couldn't use his car radio to report the news that the station wagon had been found. He also knew that the first order of business was to contact Washington immediately. J. Edgar Hoover insisted on being first to inform the president of breaking news in a major case, and then making the press announcement personally.

More important to the investigation, however, was the FBI's desire to keep Neshoba County law enforcement out of the information loop. They suspected that the sheriff and deputy were not telling them the whole truth, and had learned from a highway patrolman that the two had probably been involved in the disappearance of the three young men.

THERE'S A PHOTOGRAPH of Bogue Chitto in *Life* magazine from July of 1964. It's taken from the bridge that Jimmy and I crossed over thirty years later. In the swamp and at its edges, navy reservists in boats with nets, and others wading in high boots are dredging the swamp in search of the bodies of the civil rights workers. On the bridge stands a group of clean-cut young men in button-down shirts, dark trousers, and penny loafers. They sport crew cuts, their clothing is pressed and immaculate, and they are all white. But their faces are contorted as they jeer at those who are looking for the bodies of Goodman, Schwerner, and Chaney.

"Hey, why don't you hold a welfare check out over the water," a local is reported to have shouted out to a boatful of FBI workers. "That'll get that nigger to the surface."

ONE OF NESHOBA County's main attractions now is the casino on the Bogue Chitto Reservation. Before visiting Nanih Waiya, my father and I stop for lunch there, at an all-you-can-eat buffet for six dollars. We sit in an orange plastic booth under harsh fluorescent lights; our plates piled high with roast beef and mashed potatoes, turkey and dressing, butter beans, corn bread, and iceberg salad with western dressing. We eat in time to the sound of the slot machines in the next room. My father goes back a second time for ham, au gratin potatoes, and a slice of German chocolate cake. The *bing bing bing* from the slots ricochet against the cafeteria walls like the sound of the pinball machines at the state fair arcade.

After lunch, my father buys two rolls of quarters and dumps them into a couple of plastic buckets. I look for a machine that feels lucky and sit on a stool in front of one whose name is Double Diamonds. I insert the quarter and push the button. The tumblers spin. Two pink flamingos and a cherry. Nothing. You need three sevens, three bunches of grapes, or three diamonds to make it big. Three clovers is okay. I hit three clovers a couple of times and ten quarters jangle out into the bin below me, midmachine. It's teasing me, wanting me to spend all my quarters, so from time to time (every ten to twelve tries, I figure), it lets go a small bundle of change. When my quarters are gone, I get up from my machine and hunt through the casino for my father. His machine is hot, his bucket full. His eyes are transfixed on the tumblers, his hands busy dumping quarters in the slot, pushing the button. I tap him on the shoulder and he startles. "Ready to go so soon?" he asks, and I turn my empty bucket upside down in reply. "I'm hot," he says. "Give me a minute or two."

So I go to the lobby, to the information desk, and ask a young woman if she has any written information about the history of Bogue Chitto. She looks to be around twenty, wears blue eye shadow and heavy black eyeliner. She sits cross-legged on a high stool. "Is there anyone I can talk to?" I ask her. She looks at me sideways, chewing her gum thoughtfully. "I'd like to get in touch with some-one from the tribal council," I say. "Someone who keeps records. Is there a library? A tribal historian?"

From the look on her face I can tell that she thinks I'm crazy. I feel crazy. She blows a pink bubble the size of an egg and wraps her lips around it until it pops. Her jaw moves up and down over the wad of gum and she hands me a small brochure. "Is this about gambling?" she asks.

LAST NIGHT I had a dream. I stood in the center of a cavern with a woman I've never met. She pointed over our heads. Above us was a narrow crevice in the ceiling where normally the light would shine through. But the crevice was filled with the underside of a car—my father's car—wedged there, wheels spinning, completely stuck.

I woke up and in the dark, I saw my father from where I stood yesterday at the top of Nanih Waiya. Under my feet lay thousands of bones. Between the hill that held the bones and the swamp that surrounded it, my father leaned against the car, drinking Coca-Cola from a red can. He is seventy-seven years old; he is sick. His lungs are disintegrating from fifty years of smoking, from the grain dust he inhaled in other people's barns as a boy, from the asbestos that lined the troop transport ships that carried him, homesick, to the South Pacific in 1942. The deprivation of oxygen makes him sleepy and ornery more often than usual. He doesn't have much patience and talks over people as if he were the only person who had anything to say.

According to Choctaw tradition, the dead are placed on a bier held up to the sky by stilts. The corpse remains there for several months, decaying, while family members gather daily, enduring the smell of rotting flesh, to lay flowers, corn, and clay pots of smoking herbs at the base of the stilts to ward off evil spirits. When most of the flesh has decomposed or been carried away by birds, the medicine man or woman is called. With long fingernails grown especially for this purpose, the holy man, known as the bone picker, scrapes away any remaining flesh and burns it with herbs, praying over smoke that vanishes into spirit. The bones are scrubbed clean and given to the family, who keep them in a bone house. Then once a year the tribe carries its dead to the communal burial ground, Nanih Waiya, the Mother Mound.

Beyond my father lay Bogue Chitto, at the southern edge of the Choctaw Reservation. At the edge of the water, sinking into the mud, a crooked sign rose from the reeds, warning people to stay away from the alligators and water moccasins.

On the weekends, Choctaw men act as guides for fishermen from the city who come to Bogue Chitto looking for catfish. I saw a short man with a round face at the other end of the swamp, standing in a flat-bottomed boat, poling his way across; seated beside him was a middle-aged man in a baseball cap stuck through with hooks and lures. My father turned his back to me and faced the swamp. His jaw was set as if in stone, and I wanted to carve an epitaph into it so that I could remember the moment forever.

IN DECEMBER OF 1964, *Life* magazine ran another story, with a photograph from Neshoba County. In it, two law enforcement officers, Sheriff Rainey and Deputy Sheriff Price, during their arraignment for the disappearance and murders of Goodman, Schwerner, and Chaney, sit back in their courtroom seats with an air of supreme confidence, smiling broadly, cheeks bulging with chewing tobacco. After their arrest, which took place in early December, the two had found their approval rating in the community exceptionally high. "It took me an hour to get to work this morning," Price had told the reporter from *Life*, "I had to shake so many hands."

Local newspapers continued to defend the sheriff and his deputy, despite their arrests. Jack Long Tannehill, editor of the *Neshoba Democrat*, used the following statement to defend Rainey: "When he sees a drunk nigger on the street, instead of just grabbing him, Lawrence will say, 'Now, boy, you get on home 'fore I have to run you in.' That's the kind of man Lawrence Rainey is."

Nine years after the murder of Emmett Till—and in no small

part because white boys had been killed alongside a black—national publicity began to influence public opinion. The photograph of two smiling police officers, smug in the face of murder charges, shocked even readers who'd become accustomed to images of an angry Bull Connor and a resolute George Wallace.

"Philadelphia," wrote David Nevin, the *Life* reporter, "is barely willing to admit that an inhuman crime did take place and it is quite unable to feel any collective guilt. It is . . . a town which has deluded itself endlessly and is still doing so."

THE STONE from Nanih Waiya doesn't really speak to me, but it draws my hands to it, cool and solid in my pocket, on my desk, beside me now as I write about it. It reminds me of things as though it had voices, worried voices that echo with the relentlessness of water: dripping from a hole somewhere down an interior wall. Voices that sound like ghosts and send my father—then a little boy—and me—now a grown-up woman—running, divided by the darkness of seventy years, past a pair of stone-faced angels, through the narrow, anxious opening of the burial mound and into the un-finished business of the day.

CHAPTER 18

Grave Markers

M Y FATHER is hospitalized in early 2001 with his annual bout of bronchitis. I've brought my tape recorder, but when I enter his room, he's asleep. His legs are too long for him to fit into hospital beds, and his feet always stick out at the end of the bed, uncovered by the blankets.

From earliest memory, my father's feet have traumatized me: hard, white feet lined with a road map of red and blue veins. Frankenstein feet that lost their original shape after the basketball accident that saved his life during the war (he didn't have to go to Iwo Jima), at the cost of his feet. Feet that smelled like a wet saddle when he took off his shoes at the end of the day. Feet that burned like ice against my legs when I crawled into bed between him and Mom in the middle of the night.

His feet looked like slabs of frozen meat, standing on the bathroom tile when he shaved. I often thought that rather than the floppy slippers he wore when he fried the bacon on Sunday mornings, his feet should be wrapped in white butcher paper. Calloused, reptilian feet with unclipped yellow toenails. Feet that humiliated me in front of my friends when he wore strappy leather sandals in the summertime, as if he'd put a harness on a pair of bloodless lizards.

In the only home movie I've ever seen of myself from when I was little, a black and white super eight reel, I am knee-deep in Lake Harriet, clinging to my father's ankles and screaming with terror. He's shaking me off his leg as if he were a dog and I were a squirrel, and I won't let go for anything. I don't remember the incident; in the movie I look to be about three.

But the image of my father's white foot lifting out of the water, the calf tan above the sock line, with me clutching the hair on his legs, makes me remember my childhood traumas: putting my face in the water, the taunts of other children, and the sight of my father's feet.

I am forty-eight years old, and remnants of my childhood fears remain. I am still afraid of the dark, and need a light on somewhere in the house when I sleep. I'm afraid of enclosed places, and nervous when I'm with someone who can't stop talking and I can't get away. I get woozy and light-headed; I need to know that I can get out at all times.

Which is how I feel now, sitting at my father's bedside in the hospital with his bare feet sticking out from the end of the blanket. The volume on the television set is so loud that I wonder how my father can sleep through Wolf Blitzer's shouting. We probably won't get much tape recording done today. He gets crabby when he doesn't feel well, and starts to growl and complain. Then he becomes melancholy and talks about how he fell in love with his nurse in New Zealand during the war and if he had only married her, things might have turned out differently.

But he didn't marry her and his ankle never healed, and as it turned out he still has feet that traumatize his children and grand-children when they visit him in the hospital fifty years later. Which is why the next day I have to go to Mississippi by myself. After months of research into the dark side of the story, I need to resurface. I'm hungry for biscuits and chicken and sweet potato pie.

TRAVELING to Mississippi without my father for the first time in my life, I stop en route in Atlanta to spend the night with Aunt Jane, youngest of the three surviving Lind Girls. Aunt Jane has been widowed twice, but of the Lind Girls, it seems to me, she has always had the sunniest outlook on life. Before dinner she mixes us a drink and I join her in smoking a cigarette, both of us feeling guilty for smoking in front of the other. She has congestive heart disease and shouldn't smoke. My father is in the hospital, an oxygen tube in his nose, gasping for breath after a lifetime of smoking. But we shrug our shoulders, light up anyway, and clink our glasses together.

One bourbon and water leads to another, and soon we're gossiping about relatives on the Lind Girl side. Some of us are highly successful, some of us are living quiet lives, and some of us are downright crazy. After dinner she shows me a black-and-white home movie of Aunt Louise's wedding from sometime in the 1930s, and I see my mother as a teenager, laughing and running to the door of the car to throw rice. Her hair is dark and her eyes are bright and she smiles happily, waving at the camera. I think of her now, at home, after two heart attacks, slightly stooped and tinier than she ever was, having shrunk from osteoporosis. With silver hair and a pale complexion from poor circulation, it's difficult to believe that this vibrant young woman now sits alone in a hospital room with my father, who is seriously ill.

The next day I rent a car and drive across Alabama to Meridian, a five-hour trip. When I arrive, Auntie Lu greets me with a kiss. Lunch is ready and we sit across from each other at the kitchen table. She's fixed chicken salad sandwiches with grapes and apples and a tangerine salad. There's a knock. Pearl comes through the door and hands Lumiere a pecan pie covered with foil that is still steamy in the middle.

"We bring things to each other when we have company," Lumiere says. Pearl and Nelson live around the corner and across the street. They can see Lumiere's place through their back windows. Since Lumiere's been alone, they watch the house and ask if there's anything she needs from the store. Later on the phone rings. Another neighbor sees my red rental car in the driveway and calls to make sure that everything is okay.

The pie is warm, and we eat small slices after lunch with a dollop of fat-free Cool Whip. It is crunchy on top and smooth underneath.

Lumiere doesn't seem to change. Her eyes still sparkle, and she smiles easily. She likes to work and busies herself in the kitchen. After lunch she gets up, goes to the sink, and turns on the tap. She washes and I dry.

We discuss in detail my father's breathing problems. I mention grain dust in the barns and the asbestos that lined the troop transport ships and the smoking. "Don't forget about the insecticide," she reminds me. "It came down from low planes. Lafe spread it out himself behind the tractor."

I stack the leftovers in the refrigerator and notice a coconut layer cake on the top shelf. "Darla and William are comin' for dinner tonight and that cake is William's favorite," Lumiere says. "His daddy's too. Why, the last time I made it he carried half the cake home with him and made me promise to make him another one."

On Friday afternoon we drive out to the farm to visit Susie Lee and Frank. Once we're past Meridian and the white-pillared house with the Winstead Realty sign out front (home of the other Wilbur Winstead, another of my father's cousins), the highway narrows, and a windbreak of tall pines lines the road. Through the occasional clearing, we begin to see low hills, farmhouses, and neat fences beside grain-filled silos.

Our first stop is the cemetery of the Pine Grove Church. We pull into the church's gravel parking lot and get out of the car. I open the gate to let Auntie Lu walk through first. This is where

Grandma and Grandpa Collins are buried, along with Daddy Bob and Grandma Ora, Ruby and Lafe and their son Brady.

Mississippi in late January reminds me of Minnesota in early April, when a cold wind comes in from the north. People in other parts of the country don't realize how much cold weather travels down the Mississippi Valley, all the way from Minneapolis to Meridian. The gray sky, empty of birds, hangs low like a canopy, and the heaviness of intermittent rain permeates everything. Each footfall sinks a little into the sod, the grass brown but nevertheless saturated at the roots. Soon my tennis shoes are soaked. The dampness seeps down through my jacket, sweater, and shirt. Soon my skin feels clammy, my bones chilled.

"Now let's just go row by row," Auntie Lu says, motioning with her arm for me to walk up the hill. All around us, tombstones rise up at the heads of graves, covered with a network of vines that soon will bloom into moss roses. As we climb to the top, the oldest headstones round the slope in uneven rows: marble, granite, and limestone; black, gray, and white. "You take one and I'll take the other," Lumiere calls over to me. She takes short, brisk steps and moves quickly to where the farthest headstones lie hidden, some broken, by the back fence in the tallest grass. "We'll see better if they's kin."

And so we begin our inspection: one by one, the way a gardener inspects the progress of a flower bed, kneeling down in the loam, patting the earth with gloved hands, pulling a weed, or clipping a top-heavy blossom whose petals have fallen to the ground.

I must be related to everyone in this cemetery in one fashion or another. There are Winsteads, Collins, Portwoods, Peebles, Rushes, Hesters, and Killens. The wind whines around the headstones. The tips of my fingers tingle, my left ear aches.

"Mercy, that wind is cold."

I feel uneasy walking over the spongy earth that lies in front of each headstone, as if the ground were unstable and might give way under my weight. Here's a new grave, a caked, cracked rectangle of dirt that's sunk in an inch or two; not yet sodded over. I take pains to walk around its perimeter. "Here's someone. Do you know a Crenshaw?"

"Yeah, that's kin," Lumiere says. "Come over here."

I walk over to where Auntie Lu stands, in front of Grandma Ora and Daddy Bob's double marker. "See," she says, "I'm 'own bring me over a bucket, some rags, and a spray bottle of Clorox." She runs her hand over the etched marble, which is blackened with dirt. "I cleaned Ed's that way. Just sprayed it on. Nelson helped me. It turned out so pretty. Maybe I can get Frank to come over and make Mama and Daddy's markers pretty again."

I find a certain comfort in pacing up and down these cemetery rows. Nowhere else in the world am I surrounded by people to whom I so essentially belong. People I'll never know, people who were never even aware of my existence, but with whom I share a kinship that can't be broken. Before me lie grandparents, great-grandparents, and great-greats. People who have lived and died in this county for two hundred years. There are aunts and great-aunts, uncles and great-uncles, cousins and second cousins. Their headstones read like the beginnings and endings of unwritten stories.

Tall pines surround us on three sides; the eldest buried here probably cleared this acre themselves. Standing beside Aunt Lumiere, I look at Grandma Ora and Daddy Bob's dirty headstones. I wish my father were here, and my mother, and my brother and sisters. I imagine my nieces and nephews crowding around us, my two sons and my daughter.

"I'll help you clean these," I tell Auntie Lu. "Next time I come."

It's getting colder and we have one more cemetery to cover, so we close the gate and climb into the car, out of the wind.

We stop in the parking lot of the Mount Olive Baptist Church, about two miles away from Pine Grove. This church is smaller, the shingles missing in places and some of the windows boarded. Pappy and Donie are buried here, and most of the Winstead kin. Lumiere and I stand before the graves of my great-grandparents, blackened with age and neglect. Auntie Lu sighs and turns to me. "We'll Clorox their graves too," she says. "Next time you come."

ON SATURDAY, August 1, 1964, after forty-four days of searching for clues as to the whereabouts of Goodman, Schwerner, and Chaney, a paid Klan informant, under the protection of strict anonymity, notified the FBI that he would tell them the location of their unmarked grave.

Their station wagon had been found fifteen miles northeast of Philadelphia, which was where the FBI had then focused their search for most of the summer. Bogue Chitto swamp teemed with mosquitoes, snakes, and chiggers, which, in the heat of a Mississippi summer, must have made the search especially miserable. One of the murderers is alleged to have expressed delight at the thought of federal agents dragging through the swamp, especially when he knew that the bodies had been buried nowhere near the place where the car had been burned.

A few days after the car was found, Preacher Killen paid another visit to his friend Wallace Miller. This visit was different from the last, Mrs. Miller remembered, when the two had sat at the kitchen table and talked. This time, Wallace had suggested that they go into the bedroom and shut the door before he and Preacher had their conversation.

Wallace Miller later testified that he and Preacher Killen sat on the bed and discussed the civil rights workers. Preacher then told him "that they had been shot, that they were dead, and that they were buried in a dam about fifteen feet deep."

It was the last time Preacher paid a visit to the Miller home, Wallace's wife recalled, many years later, in newspaper interviews. The murders were more than Wallace had bargained for, that night in April when Preacher had administered the Klan oath to him in his dining room. Shortly after his last meeting with Preacher, Wallace began to meet in secret with the FBI. During those sessions, he told them everything that he knew about what had happened, and gave the names of those he knew to have been involved. The information he provided led the FBI to James Jordan, who then confessed.

When Preacher Killen and twenty other men were arrested in December on charges of conspiracy in connection with the murders, the Klan began to suspect that Wallace had informed the FBI. From that moment on, he became a marked man. For the next three years, until the trial actually took place, and for months afterward, the Millers endured death threats and threats on the lives of their children. Wallace was harassed at work. When he and his wife went out for lunch or shopping, people in restaurants and other public places would humiliate them, calling Wallace an SOB, a "nigger lover," and a traitor. They owned a small grocery store. It was burned to the ground.

The informant, who remains nameless to this day, led the FBI's chief investigators to an earthen dam, six miles southwest of Philadelphia. Finding the heavy equipment they'd need would delay their search, but once the agents found a bulldozer and a dragline, they began to dig.

Tuesday, August 4, dawned hot, even by Mississippi standards for late summer, and the temperature that morning climbed to 106 degrees. The agents worked for several hours, and at eleven one of them noticed an unusual smell, "the faint odor of decaying organic material," he wrote in his notebook. The smell grew stronger as the shovel dug deeper into the dam. At three in the afternoon, "the pungent odor of decaying flesh is clearly discernable," the agent wrote. Greenish blue blowflies swarmed in the pit where the shovel was digging, and buzzards had begun to circle overhead.

Fifteen minutes later, the heel of a man's boot appeared. The bulldozer was halted and agents jumped in with spades and shovels, carefully scraping away the dirt until the outline of a man's body appeared, completely covered with clay. The stench was overpowering; the heat brutal. Several of the agents crawled from the pit and vomited.

They took turns digging, each man either wearing a surgical mask or covering his nose and mouth with a handkerchief. After two hours of careful digging, the man's body emerged. He was wearing blue jeans and was naked from the waist up. The agents reached carefully into the back pocket of his blue jeans and lifted out a wallet. The draft card inside belonged to Mickey Schwerner.

Shortly after five, the agents found another body, facedown. One arm was outstretched; the other was draped over Mickey's body. The left hand was clenched into a fist that held a lump of hard clay. This body was also naked from the waist up, but beneath the hips agents found a bloodied shirt. A wallet was carefully removed from the back pocket of the slacks he wore. Inside, the identification belonged to Andy Goodman.

Fifteen minutes later the body of James Chaney was found. He was on his back, barefoot, and fully clothed. Each of the bodies was in an advanced state of decomposition, and their facial features had nearly vanished. But since the other two bodies had been identified as J. E.'s companions from the night of June 21, the agents had no doubt as to the identity of the third.

At this point the investigators began to understand why the Neshoba County suspects had been so smug. In the middle of the night, using shovels and bulldozers, the lynch mob had buried these young men beneath ten tons of earth, fully intending that their carefully concealed burial place would never be found.

In this place of lovingly tended grave sites, the Klan had decided that the families of Michael Schwerner, Andrew Goodman, and James Chaney would spend the rest of their lives with no final resting place for their loved ones. It was as though they had murdered them twice: first by shooting them in the middle of the night on the Rock Cut Road, and then by trying to rid the world of their memory by placing them in an unmarked grave.

How small the world must have seemed to those men; how close the circle in which they carried out their plan. As if Andy, Mickey, and J. E. had belonged to no one. As if there were no families who would come forward and wonder where they were. As if the agony they inflicted on those who loved these young men didn't exist, wouldn't take place, or worse, didn't even matter. And yet, the very narrow-mindedness of their malice would ensure that the victims, whose claims were infinitely larger, would attain the very immortality that their murderers had tried to prevent.

Having failed to gain the support of state and local authorities in bringing murder charges against those they had suspected of the killings, the FBI could not act until December and then, only on charges of conspiracy. But they moved quickly, and on the morning of December 4, 1964, arrested twenty men. The Neshoba County sheriff and deputy sheriff were among those arrested, as was Imperial Wizard Sam Bowers and Preacher Edgar Ray Killen.

When the preliminary hearing took place a week later, however, U.S. Commissioner for the Southern District of Mississippi Esther Carter dismissed the charges. In a move that the Justice Department called totally without precedent, Judge Carter had ruled that the FBI's sworn reading of a confession by one of the conspirators was inadmissible evidence. A photographer from *Life* magazine snapped the defendants' picture as they laughed and congratulated one another in the courtroom. A few moments later, Preacher Killen and his friends left the courthouse, free.

THE ROAD to Susie's is narrow and serpentine. After our visit to the cemetery, the landmarks along the way seem nothing less than a continuation of the family graveyard. First there's the old Masonic hall on the right. It's a white clapboard building that looks like an old-fashioned one-room schoolhouse. "Daddy helped found that Masonic hall," Auntie Lu says. "He was always at lodge meetings. When he died, they gave 'im a Masonic funeral."

What once was Cliff's store is fifty yards or so down the road. The windows are cloudy, and someone has taped newspapers over them, and there are only two metal chairs on the porch. It looks like it's closed, but the door is open, and on the stoop there's a rack of dresses and blouses that look like they're secondhand.

Next is a shack on the left side of the road whose collapsed roof is covered with a tangle of kudzu vine. Here Grandma Donie lived with Aunt Jenie until Donie died in 1953, then Jenie lived alone until her own death.

Next is the auto salvage yard that takes up several hilly acres. The bodies of the battered cars have been neatly stacked in parallel rows up and down the hillside. I've never seen junk displayed in such an orderly way. Then we pull up the narrow drive to Susie's one-story brick house. Susie won't be home for another hour, so we go inside, sit in the family room, and begin our visit with Frank. Our talk runs from family, to politics, and back to family. The television is on in a corner of the room, but when the conversation lapses, the TV becomes a focal point that we all can share. With the remote, Frank flips from CNN to ESPN to the History Channel, the Country Music Channel, and back.

With his customary hospitality, he has offered us something to drink. Settling back into his recliner, Frank says to Auntie Lu, "Looks like they're about to reopen the civil rights case and your kin may be in trouble again."

"We don't claim him as kin," Lumiere says.

"I read about that," I say. "In fact, I sent an E-mail to the Mississippi attorney general's office, but they didn't offer me any information."

"Well, they never could prove that it was them buried in that dam. Nobody really saw who it was when they hauled the bodies out," Frank says.

I'm never comfortable contradicting others, but this is too much. I can't believe what I'm hearing. Is he joking?

I've read too much about the case to let Frank's comment just float in the air. It's like an unfinished sentence that needed to be completed forty years ago and is just now coming up for air. I take a deep breath and speak.

"I read that they found identification on them and that they matched dental records. It sounded pretty positive." If I don't look at anyone, it'll be like I'm speaking to myself. There is no other sound in the room, and my words fall to the floor with the thud of an unopened dictionary.

What am I so afraid of? I've known these relatives since I was thirteen years old.

It occurs to me then that my father provides me with a buffer. As long as he is with me in Neshoba County, I belong. Without him, I question my own legitimacy.

"Well, that ol' Edgar Killen, he's a nut, and we don't claim him," Auntie Lu repeats. She pushes herself back in the reclining chair and her legs go up.

"Besides," she says. "Those people were white trash."

I startle at her words. The ease with which they come out of Lumiere's mouth jolts me. It is like watching *Gone With the Wind*, only the soundtrack is all wrong. Instead of Olivia de Havilland's voice coming out of Miss Melanie Hamilton's mouth, it is the voice of George Wallace.

At this moment, I see that my Mississippi kin and I don't really know one another at all. I feel weighed down by a discomfort that is as familiar to me as it must be to them. We've been cordial because of blood, but right now our unarticulated differences are creating a wedge between us. Without my father, I have nobody behind whom I can safely hide, and I don't feel ready to stand on my own.

My mind wanders down the road to Ruby's deserted house, which still looks as through somebody inhabits it. I feel a sense of loyalty to a lingering presence, an emblematic charge that travels out into the community. As long as I'm here, I am to keep doors closed and everything that is inside unused and just the way it always was. The shells of the dead remain behind, as on a beach where they have been emptied of life. Yet behind all these closed doors and covered windows, the past is not a void, but is a full reality that has been protected at the cost of the very history that memory is meant to preserve. I think of the day four years ago when Jimmy took me into his mother's house, closed up and musty, everything still intact the way it was the day Aunt Ruby died. Susie Lee can't bear to go down there, and so Jimmy took me inside to show me the family photograph albums and help me find the Marine Corps portrait of my father that Grandma Ora held over her heart when she died.

The place had an eerie feeling, not of lifelessness, but of something that was holding its breath. Everything was covered with dust, and the windows had remained shut for a couple of years. It seemed to me that unless someone opened them up and let in some fresh air, the voices that waited inside the house would remain silent forever.

On January 11, 1965, Judge Harold Cox reconvened the federal grand jury. Four days later, the jury returned two indictments against eighteen defendants. The indictments were brought under two sections of legislation from 1870. One charged the group with a felony: conspiring to deprive Goodman, Schwerner, and Chaney of their federally secured rights. The other charged the group with a misdemeanor: conspiring with law officers to inflict "summary punishment" on the young men "without due process of law."

On Saturday, January 16, seventeen of the eighteen men were arrested for the second time. (The name of Philadelphia police officer Richard Willis had been added to the list. Willis had been on duty the afternoon of June 21, had come to the scene of Mickey, Andy, and J. E.'s arrest for speeding, and had accompanied the deputy sheriff when he followed their car to the city limits that night.) The men were released the same day on bond of $5,750 each.

The grand jury reconvened February 1, and Judge O. H. Barnett (cousin of former Governor Ross Barnett) charged the jury with sentiments that echoed his earlier charge the previous September, when the jury had returned indictments having nothing to do with the murders of Goodman, Schwerner, and Chaney, and the federal judge had dismissed the FBI's case:

Because of this unlawful and dastardly deed of a few persons, the entire citizenship of Neshoba County has been indicted and tried before the whole world by such irresponsible organizations as the NAACP, the ADA, COFO, the National Council of Churches, the communistic party, the socialistic minded liberals and both the Democratic and Republican parties and the irresponsible press and news media, but I want it clearly understood that not all of the press and all of the news media are irresponsible, but certain elements are. . . .

The citizenship of Neshoba County nor the State of Mississippi does not condone, encourage or defend the unlawful taking of human life and it is time to rise up in righteous indignation and disgust to stop the unlawful taking of human life, to find the guilty and to proclaim to the world this is not acceptable to the citizenship of Neshoba County nor the citizenship of the State of Mississippi. . . . this is the tribune for those who have been loudest about the matter to come forward and tell this grand jury all they know. Now, Mr. Foreman, is the time to put up or shut up.

Judge Barnett had gone on to tell the jury that they would have the assistance of the "most courageous sheriff in all America, Lawrence Rainey." Because the FBI had not wanted to jeopardize its case by turning over the records of its investigation too soon, the indictments that September failed to address the actual crime that had been committed.

By February, the FBI was still holding on to evidence that they wanted to protect from premature release, and refused to come before the jury to testify. Judge Cox dismissed the felony counts of conspiracy yet again, leaving the killers facing nothing more than a misdemeanor.

The federal government then appealed the case to the United States Supreme Court.

———

I'VE ALWAYS ENVIED Susie Lee: she and Frank looked to me like the bride and groom on the top of the wedding cake. Their handsome sons like to come home on weekends to visit, and it isn't unusual to see the boys sitting beside their mother with their arms around her.

The boys have stories to tell, too, stories that will stop when I begin to ask the wrong questions. So I feel intrusive now. I'm writing a book that brings the private conversations of family members I hardly know onto the page.

There is a strange silence around all this, a kind of cemetery hush, as if discussing it would evoke the ill powers of the dead.

I looked into the soundless flames in the gas fireplace. "Isn't Edgar Killen a preacher?"

"Yeah, he sure is. Don't know where, though," Frank replied. He went over to the sofa and stretched out. Frank is a big and powerful man. "I just saw him yesterday over at Wal-Mart. If you do ever see him, don't tell him you're kin, 'cause you'll never get rid of him."

"He likes to talk?"

"Sure does," Frank replied with a laugh.

I wonder now if it would have been possible for me to stake out the Wal-Mart. Maybe I would have simply run into him and let him talk my ears off.

"How does something like that happen? How does someone become a Klan member?" I asked. Another mistake.

I've never had such an uncomfortable conversation in my life. I was swamped by everything I didn't know and all the questions I didn't feel free to ask, including why this subject feels taboo and *why* I can't ask questions about it. If there's nothing to hide, why the secrecy? If there's embarrassment, what for? If everything is all right, then what's the matter? I felt like I was going crazy.

I'm not really sure I understood his response either. "How does someone get involved in drugs?" he asked by way of reply. "You experiment, and pretty soon you're hooked." The subject was closed.

CHAPTER 19

Kinfolk and More Kinfolk

That evening, we go for supper at the Bloomo Junction, a café that I remember from a couple of years ago, when Susie and Frank brought me here to eat catfish. The walls are covered with photographs of the old Bloomo School, its faculty, and graduating classes from over the years.

Bloomo Junction is full of people who are related to me. Everywhere we look, people are waving hey to us from where they sit, eating pulled pork, fried catfish, or hamburger steak with mushroom gravy. People come over to the table, and Susie introduces me as Chub's daughter from Minnesota. There's a smile and a flash of recognition in their eyes. She gets up once or twice to go over to someone's table to say hello; so does Frank. This person is so-and-so's cousin. That person's daddy is so and so. Pretty soon I'm completely overwhelmed. The names sound alike and it's like being in the cemetery again, only these people are still above ground: Peden, Reynolds, Akin, Posey, Rush, Killen, Portwood, all descended from or married into the old Winstead and Collins clans, kin and double kin, cousins, second cousins, and relations for which there is no simple connection.

The next morning I wake up to the smell of Susie's biscuits. I have had a heavy sleep, with one vivid dream following another, and I stagger into the kitchen in my gray flannel pajamas. There's a cake pan full of hot biscuits on the stove. Susie is scrambling eggs and puts a plate of bacon in the microwave. Frank pours me a cup of coffee, for which I am grateful. Then he slices each hot biscuit in half, melts a pat of butter between the top and bottom of each slice, and puts a jar of Lumiere's homemade fig preserves on the table. This is Ruby's recipe, and they taste of milk, flour, butter, and something I can't put into words. Last night I'd asked Susie to bake them for me, and of course this morning she has.

Any accolade you may hear in praise of southern biscuits will do them disservice. They are so light, flaky, and tender that it feels impossible to describe them without resorting to cliché or sounding like a television commercial for the kind of biscuits that come in a can and are a sacrilege by comparison. I can't think of any other food I'd rather eat in the whole world.

It's a sunny Saturday morning, and after breakfast, we have an appointment to visit with my father's cousin on Daddy Bob's side. Fannie lives near Union, just ten minutes or so from Susie's, in a neat brick ranch-style house, on a hilly piece of property bordered by a small patch of woods. We go through the garage and knock. "Back door guests are the best," Susie says.

Fannie meets us at the door and invites us in. Auntie Lu, Susie, and I sit around her kitchen table talking. Fannie has emptied her attic and closets of photograph albums, newspaper clippings, letters, and framed certificates for me to look at. A plate of chocolate chip cookies sits on the counter behind me. There's coffee on the stove.

She pulls out a newspaper clipping of a letter that had appeared in the *Neshoba Democrat*. The letter had been sent to Pappy's daddy to inform him of Uncle Henry having been killed in the Civil War.

"You see, the Union Army camped near Union," she said. "And took everything they could. Pappy watched 'em from up in a tree. He was thirteen years old."

My father has told me this story many times. It's one of the stories Pappy used to tell him when they went hunting together when he was little. Then she reveals a detail I hadn't heard before.

"They took everything there was to eat," Fannie goes on. "Then," she says, "they went back to the house and gave back the food they couldn't finish." At this her eyes fill and her voice catches. "Times was so hard." There is so much emotion in her voice that if it wasn't February of 2001 I'd swear she'd been there.

Here the conversation stops for a moment while the two cousins seem to leave the room and go back in time. "My mother was fifty-four when she died." Lumiere looks at Fannie.

Fannie speaks softly. "You know, Aunt Ora was one of the first I knew about, anything about cancer."

"You made my day the other day when you said something good about Mama," Auntie Lu says. "It makes you feel good when somebody says something nice about your mama."

"Oh, my goodness, I thought the world of Aunt Ora and Uncle Bobby." Here Fannie smiles. "We used to go over and stay with 'em. Uncle Bobby believed in goin' to the lodge. Man, he didn't miss a lodge meetin'."

"My daddy helped found that lodge," Auntie Lu says. "When he died, they gave him a Masonic funeral."

"Y'know, when Uncle Bobby said somethin', it was funny. And he wouldn't even crack a smile. He didn't mean to be funny, he was just funny. And he could just say it and never laugh, you know. It'd just tickle you to death.

"But, honey . . . I never will forget goin' over there, to Uncle Bobby's," Fannie continues. "Now he would go to his lodge meetin', and Aunt Ora would have to have me or my sister to come over and spend the night. She was scared. Even though he was goin' to be comin' in an hour or two. But we had to go spend the night.

Doors and things didn't know what locks was, y'know back in them days. There wasn't nothing comin' to bother us in the first place. But scared? She was scared to death when night come. And we got every ol' kitchen chair that there was and ol' straight chair, and we blocked the front door. I tell you, if there'd been a fire, I don't think we would've got out of that place." Everyone is laughing now.

"Oh, Lawdy," Lumiere says, and pauses again. "You know, that's one thing I hate. I don't wanna go back to the old days where you peeked through a crack in the wall. But people, I do hate that people quit carin' about one another. Y'know, when we grew up everybody cared about one another."

"Oh, no, I don't think we'd want to go back to the old days, livin' like we lived," Fannie says and shakes her head. "But I wish we could visit more," she goes on with a wistful chuckle. "And enjoy bein' with people more." She walks over to the closet in the front room and from the upper shelf pulls down a quilt. "I'm doin' this for my grandson," she says. Susie Lee takes one end, Fannie the other, and they spread it out over the sofa. The quilt is white with red stitches. "Chicken scratches, they're called," she says.

"People are too busy now," Auntie Lu says, touching the star pattern that Fannie has made from the red chicken scratches.

"But see, we wait till we get old to realize that," Fannie replies as she and Susie refold the quilt.

While she places the quilt in a plastic bag, I ask Fannie if she remembers anything special about my dad from when they were growing up. I find out from her that a black man named Doode Thames scared my father one evening when he was walking home from basketball practice in the twelfth grade. When Fannie says Doode Thames's first name, a thrill of recognition comes over me. For all the times my father and I looked at the sharecroppers who stood in the background of Grandma Ora's funeral photograph, he'd remembered their last names: Thames and McCormick. But I'd never known anybody's first name.

"Well, it was my daddy that carried on with Chub the most,"

Fannie went on. "Chub would go at night to practice basketball over at House. And so he's comin' back one night, and he gets down there in that holler, down below our house, past Ruby's, where Uncle Bobby and them lived."

"How was he getting home?" I ask, and take a bite of one of Fannie's homemade cookies. It's warm from the oven and the chocolate chips are still slightly melted.

"He was walkin'," Fannie says with a laugh. "We didn't have no way of ridin.' He had walked in from House and got down in that holler and somethin' scared 'im. He said he saw a bear, that's what he tol' my daddy."

"Mercy!" Auntie Lu exclaims.

"See, I was younger than Chub, so y'know Daddy was the one who was always kiddin' him and frolickin' with him and Arby. Daddy told 'im, said, 'Chub that wasn't nothin' but ol' Doode Thames,' an ol' black man who'd been in a crap game and was crawlin' through the bushes on his way home. And Chub didn't b'lieve him so he ran all the way home and they said that he was teetotalin' out of breath."

Though my father is back home in Minnesota, it is as though the picture he always carried of Grandma Ora's funeral is before me, in the stack of photographs that Fannie has collected for us to sort through. As though for the tiniest moment a bit of life has been breathed into the silence of the still frame. As though in that breath everyone becomes human and memory reanimates the scene. Grandma Ora is afraid to be alone. After a crap game, Doode Thames comes forward, named.

A week later, when I tell my father this, he remembers another name, and I turn to the photograph albums that my mother has organized on shelves in the den and page through until I find the funeral picture. "Doode Thames," he says. "Come to think of it, now, Doode had a brother by the name of Goode Thames too," he says. "Doode and Goode." He chuckles, and pauses in his reclining chair to adjust the oxygen tube in his nose. "A Baptist preacher. He used to have breakfast with my father on Sunday mornings. He'd stop by the back door and sit at one end of the kitchen, my father at the opposite end. It was a big room, but blacks didn't sit at the same table as whites in those days.

"Ol' Goode used to say 'I made the devil steamin' mad today.'

"And Daddy Bob'd ask 'im what he meant. Meanwhile, my mother was cooking breakfast at the big stove in the middle of the room. At that, Ol' Goode turned to Daddy Bob and slapped his knee.

" 'This mornin' I baptized me another big ol' nigger,' Goode said, shakin' his head and laughin'. And my father laughed right along with him, all the way from the other side of the room."

After meeting with Fannie, we drive to Philadelphia, where we'll have lunch in a new restaurant that has a soup and salad bar. In the car, we talk briefly about race relations.

"We played with the colored kids when we were little," Susie Lee says. "Mama and Daddy treated them real good. They lived right behind the house, and I always had someone to play with. We loved Lil. She made the best pies and cakes, and she took good care of Mother."

"That's interesting," I say. "Maybe I should talk to her."

"Oh, no," Susie Lee quickly replies. "She wouldn't know anything about the family."

When I visited Neshoba County in 1997, I wandered around Ruby's yard early one morning, having stayed the night with Susie. I wanted to stand in the backyard and remember the afternoon when Lafe had deep-fried that unforgettable chicken more than thirty years ago. I wanted to remember how Ruby looked the first time we drove up to the house. But something caught my eye this time that I hadn't noticed before: a small two-room cabin behind the house. I tried to peek into the windows, but they were covered with dust and too high for me to really see into. The place was falling into ruin and looked unsafe, but I stepped onto the narrow front porch and opened the door anyway.

Inside, in the middle of the small front room, stood a narrow desklike table, with a chair that had been pushed back slightly from underneath. The light from the window shone softly across the tabletop, illuminating a book that lay open there. It was as though somebody had been studying one day long ago, had been called away and left the book open to continue reading, but had never returned. The room had the hushed quality of someone who anticipated coming back and finishing a day that had been interrupted suddenly. It was as though time had stopped and was waiting for this person who'd been reading—who was it?—to walk back through the door and start the clock again. It took me a moment to realize that I'd stopped breathing.

I backed out of the room, feeling that I'd walked into a scene from someone's intimate family life and that I didn't want to intrude.

This must have been Lil's house. There were two small rooms, front and back, equal in size, the walls unfinished, the floor a little slanted, a cupboard hanging precariously from the side of the back room that faced the front door. I don't remember a bathroom. When I read Anne Moody's memoir, this was the place I imagined. When I read Richard Wright, I thought about this cabin.

Before lunch, Susie and I stop to make a photocopy of one of many newspaper clips that Fannie had saved from the trial in 1967 and had taken out to show me. It's an unwieldy clip and takes us several tries. "That must have been an awful time," I say.

"It was tense around here," she replies. She gathers up the copies we can't use. "I'm own shred these," she says. "I know somebody who's related to one of the men in this picture, and I wouldn't want anybody to see it and feel bad."

IN EARLY JUNE OF 2001, I traveled to New York to meet Mrs. Carolyn Goodman, Andy's mother. I first decided to call her when time and again I'd heard the fate of her son and his companions reduced to a legend, the kind of event that gets pushed back into the murky recesses, rather than acknowledged outright.

Mostly I wanted to meet her because I wanted to know about Andy. I wanted to hear what losing a son this way has meant to a mother. Mrs. Goodman agreed to meet with me in her apartment on Manhattan's Upper West Side when I called from Minneapolis in May. I told her about my memoir, how it had begun, and how it had changed; and she invited me into her home. "Not only am I comfortable talking about it, but I feel that it's very important, as I suspect you do," she said. "Because it was a very important time in our nation's history, and for a long time not very much was said about it at all."

I thanked her for agreeing to meet with me and asked how she felt about discussing her son. "Not very much has been written about it," she said. "It's almost as if it's been hushed up."

When she greeted me in the foyer of her apartment, I was surprised at her youthfulness. At eighty-six, she is intellectually intense and personally vivacious. I'd read that she'd recently demonstrated against police brutality in the wake of Amadou Diallo's murder in New York City. After her arrest, she'd told reporters that she knew firsthand the horror of corrupt law enforcement.

She showed me into her sitting room, where we sat facing each other with the tape recorder between us. Mrs. Goodman has lived in this apartment for more than fifty years; this is where she raised her family. The sitting room is situated off the foyer and is centrally located between the living room, where a grand piano is covered with framed photographs; her office, where she conducts the business of the Andrew Goodman Foundation; and a dining room that looks like it would easily seat large groups of people. "I love to entertain," she said. "We used to fill our home with interesting people. I still do, when I can."

Andy comes to mind at every turn, for there's a wall in each room reserved for a portrait of him. "There are young people now who are more concerned and are talking about it," she said when we sat across from each other beside a large window.

"Have you met those young people through the foundation?"

"Yes," she said. "Through the Andrew Goodman Foundation, which my husband, Robert Goodman, and I founded two years after Andy was killed. We wanted to support youth activism wherever young people were organizing for those things that Andy believed in."

Mrs. Goodman listed some of the projects that have been funded in Andy's name: voter registration, peer counseling, quality education, gay and lesbian activities, and prison reform. The list was comprehensive.

"When my husband was killed . . ." Here Mrs. Goodman pauses. "He died, actually. I said he was killed. Perhaps somewhere in the back of my head I believe that the trauma of Andy's death killed him. He was a very sensitive man. He was by training a civil engineer, but by temperament a poet. He wrote beautiful poetry. He died very young. He was fifty-five. Five years after Andy was killed.

"He was quite a remarkable and wonderful man. I married again, years later. We were married for twenty years. He died nine years ago. So I have had many losses."

As Mrs. Goodman described Andy, she spoke of the ways in which he resembled his father. Andy was sensitive, like his dad. "I can remember in the early days of Lincoln Center," she said. "Bob would be standing and applauding at the end of the concert with tears in his eyes because of the music. That's the way Andy was."

When she related the first of many anecdotes about Andy, her voice took on a different kind of energy. She began to laugh, and the memories had a kind of buoyancy that livened the conversation and brightened the room. "We had a summer place in the Adirondacks," she began. "I remember once that I was driving home with the kids in the backseat, and I must have been speeding because I was pulled over by the highway patrol.

"He leaned into the car and looked at me.

" 'Lady, do you know how fast you were going? And with all these little children in the car. You could go to jail for this. I could put you in jail for six months for driving at this rate of speed.'

"All of a sudden I heard this snuffling in the backseat and the officer said, 'Okay, I'll let you go, but don't drive so fast.'

"So I turned around, and there was Andy, crying. 'Andy, why are you crying?' I asked him.

" 'Mom, I don't want you to go to jail,' he said.

"That was Andy. He was very emotional. He walked like his father, he talked like him, his whole body build was like him."

After graduating from Walden School, Andy had attended the University of Wisconsin at Madison. "There was a program at the time call integrated liberal studies," Mrs. Goodman said. "Where students studied a period of history and its art, drama, music, math, and sciences.

"There's a plaque on the campus there, dedicated to Andy, in one of the bigger administration buildings. I went to its dedication not too long ago."

Andy was the middle son of three. As Mrs. Goodman described him, she paged through the family photo albums whose pictures of Andy stopped in 1964.

I couldn't help but put myself in her place. My own middle son, Joe, is an English major at the University of Wisconsin at Madison. Like Andy, he has dark hair and dark eyes and loves the arts. He also has a sense of adventure like Andy's, which pushes him forward to make a difference in the world. He tutors in an inner-city middle school and has applied to a program that would permit him to work for a time in an orphanage in Kenya.

Andy was twenty when he was killed and would have turned twenty-one the following November, just like my own middle son. I think of the terrorist bombings in Nairobi. I think of those who hate America enough to attack its embassies abroad and the buildings that symbolize its power at home. I think about the civilians who have been killed. I want to say to my son, "Don't go. Don't risk it."

Two weekends later, Joe and I are in Madison, the two of us searching the campus for Andy's plaque. We find it in the Red Gym, the old armory that now houses campus orientation activities and overlooks Lake Mendota. It hangs in an assembly hall beside a signed photograph of Dr. Martin Luther King Jr. On Andy's plaque is the familiar photo of him that appeared on the ubiquitous FBI posters that summer of 1964. I don't tell Joe not to go to Africa, though everything in me wants him to change his mind.

Andy contracted pneumonia when he was at Madison. He had to go home to recuperate and didn't finish his freshman year in Wisconsin. He took a semester off and went to work at his father's engineering firm.

"Here's an interesting story about Andy," Mrs. Goodman went on. "My husband's engineering firm was working on the Alexander Hamilton Bridge at the end of the Cross Bronx Expressway. Andy worked on that bridge the summer after he was ill. Now something happened when he was working on that job," she said.

"One of the workers was a big man, an African American man, and while he was working he slipped and held on, literally, with his fingertips. Andy, who was nowhere near as big as this man who had fallen, pulled him to safety. If I remember correctly, the man's name was Roosevelt.

"And so here's this kid who had the strength to pull a man from his death over the East River. That was Andy, too."

Andy enrolled at Queens College in the fall of 1963, where he studied dramatic arts. He acted in the Thirteenth Street Theater, an off-Broadway theater in Manhattan. "Andy was always something of a ham," his mother said. "He loved acting. Even when he was little, he was the one who organized all the other kids at our place in the summer and put on a play. He loved it. In high school he wrote a play that was performed at his graduation.

"He was also a musician," she went on. "He played a marvelous clarinet."

Her tone became serious and her voice slowed down, as if remembering her son's life had the power to animate, and remembering his death had the power to extinguish. "The following April, Andy told us that he wanted to go to Mississippi. We knew that SNCC had been recruiting on campus for the Mississippi voter drive, and that Andy had been listening to speakers all spring."

"Did you have to suppress the urge to tell him not to go to Mississippi?" I asked.

"Oh, yes. His father and I were very conflicted. On the one hand, we'd been discussing what was happening in the South at the dinner table. In Alabama, with Bull Connor, the riots and the bombing of the church that killed the four little girls, and Medgar Evers the year before.

"In our home, we talked about the horror of all this. We'd said that we needed to fight it on every front, and that we supported the efforts of the civil rights movement.

"Yet here was our son wanting to go into the belly of the beast. My husband and I looked at each other over the dinner table and said silently to each other, How can we possibly say no? We couldn't just pay lip service to the struggles that were taking place in the South for equal rights.

"Andy wasn't yet twenty-one, so he needed parental permission. And we gave him permission, of course."

Mrs. Goodman got up and walked across the foyer to a portrait of Andy that hangs beside the front door. "It was right here that I saw him for the last time and held him in my arms," she said. "It's funny what you do, as a mother. I was worried about him, naturally, and so I went into the bathroom before he left, opened the medicine cabinet, and took out bottles of iodine and Mercurochrome and a box of Band-Aids for Andy to put in his duffel bag, just in case."

Mrs. Goodman took a breath and paused. "So, of course Andy went, first to the training in, where was it? Ohio, where Michael

Schwerner, who was a social worker from New Rochelle, and James Chaney, who was from Mississippi, were helping. Andy had only been there a couple of days when they got the call that the church had burned. Well, Michael had tried to start a freedom school there, so he felt a tremendous sense of responsibility for what happened and knew he had to leave the training early, with James. So they asked for volunteers, and Andy volunteered.

"Later his brother said, 'If anyone was going to volunteer, it would be Andy.'

"Andy's grandfather, Charles Goodman, who was an important part of our family, always said, 'Be a doer. If you're going to believe in something, don't just stand there, do something.' That was Andy. Andy was a doer. His grandpa had inculcated that into his grandchildren. Every summer, when we'd all gather together in the Adirondacks, Grandpa Goodman had a profound impact on all of us."

As she spoke, I imagined the awful clash that awaited Andy in Mississippi: it was a clash of the *doers* on either side of the voting rights issue. I thought of those on the sidelines who didn't do or say anything. I thought of how those who were intent upon murder needed the inaction and the silence of others in order to secure the success of their mission, and how desperately those who were intent upon voter registration needed the onlookers to act.

"Andy would have stayed and completed the training had the church not been burned, so he jumped in the car with the others and they drove all night to Mississippi."

"Did he call to let you know that he'd arrived safely?" I asked.

"No," she said. "He'd told us that he'd probably write but wouldn't have time to write letters, so we'd sent him away with lots of postcards, so he could jot us a quick note, you know, 'everything's fine,' that kind of thing.

"Two days after we got the call that Andy was missing, his first and only postcard arrived in the mail—I still have that card. I know it by heart—'We arrived safely. The weather's fine.'

"First, SNCC called to tell us that he was missing. Then they called and said they'd been arrested and were in jail, which didn't necessarily mean anything, because they picked up lots of people. They were after Michael Schwerner. He was the target. And the fact that there was a black person in the car. They put them in jail so that they could round up the other Klansmen. There was a road-block when they let them go, then they shot them dead."

What must it be like for a mother to have a sentence like that in her repertoire, written indelibly onto her life's script by someone who murdered her son? "Those six weeks of not knowing . . . What did your instincts tell you?" I asked.

"I denied it. I couldn't believe they were dead. The worst I thought was that they were languishing somewhere in some southern jail, which was bad enough. Then, when they found the car . . . I think I was here." She points to the phone on the table.

"We had gone to Washington with a wonderful friend who was a lawyer, and we'd met with the president."

"What was Lyndon Johnson like?" I asked.

"Oh, he was wonderful. He said he was going to do everything possible. While we were sitting there, he pushed a button and said into the intercom, 'I want all the marines out. I want the army out. I want the navy. I want them to go through the marshes, to dredge the Pearl River.' He did everything he could possibly do.

"So we walked into the house and the phone rang and they told us they'd found their car and I screamed. I knew that if they'd found the car that something horrible had happened.

"And then all those weeks of waiting. We had the FBI here, they set up a special line, they tapped into every call that came in. There were terrible crank calls. People were saying, 'We have your son. Just drop five thousand dollars in such and such a place.' You just wouldn't believe it. People prey on pain, on grief. One person called and said, 'We kidnapped your son and we know you have diamonds, so if you'd just drop off your diamonds. . . .' "

"How often did you get updates?"

"They kept in touch with us and our attorney, and the attorney general, Nicholas Katzenbach, and Bobby Kennedy, everybody wanted to help, but there was nothing anyone could do because, of course, they were all buried under an earthen dam. Nobody knew until the FBI offered money and an informant came forward. There's no honor among thieves.

"We were at the theater when we found out. We'd had people here all the time for six weeks and I didn't want to leave. Finally someone said you've got to go out. I had been glued to the phone. I wanted to hear everything, every scrap of information, any lead, however scanty. My whole life was about waiting for something, any news of Andy.

"But we went to the theater for my husband's birthday. People knew exactly where we were all the time, and someone came to the theater.

"It was almost . . . I was just so drained by that time. People said I was the only one who thought he was alive, everyone else knew except me. I guess I really knew. Well, I subsequently learned that when people near to a person die, they don't seem dead. Sometimes you even hallucinate.

"When Andy's coffin came back, it was at the Riverside Memorial down on Seventy-sixth Street," Mrs. Goodman explained. "I walked into the memorial and I saw him, five years old, dressed up to perform for the family, sitting on top of the coffin, which, of course, was closed. He had been buried for forty-four days. But there he was. I still see him there, even today.

"I'm a psychologist and I know that the mind works in strange ways. You don't control your own mind.

"I will tell you that not a day goes by when I don't think about Andrew, not a single, solitary day. But not in a morbid way. There is nothing worse than losing a child. It's a pain that's almost indescribable. Under normal circumstances we expect to outlive our parents, but we don't expect to outlive our children. As a mother, you've got these two grown sons and one who didn't get to become an adult.

"I knew a couple who lost their son and had his room draped in black. It was terrible to see that kind of grief."

Mrs. Goodman then got up and invited me to follow her into her living room. She walked across the carpeted floor to a small table that, like the grand piano, was covered with framed photographs. She held one in each hand and showed them to me. "There's a picture of him beside a picture of his father. His father is twenty years old and Andy is twenty years old. And the reason I have them there is because of the incredible resemblance.

"My older son and younger son look just like me," she said, and picked up two more photographs. "Here's my youngest son with his son, and as you can see, they look just alike. I showed someone this photo of my older son just recently and they said, 'My God, this is you.' Of course he's in his sixties now and has gray hair. He is a Juilliard grad, a brilliant musician and director. He plays piano and trombone, but mostly he does conducting."

"Have you ever visited Neshoba County?" I asked when our time was drawing to a close.

"Yes, once a long time ago, but that is so fuzzy, and once very recently.

"I was in Mississippi last winter to visit Stanley Dearman, who was the editor of the Neshoba County paper for more than thirty years and has become a dear friend. Stan was about to retire and had sold the paper. The new owner called and asked if I'd write something on the occasion of Stanley's retirement. So I wrote it and then I got the idea—I don't travel much, nor do I travel well any-more—so I called a friend and asked if she'd go to Mississippi with me, all expenses paid. She said she'd go with me.

"Then I called Stan's wife, who has the same name as me—a wonderful woman—has written a cookbook, no less, and she said, 'Let's surprise him.'

"They were having a reception for Stan at the public library in Philadelphia, and Stan's wife told me when to arrive. So in I walked, right in the middle of the party. I saw him before he saw me and when he did we fell into each other's arms and we just wept.

"It was beautiful, a beautiful moment.

"Stan got up to speak," she said. "I was so moved I can't remember what he said, except that it was too much. I even said that to him, 'Stan, this is too much,' and he said that it wasn't enough. It was wonderful, it really was."

Then Mrs. Goodman gave me a gift. During Stanley Dearman's reception, many Neshoba County people came up to her and said hello, she told me, and thanked her for coming. After the conversations I'd had with family members, this anecdote was the first little glimmer of hope that I'd had, and I realized that in spite of everything, healing happens.

"Then, one woman came up and said her name was Mary Lou Killen." Mrs. Goodman paused here. "My heart stopped. You know, everyone is related to everyone else there. I think she was his sister. He was a horror, but she was a very lovely woman. After all, everyone was there to honor Stan.

"You know, there are three ethnic communities in Neshoba County: blacks, whites, and Choctaw Indians. All three were represented at Stan's party, and it seems that now all get along in harmony, if the feeling at Stan's gathering was any indication."

"You know, Edgar Killen is my father's cousin," I tell her. I'm scared.

"What? The Preacher?"

"Yes. I've never met him, but he's kin, and someone that nobody wants to claim."

"Well, Stan put his life in his hands when he starting writing in that paper that the Klan committed the murders. So he exposed them. I think it's important to speak out, even when we disagree."

"I'm having some trouble with my father's family on that very issue," I told her.

"Why wouldn't they want you to speak out?"

"I'm not entirely clear. I think they're afraid of guilt by association, but that's not what they say. Embarrassment, maybe. I haven't talked to anyone for a while."

CHAPTER 20

Who Owns History?

I N APRIL of 2001 my publisher and I discussed the possibility
of contacting Edgar Ray Killen; perhaps the climax of my book
would be a conversation with him.

I didn't want to do it. Everything in me resisted it. But I had
to try, so I sent my cousin Troy an E-mail. He had told a story,
once, about Edgar Ray Killen paying Aunt Ruby a hospital visit.
Perhaps he, like Jimmy, would find this interesting and would help,
perhaps protect, me. I was afraid to go it alone.

Troy didn't respond. I left him a phone message. He didn't
return my call. A few days later, I received a long E-mail that didn't
make much sense but communicated a clear message: he, Susie Lee,
and Auntie Lu had decided that I was writing a book about civil
rights, that I'd been hiding that fact from them, that Aunt Ruby
had never had a hospital visit from Edgar Ray, and how dare I try
to malign Auntie Lu, who is an angel. His mother felt betrayed,
embarrassed that I'd mentioned it to the ladies we'd visited. Finally,
they have to live there after the book is published, and I don't.

This was when the stories in my memoir would include a story about my memoir.

Eventually, I received Edgar Ray's telephone number from Jerry Mitchell, a reporter for the Jackson *Clarion-Ledger*, who has researched the case and written about it extensively. But I never was able to reach Edgar Ray. Over the past decade, Mississippi has successfully brought to justice two civil rights murderers from the 1960s. In 1994, Byron de la Beckwith was found guilty in the 1963 murder of Medgar Evers. In 1998, Sam Bowers was convicted of murdering Vernon Dahmer in 1966.

State Attorney General Mike Moore is now watching Edgar Ray Killen's movements in hopes of convening a grand jury that would bring murder charges against him. Other conspirators from the 1964 trial who are still living are also under suspicion, but new evidence has surfaced that points to Edgar Ray. He is the prime suspect, and he doesn't pick up the phone. If he had, I'm sure he wouldn't have talked, even to kinfolk, knowing that it would be on the record.

As far as I was concerned, whether he and I talked didn't really matter anymore, because I didn't need him to provide me with a climax to my memoir. My father's family provided that for me, and did it in a way that began to shed light on issues that had been nagging at me since I discovered that Edgar Ray was kin in 1997: *How could this have happened?* And *Why didn't we know?*

Nobody in my father's family had seen a single word of my manuscript, so I sent twenty pages to Auntie Lu and Susie Lee to show them that I was writing a memoir about my dad and about our family. The only comment I heard came secondhand through my father: change the name of the great-uncle who embezzled money in 1929 because his family will feel bad. I asked my father if they said anything else. Did they like the story? "They didn't say," he said.

"Okay, so I'll change the uncle's name to Titus," I said. "How long has he been dead?"

"Who knows?" my father said. "A long time. He was older than Daddy Bob."

"Would anybody know who I was talking about anyway?"

"I doubt it. I doubt they'd know me from a load of hay. Better change all the names, though. Lumiere's been upset with me, and I'm afraid I'll lose her. Do what you need to do, but be careful and remember to change the names," my father said.

"Why would Auntie Lu take it out on you?" I asked, surprised.

"I guess everyone thinks that I should be able to tell you what to do," he said with a little chuckle. "Guess they don't know me. Or you."

"Yeah, but I still don't understand why anybody'd be mad at you," I said. "You haven't done anything. And besides, there's the whole emphasis on kinfolk and all."

"Listen," he said. "I've lived in both the North and the South, and I understand where they're coming from. They bury everything. You want to unearth it. It's breaking a big rule."

IN MARCH of 1966, a full year after the felony charges against the alleged killers had been dismissed in federal court, the United States Supreme Court unanimously reversed all of Judge Cox's dismissals. Most importantly, the Court ruled that the rights of the three victims not to be denied life and liberty without due process of law were protected under the Fourteenth Amendment. The felony indictment was reinstated and the government's case strengthened.

In September, however, Judge Cox dismissed the indictments again, this time on the grounds that the grand jury panel had not included Negroes and women. The Justice Department agreed. The charges were dropped and the defendants were once again completely free.

In February of 1967, a new and legally constituted federal grand jury brought the final felony indictment for conspiracy against nineteen men. The trial was set for May 26 but was delayed until October 9 due to a technical violation involving jury lists.

As October approached, it became clear that a trial would actually take place. The stakes were high: not only were elected law enforcement officers about to give sworn testimony in open court regarding the deaths of Goodman, Schwerner, and Chaney, but this was also the first federal prosecution of the White Knights of the Ku Klux Klan. Many people expressed serious concern about whether the federal government could succeed in prosecuting members of the Klan before a Mississippi jury. All knew that the result would have an impact on future prosecutions, not only in the state, but also anywhere that lynchings had taken place and the killers had enjoyed legal protection under local officials and jurisdictions.

For eight days the federal courtroom in Meridian was packed. The prosecution was well aware that Judge Cox, who was to preside over the case, was considered unsympathetic toward civil rights workers and their attorneys. Cox, whose attempts to dismiss the charges had ultimately failed, had several years before referred publicly to a group of black voting registrants as "a bunch of chimpanzees."

Three attorneys represented the federal government for the prosecution: John Doar, assistant attorney general who headed the Civil Rights Division of the Justice Department; another Justice Department attorney; and the federal attorney for the Southern Mississippi District, a Mississippi native.

Twelve lawyers represented the eighteen defendants. The entire practicing Neshoba County bar defended the Neshoba men, with the exception of the county attorney. They were Herman Alford; Clayton Lewis, mayor of Philadelphia; Montgomery Mars; W. D. Moore; and Laurel Weir. A Jackson attorney represented Sheriff Rainey. Five Meridian attorneys represented the Lauderdale defendants. Attorney Travis Buckley represented Imperial Wizard Sam Bowers.

The defendants appeared relaxed throughout the trial, at times embarrassing the defense team as they joked with one another and friends during recess. The jury had been chosen on the first day and comprised five men and seven women, mostly working-class citizens, all of them white.

The defense had planned a strategy that would position Judge Cox as an ally who would eventually support them in decrying the government's case and denouncing its paid informants. The prosecution knew that it would gain nothing by harassing defendants who were well known in the community, and did not want to risk turning a Mississippi jury's sympathy toward the alleged killers. Their strategy was to go forward slowly, allow the defense to make mistakes, and show the utmost respect for the court.

It didn't take long for the defense team to blunder, a forced error that immediately placed the prosecution in a favorable position. After several maps had been introduced as evidence, lead prosecutor John Doar called a witness, the Reverend Charles Johnson from Meridian. Johnson, a black minister who had known Mickey Schwerner throughout early 1964, was called to provide background information about Schwerner's activities in the area that spring.

Then the defense stood to cross-examine the witness.

A lawyer from Philadelphia, Laurel Weir was in his midthirties and had built for himself a local reputation for homespun humor in the courtroom. "Now, let me ask you," Weir began, using what those who attended the trial would call "his most down-home accent."

"Let me ask you if you and Mr. Schwerner didn't advocate and try to get young male Negroes to sign statements agreeing to rape a white woman once a week during the hot summer of 1964?"

The strategy backfired. First, Judge Cox informed the defense that they had stepped over the line. Second, he allowed the witness to answer the question.

"No, never," the Reverend Johnson replied.

Then the judge set the tone for the trial. He told Weir that he found that question "highly improper" and demanded to see some basis for it, for the record. Startled, Weir looked to his colleagues. He then replied that a note had been passed to him from one of the defendants.

"Who is the author of that question?" Cox was adamant.

Everyone was silent for a moment. Then Herman Alford, another of the defense attorneys, spoke. "Brother Killen wrote the question, one of the defendants."

Judge Cox shot back at the defendants and their attorneys seated before him, "I'm not going to allow a farce to be made of this trial and everybody might as well get that through their heads, including every one of the defendants, right now. I don't understand such a question as that, and I don't appreciate it, and I'm going to say so before I get through with the trial of this case. I'm surprised at a question like that coming from a preacher, too. I'm talking about Killen, or whatever his name is."

Weir's blunder undermined the defense for the remainder of the trial. "The judge got mad that first day, and stayed mad for the rest of the time," reflected a member of the Neshoba County board of supervisors. Apart from the judge's emotional response, Doar realized at that moment, "If there had been any feeling in the courtroom that the defendants were invulnerable to conviction in Mississippi, this incident dispelled it completely. Cox made it clear that he was taking the trial seriously. That made the jurors stop and think, 'If Judge Cox is taking this stand, we'd better meet our responsibility as well.' "

I THOUGHT about Troy's letter for a while and slowly began to sort through many of my unspoken discomforts and fears. If they could round up a posse, I could too. I talked to my sisters about it: they'd experienced the same feelings, only at different times.

Through Troy, Susie Lee had communicated that I'd embarrassed her by asking Fannie and others about the murders. I listened again and again to my taped interviews. I'd asked nothing about the

murders or about Edgar Ray Killen. Fannie had offered me newspaper clips that she'd saved over the years. This felt too crazy to be
true. Why would Susie Lee say that?

I had violated a tacit rule, a value that placed another person's
feelings ahead of the truth. But it took me a while to identify the
rule, because for some reason, the feelings to be protected were not
mine. I was no longer kin; I was something else: an interloper, even
an outside agitator. I was being told to know my place and stay in
it, or I would not enjoy the relationships I had always known.

It became increasingly clear that Cousin Troy had begun to defend the Mississippi kin against charges nobody had made against
them; but when it came to defending me, I was on my own.

I'd asked Troy if he had any ideas about how to contact Preacher
Killen. I'd hoped that he, like Jimmy, was as curious as I was and
might even figure out a way to protect me if I had to talk to him.
But I should have known from the start; indeed my instincts were
telling me all along that when it came to telling the family story,
there was acceptable information and unacceptable information. For
both sides, North and South, loyalty to family did not cross the
Mississippi state line. Troy never did talk to me directly, nor did he
write me again. He didn't really have to.

With the five words *Auntie Lu is an angel,* Troy dropped the
gauntlet. The battleground was no longer his discomfort over what
I may or may not be writing; the battleground was now Auntie Lu's
honor. It was a shrewd move, but not impossible to argue against.
Somehow, in a way I do not yet understand, my discussion of the
1964 murders and of Edgar Ray Killen, who is related to half the
residents in Neshoba County, would compromise Auntie Lu.

Rubbish. How could the family's black sheep, someone Auntie
Lu says she's never even met, compromise, even for a moment, the
loving complexity that is my Auntie Lu? Yes, *my* Auntie Lu. Who
has spent her life caring for her loved ones more tenderly than I
could ever hope to and who, like the rest of us mortals, makes
mistakes.

Edgar Ray Killen casts a dark shadow over all his kinfolk, but no darker a shadow over Auntie Lu than he does over the rest of us. In fact, the darkest shadow lies over those of us in the younger generations. We've lived outside the system, have gone to college, and have grown up at a time when the racial status quo was changing all around us. Our silence weighs more heavily, I believe, because we've had our formative years to help us see the other side.

Unless, of course, there is something that everyone is hiding; something that I got too close to: is that the issue? Troy doesn't want me to write about this, and he's resorting to false chivalry instead of telling me directly how he feels. Auntie Lu doesn't want me to write this, and so she's upset with my father, her only living brother. It's not just Aunt Lumiere upon whom the battle is being fought, it's the older generation. Troy is protecting something, and he wants me to believe that it is the women and the old gentlemen and the firesides of Neshoba County. But I wonder if it is something else.

What that something else is, remains a mystery. I hold all these questions now, and all I can do is string them together. Perhaps this reaction is simply fear that I will make connections that aren't relevant and will bring shame to innocent people. Perhaps there is something the older generation knew or did or failed to do. The Masonic lodge, the walkie-talkie, the hospital visit, the time and place, the proximity, the closed ranks, and the anger. There are historical details that I have gotten close to, and Troy has coiled up, ready to spring if I come any closer.

I am surprised that a young person, five generations removed from the rhetoric of the Old South, would resort to this kind of antique ploy. He's challenging me: *write this and I'll accuse you of compromising Auntie Lu. Write this and it will destroy Uncle Chub's relationship with his sister.* He wants to silence me by turning our beloved aunt into someone whose character is now in question. He wants to silence me by threatening to hurt my dad if I speak out.

It's like the old days of the civil rights movement, when everyone pointed fingers at the volunteers and the federal government, and neglected to look at the system they were trying to change. Only this time, the villain is no longer Edgar Ray Killen, a member of the family who will probably be tried soon for a murder that the evidence shows he planned from start to finish. The villain is me, who wants to write about it.

We all live at the base of the triangle: those who commit evil acts depend on our silence and those who try to stop them depend on our support. We're all in this together.

There were so many things that I couldn't quite decipher. So I called Auntie Lu.

"I got an E-mail from Troy that I don't understand," I said.

"Why didn't you tell us you were writing a book about civil rights?" she asked.

I got defensive. "Because I'm not writing a book about civil rights," I answered.

"Then how come you weren't taking down notes in the cemetery?" she asked. I'd been to the cemetery on several occasions over the years. With the exception of one or two people, I had plenty of notes already, and I told her this.

"I don't want to be ugly," she said. "But I don't want my name associated with a book that is about civil rights."

"But it's not about civil rights," I said. "It's a family memoir."

"If it's not about civil rights, why do you want to talk to that ol' Edgar Killen? I've never even met him. Jimmy's wife said the other night, 'You can't be responsible for what your kin does.' "

Why, then, was everyone taking responsibility?

My father suggested that I not call my southern kinfolk again. "I'll take care of this," he said. "They're all riled up and they won't listen to you anyway."

And it was just as well. For weeks, my feelings about my Mississippi kin narrowed my perspective. I found myself trying to create an outward picture of my life that others would approve of. I spent Saturdays patching the brown spots my dogs had left on my suburban lawn, planting flowers and shampooing my carpets, unaware that I had become more concerned with what the neighbors thought than I cared about working on my manuscript. I wrote long, cloying, and apologetic letters to my southern relatives, responding to fears that I had only heard about secondhand. The book is not about civil rights, I wrote.

I was angry and defensive. I wanted it to be their fault for not understanding what I was doing. I was mad that everyone had been talking about me behind my back and making assumptions about me that weren't true.

Then it occurred to me. Why was it so wrong to write a book about civil rights? Why was I so insistent that I wouldn't write a book like that? What—or who—was I really fighting against? At this point, it was clear that it was no longer important to rail against my Mississippi kin. I read the letters and tore them up once I saw that I was making promises that I couldn't keep. At this point, it was clear that it was more important to look at myself.

OVER THE NEXT FEW DAYS, in October of 1967, the government introduced some of the gruesome physical evidence related to the crime, began to establish the defendants' membership in the Klan, and presented details of the plan to kill Schwerner and a step-by-step chronology of the murder itself.

The first Klan informant was Wallace Miller, who testified that Preacher Killen had sworn him into the Klan in April of 1964. He provided evidence to show that Killen had organized the Lauderdale klavern. He had witnessed Killen's swearing-in to the Klan of six of the defendants: Frank Herndon, James Jordan, Pete Harris, Jimmie Snowden, Travis Barnette, and Alton Wayne Roberts.

The next witness for the prosecution was Delmar Dennis, whose entrance into the courtroom stunned the defendants, most especially Sam Bowers. Up until that moment, nobody had suspected that Dennis, a province titan for the White Knights of the Ku Klux Klan, was an FBI informant. For three years he had assisted the imperial wizard in administrative matters and had reported only to Bowers. Preacher Killen had sworn Dennis in to the Lauderdale klavern in March of 1964. Also present at his swearing in had been Wayne Roberts, Frank Herndon, and Peter Harris. He testified, "Edgar Ray Killen was the leader, or the kleagle, for the first few weeks as we were still organizing, and after that the officers of the local klavern were in charge." He also established Killen's ties to Klan leadership. Killen had access to information that the Klan's state officers had approved Schwerner's "elimination," or murder.

Dennis was the first witness to identify Neshoba County law enforcement officials as klansmen, having seen Hop Barnett at the Bloomo School meeting on June 16. He also testified that he had discussed Klan business with Sheriff Rainey and Deputy Sheriff Price.

Upon cross-examination, the defense asked Dennis if he had not also discussed the Klan with the FBI. Did that not make them Klansmen as well?

Dennis replied, "Yes, but the Federal Bureau of Investigation didn't give me the [Klan] handshake and didn't know what was going on in the Neshoba County klavern."

He had become disillusioned because of the violence, had become a paid informer for the FBI in November of 1964, and had been providing the federal government with inside information about the Klan's activities for almost three years.

Cross-examination revealed the amount of money the FBI had paid Dennis for his information, and Attorney Weir made one more futile attempt to humor the judge and jury. "But were you paid for that information?" he asked. "And instead of thirty pieces of silver you got fifteen thousand dollars?"

The judge was not amused. Added to Dennis's damning testimony, Weir's antics further eroded an already weak defense.

Miller's and Dennis's testimonies provided the prosecution with the evidence they needed to show that the conspiracy to murder

Mickey Schwerner had taken place over the course of several months. Over and over again, the name Edgar Ray Killen was mentioned. He had recruited a number of Klansmen into the Lauderdale and Neshoba klaverns. He had organized regular Klan meetings and had provided communication from Klan leadership that the elimination of Mickey Schwerner had been approved. His organizational efforts resulted in a well-prepared group of terrorists from whom he could find volunteers to come to his aid at a moment's notice.

The testimony that followed, during which several eyewitnesses revealed the events of June 21, 1964, demonstrated just how effective Preacher Killen's preparedness had been.

VIRTUALLY EVERYONE in Neshoba County is related to everyone else, so Edgar Ray Killen's kinship surely would be no surprise to anyone in the community. And yet, for me, it is a surprise. He embarrasses all of us, makes us feel ashamed. No wonder nobody claims him. He's the funny uncle, the outcast, the one nobody ever talks about.

But is there something more personal? Does he embody something that we don't want to claim in the family because of how different he is? Or does he embody something that we don't want to claim in the family because of the mirror he holds up to the rest of us? I can't speak for the others, but when I look at Edgar Ray Killen, what reflects back to me is fear.

My desire to be approved of, embraced, and loved was so strong that I found myself rewriting passages, doubting conversations I'd heard, feeling guilty for breaking promises that, upon reflection, I'd never even made, nor had I been asked to. I found myself reluctant to write a book about civil rights, unwilling to take a stand. I was part of the system, playing right along. I was afraid not to.

Oddly, however, here was this word: *betrayal*. Was it betrayal, or the threat of betrayal?

There was a code of ethics that nobody had bothered to articulate but that had bound me anyway. I had sensed something in my relations' unwillingness to discuss anything other than bloodlines and chicken stories, and they had sensed that something in me wanted more. And so we had pretended: I had pretended that all I wanted to talk about was the family tree; they pretended that the family tree was all there was to discuss.

I needed to reclaim my story, yet I was afraid to explore what the story was about.

I began to feel that old familiar loneliness, an ache akin to homesickness. I had become untethered from one of my moorings, the one that had connected me to my father's roots and had held me in place all my life. I had observed that the strength of kinship would triumph over any difficulty, but I hadn't looked at the entire picture. Outsider, northerner: these trumped blood ties. I was no longer the Mary that belonged to Chub, to Grandma Ora and Daddy Bob. Unasked and unconsulted, I was reduced to a stereotype. Nobody bothered to call me to find out what I was doing. Phone calls and E-mails went unanswered. Letters unresponded to.

Then I behaved in kind. My Mississippi family, whose enormous capacity to love had always baffled me and my siblings from a distance, became a stereotype as well. As soon as communication halted and our relations with each other were transformed into suspicion, gossip, and unsubstantiated speculation, they became for me the picture of the closed society that I had read about over and over again during my research. I had rejected that stereotype, using the warm welcomes and unconditional love of my Mississippi kin as evidence. I hadn't seen that there were strings attached: that love meant loyalty and gratitude, which meant keeping secrets and adhering to a status quo that I had hitherto denied.

But I saw them now, and in them I saw more fear.

They said I'd betrayed them, and for a time I believed them, until I saw that we had betrayed each other: our deepest fears of being humiliated, or exposed, or abandoned. We had betrayed each other not because we'd made and broken any promises, but because we'd always spoken using words that someone else had given us, a script about which we hadn't even been aware. We'd never really known each other and now there was a very good chance that we never would.

ERNEST KIRKLAND of the Mount Zion community testified that the boys had visited church members on the afternoon of June 21. Then Philadelphia police officer Earl Robert Poe confirmed that Deputy Sheriff Price had arrested them for speeding, and had taken them to the Neshoba County Jail at approximately four in the afternoon.

Next, Minnie Herring, the jailer's wife, took the stand and contradicted a portion of Price's alibi. According to Price, he had detained the three in jail because it had taken him several hours to locate the local justice of the peace, Leonard Warren, to fix the speeding fine. According to Mrs. Herring, the usual procedure for paying speeding tickets did not require for the sheriff or deputy to be present for the speeder to make bond or pay a fine. She then identified a carefully written schedule that had been posted in the jail by Warren, who often was out of town. When Warren arrived at the jail with Price, J. E. (who had been driving and was liable for the fine) borrowed twenty dollars from Mickey. Price then released the three, saying, "See how quick you all can get out of Neshoba County." They thanked him and left the jail.

What happened next, from the meeting at the Longhorn Drive-In with Preacher Killen to the rendezvous at the dam, was presented in two confessions. James Jordan and Horace Doyle Barnette's testimonies so closely resembled each other that the prosecution had ample corroboration for their evidence. Jordan's was the more important testimony of the two, as he described in graphic detail what happened on June 21. Jordan had collapsed the day he was to testify but appeared the following afternoon.

Jordan placed Preacher Killen at the Longhorn Drive-In in Meridian in the early evening of June 21 with two young men, who came in with him. Killen had "said he had a job he needed some help on over in Neshoba County and he needed some men to go with him. He said that two or three of those civil rights workers were locked up and they needed their rear ends tore up." One of them was Goatee, Killen had told Jordan and the others.

Several of the men made phone calls to recruit more volunteers, and others went to a grocery store for rubber gloves. The rest met at Bernard Akin's mobile home with Wayne Roberts. The lynch mob assembled, Killen said they had to hurry, and they were to pick them [Goodman, Schwerner, and Chaney] up. Killen told them that a highway patrol car would stop the three on the out-skirts of town. Killen urged them to obtain the rubber gloves and gas up the cars. He then went ahead because he said he had to make the rest of the arrangements. He had told them where to park their cars so that they could be given instructions about what to do and where to go.

When Jordan arrived at the courthouse, Killen came from around the corner, told the group that he would show them the jail and then give them their next instructions. Killen drove them around the jail and took them behind an old warehouse at the end of town, where they were supposed to wait. They then took Killen to the McLain-Hayes funeral home in Philadelphia. If anything happened he would be the first one questioned, Killen had said.

They waited at the warehouse for fifteen minutes before a city police car drove by. "They're going on Highway Nineteen, toward Meridian. Follow them." The police officer then turned back toward town while Jordan, Billy Wayne Posey, Wayne Roberts, Jerry Sharpe, and another whom Jordan could not identify headed onto the highway in two cars. They saw the deputy's car pass them, and followed it at a high rate of speed.

"We saw a little wagon in front of him," Jordan went on. "Which he pulled over to the side of the road." Price had used his flashing lights to pull the car over, Jordan testified. "We pulled up behind him, he got out and went up and told the three men that were in the car to get out." There were two white men and a Negro. Price told them to get in his car, which they did. "I heard a thump, like the deputy was rushing them to get in there or where he hit one of them."

Jordan's testimony then differed from that of Barnette. Barnette placed Jordan at the site of the murder, while Jordan himself claimed to have been left at the site of another of the Klansmen's cars, which had been disabled at the side of the road. Jordan claimed to have heard shots from a distance. Barnette's testimony placed the gun that shot James Chaney twice in James Jordan's hand.

I WOULDN'T FIND out what it had been like back in 1964 from kin who'd lived through it, so I looked elsewhere for the story.

I picked up books that I'd once started but put aside and not finished because they had been too painful for me to read. I talked to people whose proximity to the events of 1964 helped me gain new insights and perspective. I got to know people whose suffering did not go away and who understand that it will not go away just because you want it to.

I saw that I would never be able to discuss these things with my southern relatives, and that the only reason that we'd gotten along in the past was because I had, once I set foot in their homes, left myself back in Minnesota. We could be in a relationship because we could keep who we were hidden from each other. Now I had a choice of whether to take a stand or remain silent. I knew what I had to do and what the consequences would be.

I became indistinguishable from the people who hear the word *Mississippi* and color it in stereotype.

It was as though the summer of 1964 had been erased from the family calendar as something unspeakable. We avoided grief. We avoided strong feelings. We avoided confrontation of any kind. Once rebuked or publicly shamed, we fell back into ever-stricter modes of conformity—the more we fit in (or was it disappeared?) into the blandness of our surroundings, the safer we felt.

Perhaps this is why it is so horrible for me to write about Edgar Ray. We want neither a heritage nor a culture that connects us with a defiled history. The Mississippi family members are burdened in a way that I have not been.

And yet is there any history that has not been defiled?

Our injunction is silence. But I am the daughter of a man who chose to live north of the Mason-Dixon Line. I have spent my life listening to his stories and taking them into myself until they have become part of who I am. He sits in the middle: supportive of my efforts to write an important story, sad and afraid of the reaction of the family he loves. But for me, the rules have changed. I have now moved away from the safety of the center and into the riskier territory of the edge. The injunction is now to speak, and it's terrible that it took this split to discover it.

CHAPTER 21

The Double Helix

I N THE EARLY SPRING of 1864, news traveled on horseback from Meridian that Sherman had burned the city to the ground. The railroad ties had been severed, heated up, and twisted into "Sherman bow ties," cutting off the city from supplies. The couriers shouted to the farmers east of Meridian that Sherman himself was marching down the Pine Grove Road on his way to Mobile. The family farm lay directly in Sherman's path.

"Pappy," then a boy of fourteen, was ordered to take the family livestock and hide back behind the piney hills, away from the road until the Yankee troops had passed. For two weeks he camped, a mile back from the road, hidden from view by low red hills covered with thick pine forest, and separated from danger by a swamp, navigable only by a boy who knew the labyrinthine path through it, the one that took him on errands to and from his daddy's still.

In the evenings, when the mules, goats, and cattle had settled down to sleep, and when the chickens had quieted down in the covered bed of the wagon, Dempsey climbed the hills toward the road and shinnied up the closest tree he dared. From this vantage point, he watched the Union campfires flicker in the woods on the other side of the road. He could hear the soldiers laughing and singing. He smelled the smoke from the wood fires and imagined that they were eating hot food: squirrel with carrots and potatoes, spoon bread and gravy. His stomach turned with hunger and he went back to his hiding place with the animals and ate a week-old piece of corn bread so hard he couldn't bite off a corner of it. He had to dissolve it in a tin of cold creek water and spoon it out like yesterday's soup. He didn't dare build a fire and risk the sight of smoke.

When the campfires were dark a week later and the soldiers had gone, Dempsey took the animals back to find the house still standing but all the valuables stolen, the barn plundered of grain, the garden stripped. His mother lay prostrate in bed. The newly emancipated slaves joined the freedmen who followed behind the Union Army. "My daddy was too poor to own any niggers," Dempsey had told my father. "He jus' shook his head and watched 'em go."

ON WEDNESDAY, October 18, 1967, John Doar presented the government's summation to the jury. He first explained why the federal government had taken on the role of prosecutor in this case. "If there is to be any hope for this land of ours, the federal government has a duty to eliminate such evil forces that seize local law enforcement," he began. He addressed jurors' fears about federal control over the rights of the states. "The federal government is not invading Philadelphia or Neshoba County," Doar continued. "It [the presence of federal government] means only that these defendants are tried for a crime under federal law in a Mississippi city, before a Mississippi federal judge, in a Mississippi courtroom, before twelve men and women from the state of Mississippi. The sole responsibility for the determination of guilt or innocence of these men remains in the hands where it should remain, the hands of twelve citizens from the state of Mississippi.

"Members of the jury, this was a calculated, cold-blooded plot. Three men, hardly more than boys, were the victims. The plot was executed with a degree of self-possession and steadiness equal to the wickedness with which it was planned." He went on to praise the courage of those Klansmen who had become FBI informants, pointing out that the financial remuneration they had received was minimal. "They are men of convictions, both about states' rights and law enforcement . . . it is common that offenses of this type have to be proved in this way.

"Midnight murder in the rural area of Neshoba County provides few witnesses."

He then pointed directly at the deputy sheriff of Neshoba County. "Price used the machinery of law, his office, his power, his authority, his badge, his uniform, his jail, his police car, his police gun, he used them all to take, to hold, to capture, and to kill. He is responsible for this conspiracy and accountable under law and under justice.

"There are the master planners," he went on, pointing to the defendants seated at the other side of the courtroom. "There are the organizers, there are the lookout men, there are the killers, there are the clean-up and disposal people, and there are the protectors. Each of these defendants played one or more parts in this conspiracy.

"This is an important case. It is important to the government, it is important to the defendants, but most of all it is important to the state of Mississippi," Doar concluded.

Then he took his cues from Abraham Lincoln, which may have been risky in a secessionist state, but in the end it served him well. "What I say, and what the other lawyers say here today . . . will be soon forgotten, but what you twelve people do here today will long be remembered. . . . If you find that these men are not guilty, you will declare the law of Neshoba County to be the law of the state of Mississippi."

All twelve attorneys for the defense made closing arguments, most of which questioned the credibility of the paid witnesses, tried to appeal to the Mississippian's traditional resentment toward outsiders, and defamed the intentions as well as maligned the character of Goodman, Schwerner, and Chaney.

> It may well be that these young men were sacrificed by their own kind for publicity or other reasons. . . . So far as I have been able to determine they had no authority to be here, they broke the laws of that county by speeding and they violated the American constitution of messing in local affairs in a local community. Of course whatever I say about the case is my own opinion, I wouldn't no more go to New York or some other troubled area and tell them how to run their business than I would tell God how to run the universe. That is their business. Mississippians rightfully resent some hairy beatniks from another state visiting our state with hate and defying our people. It is my opinion that the so-called workers are not workers at all, but low class riff-raff, that are misfits in our own land. If the people of Mississippi need help in solving our problems, we'll call upon those who are capable of helping. We'll not send for a bum to help manage our finances or a Communist to save our government.

It was as though the state of Mississippi were an extended family. The attorneys themselves held kin responsible: if the defendants were found guilty, then all of Neshoba County would be guilty, and vice versa. Either they were all good or all bad. There was no thought of a county held hostage by the Klan, no mention of the Klan's hold on the community. It was all for one and one for all. Is this what my Mississippi kin were talking about?

On October 18, Judge Cox charged the jury. The following day they returned, claiming that they were unable to reach a verdict. Instead of declaring a mistrial, Judge Cox issued a new set of instructions, known as the "Allen charge" or the "Dynamite charge," in which he stressed the importance of reaching a verdict.

The purpose of the Allen charge was to break a deadlocked jury. Judge Cox sent them back into deliberations with the following advice. "It is your duty as jurors to consult with one another and to deliberate with a view to reaching an agreement, if you can do so without violence to individual judgment . . . if the greater number of you are for a conviction, each dissenting juror ought to seriously consider whether a doubt in his or her mind is a reasonable one."

Outside the courtroom, an officer of the court overheard Wayne Roberts say to Cecil Price, "Judge Cox just gave that jury a 'Dynamite charge.' We've got some dynamite for them ourselves." The court official then reported the incident to Judge Cox.

On the morning of October 20, the jury entered the courtroom. The foreman handed the clerk the sealed verdicts, which were torn open and read. "Western Division criminal Action Number 5291, *United States of America*, plaintiff, versus *Cecil Ray Price* et al., defendants. We, the jury, find the defendant Cecil Ray Price not guilty. I'm sorry, Your Honor, may I start over?"

Cox nodded.

"We, the jury, find the defendant Cecil Ray Price guilty of the charges contained in the indictment. We find the defendant Bernard Akin not guilty of the charges. . . . We find Jimmy Arledge guilty. . . ."

The jury had found guilty seven of the eighteen conspirators. In addition to Price and Arledge, the jury also named Sam Bowers, Wayne Roberts, Jimmie Snowden, Billy Wayne Posey, and Horace Doyle Barnett. Sheriff Rainey, Olen Burrage, and Frank Herndon were acquitted. The jury could not reach a verdict on Jerry McGrew Sharpe, "Hop" Barnett, and Edgar Ray Killen.

After the unconvicted defendants were released from the courtroom and the bond and sentencing procedures explained to those found guilty, Judge Cox excused all but Price and Roberts, whom he ordered to approach the bench.

He told them that he had denied them bond and that they were to be jailed over the weekend because of Roberts's "dynamite" remark to Price of the previous day. "If you think you can intimidate this court, you are as badly mistaken as you can be," he said. "I'm not going to let any wild man loose on a civilized society and I want you locked up. I don't think you have taken this thing very seriously and I'm going to give you an opportunity to think very seriously about it."

Price and Roberts stood silently before Judge Cox.

"I very heartily endorse the verdict of this jury," he went on. "Particularly adjudging Mr. Roberts as guilty. It would have been unthinkable to have had a verdict of any other kind against a man like that who has the audacity to make the remarks that he made, even in fun in the hall of this court."

The conviction of Deputy Sheriff Cecil Price and six of his codefendants marked the first successful jury conviction of white officials and Klansmen in the history of Mississippi for crimes against black people or civil rights workers. A trial for murder had not taken place, but it set a precedent in Mississippi courts that would write a new chapter in the history of Mississippi jurisprudence and in the attitudes of those who had once believed they could take the law into their own hands.

What happened in Neshoba County in 1964 doesn't belong to those who live there. As soon as the plan to execute Mickey, Andy, and J. E. was carried out—the moment the shots were fired and the three lay dead in the ditch—the incident belonged to America.

I feel pressure from my Mississippi kin to keep silent in order to protect an aunt who isn't guilty of any crime; a cousin to whom I've made no promises; her coworker, whom I've never met; and a second cousin who can't come out directly and tell me how he feels. I've been asked to take everything that I know, details that belong to history, and keep them hidden so that I can take care of people who feel no obligation whatsoever to take care of me.

I pull the car over to the shoulder and stop. "If it's still there, it's at the bottom of this hill," my father says, nodding to the left. We've driven all morning along rutted red roads, looking back into the woods for my great-grandfather Dempsey's shack.

"Pappy had a ring-tailed hate for Yankees," he says. "He never would've forgiven me for livin' in the North."

THERE'S SOME KIND OF URGENCY about looking for Pappy. No pictures remain of him, no clothing or bits of furniture. No wristwatch. So we're looking for his shack, if it even still exists, the one he lived in the last decade of his life, the decade of the Great Depression. "Head down that incline, Spook," my father says, pointing into the woods. "And come back and tell me what you saw."

I leave him in the passenger seat and walk into the woods alone. Tall pines border a narrow clay drive hardened into deep ruts at the bottom of a hill so steep I walk faster than I care to. Methane rises from the swamp, and the smell of rotten eggs hangs heavy in the air, pushed down against the nose like a rag soaked in chloroform. With each step I feel myself descend into a shadowy space, where the present folds itself into memory. I'm overwhelmed with drowsiness and a dream takes the shape of reality.

It's still there. Behind a tangled snarl of brush choked over with kudzu. Roof collapsing, boards the color of a sparrow's feathers and about as sturdy, foundation sinking into the sphagnum, it's still there.

Bittersweet brambles, hung with pea-size berries, wrinkled and the color of a hunter's vest, have overgrown the remnants of a sunken path that leads up to the porch. Part of me wishes for a machete to cut through the masses of tough, wiry wheels of withered vine stuck through with thorns and now and then the eviscerated fist of a sharp-edged leaf. Part of me wants simply to push through with gloved hands, step over it, and let it be. It will grow back soon enough anyway, shortly after I've gone, and after that the path and the shack, in their time, will disintegrate completely and vanish into the mire just behind.

It's a humid afternoon, the dew point holding cool moisture close to the ground in the mingling of hundreds of cattails and waist-high, spiky swamp grass. Clumps of tough weeds rise from the sponge to the tops of my ankles. A wisp of angry gnats flies in formation toward my open collar, and I wave them away with my hand. The lowest branches of the gum trees drip resin into my hair, and the overhang of the weeping willows whispers against my face, leaving my cheeks feeling brushed with wings and webs.

The porch, the size of a double bed, smells like a mattress thrown out to the swamp to mildew and rot. Its floor is of questionable stability, held up by half-sunk piles of crumbling brick. I step onto it carefully, afraid that at any moment my foot will break through to what I imagine is a nest of rattlesnakes just below boards that threaten to cave under human weight and pressure. I wade through a pile of rubbish: wooden shingles so thin with age they break into thirds and fourths, brittle when I try to pick them up. Dirt-sculpted rags that once were shirts. The bundle of a housedress, shaken out, worn to a diaphanous film by either a young girl or a woman with a tiny frame.

I step over broken glass, the remains of bottles once filled with the daisy yellow corn liquor distilled by Uncles Erb and Quill, I discover later. Yellow clay, sticky with humidity, fills a decaying tennis shoe, red and child-size. Empty mason jars, a box of ten-penny nails, half a dozen Nehi bottles, and a rusted garden rake. And on top of everything, a can of Brown's Mule tobacco full of cigarette butts, unfurled in thick, oxidated water, with bits of to-bacco expanded to look like shredded wheat.

Rain has swollen the screen door so that over time the wood has expanded to fit tightly into the frame. It sticks, and when I tug at it, the half-moon handle comes off in my hand. The screen has torn away, curls at the edges, and falls forward in half.

I feel like an unwelcome guest, and so I behave like an intruder. I slip my hand through the rent in the screen and with my palm against the interior of the door, push it toward me with a couple of sharp slaps. When it opens it almost hits me in the face. Using my shoulder, I lean my body into the second door. And with a groan, it clicks and opens.

The interior of the shack smells rusty and cool. Dim sunlight, as big as a man, falls halfway across the floorboards, as if it tripped while climbing through the broken window and never got back up to cross the room. It takes a minute for my eyes to adjust, and in that minute, I hear the rattle.

The room disappears except for a pair of yellow eyes that glitter not five feet away. I don't move. It's a diamondback rattlesnake, coiled in a pile of straw beside a striped tick pushed up against the left wall. My body jolts to attention.

I am not a student of rattlesnakes. I don't know what to do. So instinct takes over, and my hand reaches behind me for the door. I slide one foot, then the other, backward across the floor. The rattler hisses, angry at my cowardice, as if he's ready for a fight. The wire tines at the tip of his tongue slide in and out rapid-fire between predatory fangs that grin with territorial triumph. Nobody violates this space without dealing with him.

I remember the garden rake. Slowly, slowly, as though I wasn't moving at all, I reach backward through the rent in the screen and lower my body at the knees, my gloved hand groping for the wooden handle that juts out from beneath the pile of shingles. I slide the rake through the opening, handle first, my eyes fixed on his, my breath shallow, aware of nothing more than the effect of his gaze, which is a fear that pumps jets of electricity through my nervous system. My brain is supercharged with adrenaline, sending wordless survival signals out to the rest of my body. My skin tingles. I don't know what I'll do once the rake is through the door. Which it is now, steady in two hands, the seven rusted prongs pointed toward him like a row of wide-gapped teeth. If the rake were a shotgun, I'd aim at his plow-shaped head and pull the trigger.

If he springs, I want it low. I'm protected to the knee with thick leather barn boots; my jeans are tucked into them and inside heavy socks on my feet. But those fangs. Sharp enough to pierce through bone and ready to do it in his own time, which he isn't about to disclose. He rattles and hisses at the rake, glad now that I've responded to his challenge, and he leaps out at the teeth so fast I almost drop the rake for being startled and his head whips the banner of his body, thick as my wrist, through the air and in among the seven tines, weaving the diamonds back and forth through them like a shuttle through a loom. I smash the rake against the floor with his body woven thus, and trap him there. He leers up at me sideways with one eye, and with the heel of my boot I crush his head into the floor until the rope of his variegated body goes limp.

All the unspent tension rushes upward to my head seeking release. Finding it behind my eyes, it comes out in a flood of tears. I drop the rake. A wooden chair I hadn't noticed before appears on my right, and I sink into it, pull off my gloves, and sob into my bare hands. It's tension, tension, pouring out of my body in waves, leaving me limp and exhausted in the chair. I feel that I've awakened from a heavy sleep. There is a crushing stillness in the room. The wind sighs through the willow just outside. I get up, close the door behind me, and stumble, weeping, up the hill. I don't stay in the swamp long enough to discover whether there are other snakes. My whole body is shaking, the way it did after childbirth, when the nurses piled blankets on me because I couldn't get warm.

Except for flies and mosquitoes and the occasional spider, I've never killed anything before. I'm not supposed to kill things. That's somebody else's job. I've always felt that I'd left the killing, or the attempt of it, to other people.

I'd seen my brother's fists hurtle toward my face and my husband's hands wrapped around the back of the kitchen chair as part of the landscape, something that came as naturally to them as hiding behind the garage or locking myself in the bathroom came to me. In my mind's eye I'd imagined Pappy hating Yankees, and Cousin Edgar Ray sending Klansmen to firebomb the Mount Zion Methodist Church. And I'd seen my own hand, raised in anger I couldn't explain, over the head of my own frightened child, found guilty of a petty transgression.

The memories twist deep inside with the knowledge that we cannot go back in time and withdraw our hands from the acts that they've committed. We become the twin spirals of a double helix: North and South, male and female, what we're born with and what we learn. The nineteenth and twentieth centuries coil up intimately inside of us, blurring the boundaries between dream and reality, guilt and innocence, them and us. All that remains are the consequences: a legacy of anger and fear that has left its mark on us, in us, and has spanned generations despite the love, the alibis, and the amends that can't erase it from the blueprint of our beings; the outer battles little more than the manifestation of the battles within ourselves.

So it came to me easily. Killing a snake. I thought I was in danger: I reacted quickly; I defended myself. I put a kind of triumphant glaze on killing him, and I can't deny how good it felt. I did not wish I hadn't killed him. I did not feel sorry for his motionless body and the guts of the reptile brain that spilled out of his gaping mouth.

But I feel sorry now. I fought him, but I didn't outsmart him. Even dead, he kept me from violating his territory. I could have stayed and killed his whole family if I'd wanted to. But the danger— and my perception of it—wouldn't have died. There would be other snakes, coiled up and rattling, waiting for me at the very bottom of myself. Reminding me that when we are primed for it, killing comes quite naturally. It really isn't difficult at all.

EPILOGUE

Philadelphia, Mississippi, November 2001

CAROLYN GOODMAN gave me many gifts over the course of our conversations, not the least of which was the opportunity to know Stanley Dearman. Mrs. Goodman's description of the warm welcome she received at his retirement party in Philadelphia touched me with hope: hope that there has been more healing in the community than I had been led to believe.

And so, on a Saturday in early November of 2001, I'm going back to Mississippi, this time to meet Stanley Dearman. I feel very strange, however, and a little lonely. Nobody knows I'm here, not even my father in Minnesota. I'm staying with Aunt Jane in Atlanta, and I'll crisscross Alabama in one day so that I can go back to stay with her.

Friday night I traced my route, following a map of the Deep South along Interstate Highway 20, from Atlanta to Meridian. For the first time I noticed that U.S. 20 is a veritable Freedom Trail of the civil rights movement, with place-names that wouldn't have resonated as much for me five years ago as they do now.

It's early Saturday morning and the traffic is light as I drive from Decatur through Atlanta, looking for the westbound interstate that will take me out of the city. Beginning in Atlanta along the Ralph David Abernathy Expressway, I drive through western Georgia into Alabama. I pass the turnoff to Montgomery, where in 1955 Rosa Parks's refusal to give up her seat to a white man launched a bus strike that ultimately led to the integration of the city's public transportation system.

I stop for gas in Anniston, where in 1961 a Greyhound bus carrying Freedom Riders was destroyed and the activists inside badly beaten and refused treatment at the Anniston Hospital. In the center of town today is a quiet green space named for Martin Luther King Jr.

I stop to eat in Birmingham, where Bull Connor unleashed the Klan on a group of Freedom Riders on Mother's Day in 1961. He ordered police officers, using fire hoses and police dogs, to attack demonstrators in 1963.

In April of that year, Martin Luther King Jr. wrote in his *Letter from Birmingham Jail* of his keen awareness of the interrelatedness of all communities and states—a message I need to hear, even today:

> I cannot sit idly by in Atlanta and not be concerned about what happens in Birmingham. Injustice anywhere is a threat to justice everywhere. We are caught in an inescapable network of mutuality tied in a single garment of destiny. Whatever affects one directly, affects all indirectly. Never again can we afford to live with the narrow, provincial, "outside agitator" idea. Anyone who lives inside the United States can never be considered an outsider anywhere within its bounds.

Five months later, a bomb exploded in the Sixteenth Street Baptist Church in Birmingham, killing four young girls who were getting ready for choir practice inside. It took forty years before one of the killers, Thomas Blanton Jr., was tried and convicted for the murders of Cynthia Wesley, Carol Robertson, and Addie Mae Collins, all fourteen years old, and Denise McNair, who was eleven.

In a couple of hours I cross the state line into Mississippi, where at the welcome center, I'm greeted with a free cup of coffee, maps, and directions to Philadelphia. On my way out I notice and pick up from a rack of brochures a copy of the *African-American Heritage Guide*, a four-color magazine devoted to sites and monuments that document the history of black people in the state, from slavery to today.

It includes the site of "The Forks of the Road" slave market in Natchez, the statue of Medgar Evers in Jackson, and the rebuilt Mount Zion Methodist Church near Philadelphia. There's also the Margaret Walker Alexander African-American Research Center, a marker that commemorates Richard Wright, and a town-by-town tour of Mississippi's famous bluesmen, like Muddy Waters, Robert Johnson, and Sonny Boy Williamson.

As I page through, I notice that many of the antebellum estates are listed as important historical sites built by slave labor. I remember the day, so long ago, when I played in the grass at the Windsor Ruins, only now the picture is complete: the house and all its residents. It's like standing in awe before the pyramids in Egypt or the Great Wall of China. African slaves begin to take the shape of real people in the legacy of their labor, and the state of Mississippi is acknowledging it.

It's not everything, but it's something very important, and the brochure brings me to tears.

Before I reach Philadelphia, I turn off onto the Pine Grove Road and stop in the cemetery. It's a rare November afternoon, warm and sunny and golden, and I push the gate open against a wall of fallen leaves the wind has banked against the inside of the fence. The crunch of each step through them startles me; I am aware of my aloneness and my visibility. What if someone drives by and asks me why I'm here?

I stand before the graves of Grandma Ora and Daddy Bob, but without Auntie Lu or my father to stand here with me, I question my right to stand here. Without them, the place feels empty. No stories, a broken connection to my past, and a tenuous, at best, hold on any faith I might once have had in an afterlife: this is what I bring to this place now.

I'm tempted to drive down the road to Susie's, but I don't want to create a scene and make both of us uncomfortable. I also don't want my desire to make everything right again to compromise, with gratitude or loyalty or any other claims, what I need to write. My head is noisy with arguments: I am connected, I argue. These are my kinfolk too. I have a right to be here. *Why didn't you tell us you were writing a book about civil rights? I don't want my name associated with a book about civil rights.* But for all the people I'm fighting in my mind, I am alone here, like Ezekiel in the field of dry bones.

From somewhere inside, another voice emerges and says, as much to the ghosts of the ancestors before me as to myself, *I'm sorry that you feel this way.* There's no way I can make this right; the past is not mine to change or forget. I can only face down my old fears: fear of abandonment, of pain, of humiliation and separation, so that I can remember.

But it is time for me to leave the boneyard. I walk back to the gate and get into my car. I back out of the parking lot onto the Pine Grove Road, where in 1864 Pappy watched Sherman's march. I turn left onto Highway 19 to Philadelphia, Mississippi, where a century later the highway patrol watched Goodman, Schwerner, and Chaney. I won't be seeing family this time. Instead I'll talk to Mrs. Goodman's friend Stanley Dearman. Alone. Afraid. Free.

It's early afternoon when I arrive at Stan's house, a graceful red brick structure that appears through the trees at the end of a long, upward-sloping driveway. He and his wife, Carolyn, built it a few years ago, Stan tells me when we say hello for the first time, and stop to admire the view of the hills north of Philadelphia. They're still working on it, he explains; it's a labor of love.

Carolyn offers me lunch. I hadn't expected to be fed, but I'm hungry, and the hospitality feeds me as much as the sandwich does. I betray my Yankee-ness, however, when I ask for iced tea without sugar. But then I make up for it when we discuss, in full agreement, the splendor of certain southern delicacies like—to be blunt—the lard that the last generation of cooks used to make biscuits and piecrust and southern fried chicken. "I read once," I tell Stan, "that the chemistry of animal fat in the lard is what makes the biscuits flaky. Vegetable fats don't react the same way to the buttermilk and the heat."

He and I spend the next five hours together, during which—is it my need to belong to *somebody* here?—I feel that Stan and Carolyn are adopting me and filling the breach. I know within minutes that I am in the presence of people who will help and support me as I slog through family difficulties and put together my memoir.

After lunch on the back porch, we sit in Stan's library. We are surrounded by books—floor-to-ceiling books—and I instantly feel an old, familiar comfort. I am in the company of friends: Marcel Proust, Umberto Eco, Willa Cather, and of course, Eudora Welty and William Faulkner.

Stan was an English major at the University of Mississippi, and from time to time he gets up to find a quote that will illustrate his point.

I pepper him with questions, mostly to find out two things: how the community has changed over the past thirty-five years and why so many people adhered—indeed, still hold to—a code of silence.

"Well, I feel I must choose my words carefully here. What people elsewhere don't understand about this place is the desire not to hurt anybody's feelings," he says. "What people here don't realize is that what gets sacrificed is the truth."

"I can understand that," I say. "I have a cousin who wants me to keep this out of the book to protect a friend who's a family member of one of the conspirators."

"Look," Stan replies. "Everybody in this county is kinfolk to everybody else. You can't hardly write a word that doesn't bring somebody's relations into the picture.

"Besides, that man has already hurt his family," Stan goes on. "Far beyond what anybody else could ever do. You are saying something, and I feel that it's important to discuss this. Every year on June twenty-first, busloads of students come here to commemorate the deaths of those three young men. I get phone calls from scholars all the time asking for information. You're not the first person to write about this, and you won't be the last. I must say, however, that the only other book written by an insider came thirty years ago. And she really took it on the chin—Florence Mars."

"I sure don't feel like an insider."

"Well, blood is blood, and there's no taking that away. Besides, if you weren't an insider, I don't imagine your kinfolk would be so upset. Have they read anything else that's been written about the case?"

"I don't really know. Judging from the comments I've heard, I don't think many of them have read any books about the civil rights movement at all."

On the coffee table before us is Diane McWhorter's book about growing up in Birmingham during the long civil rights struggle there. I've seen her on television, after the murder conviction this year of Thomas Blanton Jr. for the deaths of the four girls in the 1963 church bombing. "She's a friend of ours," Stan explains. "And she's got kinfolk mad at her too." I'm beginning to think that in retirement, the Dearmans could run a foster home for writers orphaned by their southern families. If their hospitality is any indication, I believe they'd do it too.

"These murder trials are very important," Stan says, standing up. He paces a little, gathering his thoughts as he speaks. "I believe that until a murder trial takes place about what happened here, this community will not be able to let go and move on.

"I don't think a day goes by that I don't think about those three young men. And I don't want the history books to show that in Neshoba County, their murderers were never brought to justice. There's the shame of it. Nothing you or I or anybody else could write can shame this community. These killers running free and the courts that couldn't convict them of murder placed that mark on Mississippi, and only Mississippi can make it right by holding a trial and putting closure on it. I believe that very strongly."

Just recently, Jerry Mitchell, a writer for the Jackson *Clarion-Ledger*, did an extensive series on the murders of Goodman, Schwerner, and Chaney. New evidence has surfaced from testimony in other civil rights murder trials and from witnesses and jury members now willing to speak out. When the courts ordered unsealed the records of the now-defunct Mississippi Sovereignty Commission, additional information came to light.

Mitchell's series included a critical piece of evidence from the testimony of Sam Bowers during the 1998 trial for the murder of Vernon Dahmer. Bowers admitted in a sealed interview that he had thwarted justice in the Goodman, Schwerner, and Chaney case, and that he didn't mind going to prison because a fellow Klansman had gotten away with murder. "I was quite delighted to be convicted and have the main instigator of the entire affair walk out of the courtroom a free man," Bowers said.

"Bowers didn't name the man, but FBI confessions say Edgar Ray Killen coordinated the killings. The 1967 jury deadlocked 11–1 in favor of Killen's guilt. He says he is innocent," Mitchell wrote.

His coverage of the case included another interesting piece of information that came from interviews with several jurors from the 1967 conspiracy trial. A single juror told others on the panel that "she couldn't vote guilty against Edgar Ray Killen for one reason—she could never convict a preacher."

"I've spoken with Edgar Killen on a number of occasions," Stan tells me. "But now he's running scared. He denies everything, of course. Always has."

"That Edgar Killen has the sweetest sister," Carolyn says. "It's been hard for the family," she says, coming back with glasses of ice water.

"Tell Mary about the funeral home," Stan suggests as Carolyn sits on the love seat facing us.

"Well, I have three children," she begins. "Two living, and a little girl who died in June of 1964." She pauses, clasps her hands together in her lap, and leans forward. "The visitation was here, in Philadelphia, on Sunday evening, June 21. We'd left the funeral home early. It was an exhausting time.

"Well, months later, I got a call from the FBI asking to see the guest register from the funeral home. They were checking alibis and there in the guest book was his signature, *Edgar Ray Killen*.

"Of course, we'd gone home early and this would have been later in the evening, so I never saw him there."

"Did you know him?"

"Not really. I can't think why he'd come to our little girl's visitation."

Stan breaks in at this moment. "At first, he's just a kind of blowhard, you know, a braggart, a know-it-all. But make no mistake about it; he has a very, very dark side. One of those who preaches and believes that blacks have the curse of the Ethiopians, a kind of biblical justification for maltreatment of black people."

"Do people still hang on to that?" I ask him.

"Not like they used to," he responds. "It's one of the ways the community is changing."

"Things are obviously changing. I'm baffled about the unwillingness to talk about this," I tell Stan. "I can understand it a little— who wants to be embarrassed, time and time again, about something that happened so long ago? But why the secrecy? Why then? Why now?"

Stan described what life had been like at the time of the murders. From the spring of 1964 through the fall of 1967, he told me, the Klan had placed a stranglehold on Neshoba County that created an atmosphere of terror that brings to mind repressive, totalitarian regimes like the Nazis in Germany and the Taliban in Afghanistan.

"It's hard to admit that terrorism of this nature exists in America," Stan said. "But it did and it does."

Stan and Carolyn went on to describe from personal experience what I'd read about the Klan's reign of terror in Neshoba County. Preacher Killen had helped create a Klan-controlled network that had infiltrated all areas of life, from city government, to law enforcement, to local businesses, to church leaders, to deputized citizens. Two people standing in the checkout line at the Winn Dixie didn't dare comment on the newspaper coverage of the case.

"If you said something, anything, even 'I sure hope they catch whoever did this,' word would get back to the Klan within the hour. That day, that evening, they'd start to harrass you: phone calls threatening your children's safety, a rock thrown through your front window at dinnertime. They'd boycott your business or burn a cross on your lawn, or shoot a gun into your house in the middle of the night."

People had been publicly humiliated by the sheriff and his deputy, arrested and beaten while in the Neshoba County jail. Businesses had been ruined, people had been killed.

It was a town where no one dared speak out for fear that they would risk their children's safety, their livelihood, their home, and even their lives. If you kept quiet, you could count on their protection, they'd tell people. If you talked, then you had to face the consequences.

"There was no leadership back then, nobody to speak out and set the agenda for the community. The good people had no one to speak for them, no advocacy, no protection. When terrorists run the city, the police force, everything, you don't even have a free press.

There's an ethical void. I believe that if people from the outside had not intervened, the county would not have changed. All this about 'outside agitators' is misdirected."

"I think that's what affected me so much about Carolyn Goodman's experience here last winter. I was very touched when she described the warm welcome she got when she came to your retirement reception," I tell Stan. "Clearly there was none of that old mistrust and blame."

"Carolyn Goodman; now there is a very special person," he says. "I had no idea she was coming, and when I saw her, I admit I teared up. I was very moved." He showed me a newspaper clipping of the event. Stan had been one of a handful of people who had chosen to take a stand against the code of silence and had encouraged others to do so.

"You gave to me and my family an understanding and warmth that we needed so desperately at a time when it seemed our wounds would never, ever be healed," Mrs. Goodman had said.

"How else has the community changed?" I ask.

"Oh, in so many ways. Big things, like giving back the franchise to blacks. It's so much a part of everyday life now, there's no longer any bugaboo. But those three boys died for that.

"Once President Johnson signed the Voting Rights Act in 1965 and blacks could vote, it was amazing to see city leadership at NAACP meetings," he said. "Mail service came to the black sections, electricity, paved streets. Then, of course, when the schools were integrated in 1970, it was completely peaceful. No violent incident of any kind."

"Jerry Mitchell told me that Mississippi has more elected black officials than any other state," I said.

"The power of the ballot just can't be overestimated," Stan replied. "There were politicians all over the South who'd been in control a long time and simply didn't want to relinquish power. Some of them had to be taken to court and removed from office. That doesn't happen anymore.

"And more equitable jury selection, not just token blacks on a jury.

"Then there are the other things. When I bought the paper in 1966, there had been no wedding announcements or portraits of black brides," he said. "What's the biggest day of your life? Think about it. A wedding announcement proclaims the union, honors the parents from both sides, gives the bride her moment in the sun. Now people shake hands on the street, black and white and don't think twice about it. It's hard to believe that not too long ago, black people were denied the simplest of courtesies, like addressing someone as 'Mrs.' or 'Mr.'

"Ever since the Civil War, the South has had people pointing fingers at them and telling them they're wrong, and there's naturally resentment. Nobody likes that.

"I think that one of Neshoba County's best moments, the time I saw that the good people here just needed the opportunity to rally around a cause, came when we finally cracked down on bootlegging.

"The sheriff's office for decades had control of the liquor that came into the county. They delivered it to the little roadhouses and made a fortune. Neshoba is supposed to be a dry county." He chuckled. "But there was plenty of liquor flowing into the community in the trunks of patrol cars.

"There had been incidents, rapes, and a murder, in the roadhouses. I put a notice in the *Democrat,* asking citizens to come to a meeting and sign a petition to clean up corrupt law enforcement. You wouldn't believe how many people showed up to sign. People were just looking for a cause to rally behind. Things cleaned up after that."

I've been waiting for the right moment to ask him about his grand piano, which also brings Mrs. Goodman to mind. He tries to play every day, he tells me, picking up a mold of Chopin's hand that he keeps atop the instrument, for inspiration. He points to his compact disc collection, most of which is piano. "I'll admit it is my favorite," he says. "We've had concerts here." He crosses the room to a pair of French doors and opens them, revealing a formal parlor. "We've had as many as ninety people here for concerts. We have a niece who sings opera too."

It's growing dark, and I have a five-hour drive ahead of me, so I get up to go. But first, I ask him something that has been puzzling me all afternoon. I look at his books, the piano, the artwork and collection of music. "Why did you move to Philadelphia [from Meridian] and why did you stay so many years?"

"It's a commitment," he says. "I grew to love this community. Being the editor of the newspaper gave me the opportunity to get involved and, I hope, make a real difference." He goes to the bookshelf and pulls out a collection of essays that includes Faulkner's "Mississippi."

"This especially shows how I feel," he says, and reads the end of the essay. "'Loving all of it even while he had to hate some of it because he knows now that you dont (*sic*) love because: you love despite; not for the virtues, but despite the faults.'"

And this is how the story ends. In thinking it over, I've come to believe that Faulkner was only half right. We love despite *and* because. This, now, has become my fondest hope.

Endnotes

Works Cited

Branch, Taylor. *Parting the Waters: America During the King Years, 1954–1963*. New York: Simon & Schuster, 1989.

————. *Pillar of Fire: America During the King Years, 1963–65*. New York: Simon & Schuster, 1998.

Cagin, Seth, and Philip Dray. *We Are Not Afraid: Goodman, Schwerner and Chaney and the Civil Rights Campaign for Mississippi*. New York: Macmillan, 1988.

Faulkner, William. *Essays, Speeches and Public Letters*. New York: Random House, 1965.

Huie, William Bradford. *Three Lives for Mississippi*. New York: WCC Books, 1964.

King, Martin Luther, Jr. "Letter from Birmingham Jail," from *A World of Ideas*. Boston: Bedford Books, 1998.

Lewis, David Levering. *W. E. B. DuBois, Biography of a Race: 1868–1919*. New York: Henry Holt & Co., 1993.

————. *W. E. B. DuBois, the Fight for Equality and the American Century: 1919–1963.* New York: Henry Holt & Co., 2000.

Linder, Doug. "Mississippi Burning Trial," Famous Trials Homepage, 2001. (www.law.umkc.edu/faculty/projects/ftrials/ftrials.htm)

Loewen, James, and Charles Sallis. *Mississippi: Conflict and Change.* New York: Pantheon Books, 1974.

Mars, Florence. *Witness in Philadelphia.* Baton Rouge: Louisiana State University Press, 1977.

Mitchell, Jerry. "44 Days That Changed Mississippi," *Jackson Clarion-Ledger,* May 7, 2000–January 8, 2001.

Morris, Willie. *The Courting of Marcus Dupree.* Jackson: University Press of Mississippi, 1992.

Silver, James. *Mississippi: The Closed Society.* New York: Harcourt, Brace & World, 1963.

Whitehead, Don. *Attack on Terror: The FBI vs. The Ku Klux Klan in Mississippi.* New York: Funk & Wagnalls, 1970.

Whitfield, Stephen J. *A Death in the Delta.* Baltimore: Johns Hopkins University Press, 1988.

Prosecutive Summary of the Investigation of the Abduction and Murder of James Earl Chaney, Andrew Goodman and Michael Henry Schwerner on June 21, 1964. Federal Bureau of Investigation. (MIBURN)

United States of America vs. Cecil Ray Price et al., Criminal Action No. 5291, heard in Federal District Court for the Southern District of Mississippi in Meridian, October 11–21, 1967 (trial transcript).

Prologue

7 "Ever since he was dropped off": Cagin and Dray, pp. 41, 281; *Jackson Clarion-Ledger,* May 9, 2000.

Chapter Three

28 "Preacher Killen stopped by the police station": Cagin and Dray, p. 264; Mars, pp. 144, 236–237; Whitehead, pp. 28–29, 264–265; *Jackson Clarion-Ledger,* May 28, 2000; Miller testimony in MIBURN.

31 "Recruiting students for Freedom Summer": Cagin and Dray, pp. 47–49, 261–262; Huie, pp. 71–73, 78–80, 107–109.

33 "Michael Schwerner had come to Mississippi": Cagin and Dray, pp. 261–262, 269, 272.

Chapter Four

37 "The White Knights of Mississippi": Whitehead, pp. 22–23; Interview with Stanley Dearman.

43 "In the 1920s of my father's childhood": Cagin and Dray, pp. 37, 245; Morris, pp. 71–73; Whitehead, pp. 22–25; MIBURN.

44 "Preacher Killen's clandestine recruitment": Cagin and Dray, p. 263.

44 "One of the most infamous perpetrators": Cagin and Dray, pp. 253–255; Mars, pp. 127, 135; Morris, p. 154; Whitehead, pp. 37–38, 149–156.

48 "The state of Mississippi passed a constitutional amendment": Cagin and Dray, pp. 132–133, 136; Lewis (Volume 2), p. 557; Mars, pp. 58–59, 117–119, 163–164, 196, 280; Morris, pp. 90–91; Silver, pp. 8, 17, 21–27, 40–48, 134–138; Whitfield, pp. 62–63.

48 "In the late 1940s": Mars, pp. 162–164.

49 "The Councils also supported the appropriation": Cagin and Dray, p. 209; Whitfield, pp. 62–63.

Chapter Five

59 "Growing up in New York City": Cagin and Dray, pp. 49–53, 162–171; Huie, pp. 48–49, 94–95; Interview with Carolyn Goodman.

61 "For Michael Schwerner": Cagin and Dray, pp. 256–258.

61 "James Chaney was born in Meridian, Mississippi": Cagin and Dray, pp. 162–171.

Chapter Six

73 "In September of 1963": Cagin and Dray, pp. 259, 263; Huie, p. 61; *Meridian Star,* March 10, 1964, reprinted with permission.

77 "Yet this is exactly what the Klan was planning": Morris, pp. 153–154; Whitehead, pp. 1–10; MIBURN; *Jackson Clarion-Ledger,* May 14, 2000.

Chapter Nine

110 "Blues lovers everywhere knew": Cagin and Dray, pp. 135–136; Lewis (Volume 2), p. 298.

117 "The enemy that Sam Bowers had warned Klansmen about": Cagin and Dray, pp. 28–30, 33, 35, 276; Huie, pp. 142–146; Interview with Carolyn Goodman.

118 "A thousand miles to the south": Branch, pp. 351–352; Cagin and Dray, pp. 4–5, 29, 38–40; Huie, pp. 136–142; Mars, pp. 169–171, 240–242; Morris, p. 160; Whitehead, pp. 178, 269–273; Cole, Dennis, and Miller testimonies in MIBURN.

120 "Andy called his parents twice": Cagin and Dray, pp. 29, 34, 365; Interview with Carolyn Goodman.

120 "On their way back from Longdale": Cagin and Dray, pp. 13, 285–286.

Chapter Ten

126 "Though many clues in the investigation": Mars, pp. 89–80; *Meridian Star,* June 25, 1964, reprinted with permission.

127 "In 1964, Mississippi led the nation": Whitfield, p. 5.

128 "During the search for Goodman, Schwerner, and Chaney": Branch (Volume 2), p. 399; Cagin and Dray, pp. 371–372.

128 "In August of 1955": Whitfield, pp. 17–24.

130 "Lynching, according to some sociologists": Branch (Volume 1), pp. 181–182; Whitfield, pp. 71–73, 74.

130 "The lynching of black people in Mississippi declined after 1955": Branch (Volume 1), pp. 257–258, 818; Cagin and Dray, pp. 26, 31; Silver, p. 8; Whitfield, pp. 5, 102, 103.

Chapter Eleven

145 "In August of 1964": Huie, pp. 221–224; Mars, pp. 31–35, 107–111; Morris, pp. 66–68.

149 "The attorney general had sent": Mars, pp. 196, 280.

149 "On June 21, 1966": Cagin and Dray, pp. 380–382; Mars, pp. 207–210; Morris, pp. 205–207.

153 "But in March of 1966": Cagin and Dray, p. 441.

Chapter Fourteen

175 "Andy Goodman was fourteen": Cagin and Dray, pp. 63–64; Interview with Carolyn Goodman.

176 "J. E. Chaney had his first experience": Cagin and Dray, pp. 166–171; Huie, pp. 76–77, 93–95, 119; Linder web page, James Chaney biography; Morris, pp. 156, 159.

178 "Mickey Schwerner had been the kid": Cagin and Dray, pp. 256–261; Huie, pp. 45–64; Morris, pp. 157–159.

Chapter Fifteen

188 "In 1970, sixteen years after *Brown*": Morris, pp. 210–211; Interview with Stanley Dearman.

190 "Back in 1970, in that first class": Morris, pp. 187–188; Interview with Stanley Dearman.

Chapter Sixteen

208 "What follows are the words of a federal grand jury": Cagin and Dray, pp. 434–437; Huie, pp. 176–179; Morris, pp. 161–162; Whitehead, pp. 196–197; MIBURN; *United States vs. Cecil Ray Price et al.*

210 "After Andy, Mickey, and J. E. were released": Cagin and Dray, pp. 287–294; Whitehead, pp. 60–61, 276–277; Jordan, Poe testimonies in MIBURN; Barnette confession in MIBURN.

212 "Mickey and Andy lay dead": Cagin and Dray, pp. 36–38, 40–41, 278–281; Whitehead, p. 276; Jordan testimony in MIBURN; Barnette confession in MIBURN.

Chapter Seventeen

216 "The Monday morning after": Cagin and Dray, pp. 337–341; Huie, p. 190; Whitehead, pp. 65–69; MIBURN.

218 "There's a photograph of Bogue Chitto": *Life,* July 3, 1964.

221 "In December of 1964": *Life,* December 18, 1964; Cagin and Dray, pp. 376–377.

Chapter Eighteen

229 "On Saturday, August 1": Cagin and Dray, p. 395.

229 "A few days after": Huie, p. 267; Mitchell, *Jackson Clarion-Ledger,* May 7, 2000–January 8, 2001; Miller testimony in MIBURN.

230 "The informant, who remains nameless": Cagin and Dray, pp. 393–401; Huie, pp. 218–219; Mars, pp. 105–106; Whitehead, pp. 125–137; MIBURN.

235 "On January 11, 1965": Cagin and Dray, p. 441; Huie, p. 199; Mars, p. 129.

Chapter Twenty

257 "In March of 1966": Cagin and Dray, pp. 309, 441–443, 446–447; Mars, pp. 228–235; Whitehead, pp. 262–263; MIBURN trial transcript.

264 "Over the next few days": Cagin and Dray, pp. 430–435, 447; Mars, pp. 236–242; Whitehead, pp. 264–276; Dennis and Miller testimonies, Linder web page; trial transcripts from MIBURN.

268 "Ernest Kirkland of the Mount Zion community": Cagin and Dray, pp. 287–289, 323, 431–432, 447, 448, 449; Mars, pp. 232, 243–250; Whitehead, pp. 276–278; Linder web page; Herring, Jordan, Kirkland, Poe testimonies in MIBURN.

Chapter Twenty-one

273 "On Wednesday, October 18, 1967": Cagin and Dray, pp. 449–452; Mars, pp. 255–261; Whitehead, pp. 278–284; Linder web page; trial transcripts in MIBURN.

Epilogue

284 King, excerpt from "Letter from Birmingham Jail." Reprinted with permission.

289 "44 Days That Changed Mississippi," *Jackson Clarion-Ledger,* May 7, 2000–January 8, 2001.

294 Faulkner, excerpt from "Mississippi," *Essays, Speeches and Public Letters.* Reprinted with permission.

Bibliography

Books

Allport, Gordon. *The Nature of Prejudice.* New York: Addison-Wesley, 1979.

Ball, Edward. *Slaves in the Family.* New York: Ballantine, 1998.

Belfrage, Sally. *Freedom Summer.* New York: Viking Press, 1965.

Branch, Taylor. *Parting the Waters: America During the King Years, 1954–1963.* New York: Simon & Schuster, 1989.

———. *Pillar of Fire: America During the King Years, 1963–65.* New York: Simon & Schuster, 1998.

Burk, Robert Fredrick. *The Eisenhower Administration and Black Civil Rights.* Knoxville: University of Tennessee Press, 1984.

Cagin, Seth, and Philip Dray. *We Are Not Afraid: Goodman, Schwerner, and Chaney and the Civil Rights Campaign for Mississippi.* New York: Macmillan, 1988.

Carter, Jimmy. *An Hour Before Daylight.* New York: Simon & Schuster, 2001.

Egerton, John. *Speak Now Against the Day.* New York: Alfred A. Knopf, 1994

Evans, Walker, and James Agee. *Let Us Now Praise Famous Men.* New York: Ballantine, 1960.

Faulkner, William. *As I Lay Dying.* New York: Random House, 1940.

———. *The Sound and the Fury.* New York: Random House, 1954.

———. *Go Down, Moses.* New York: Random House, 1964.

———. *Essays, Speeches and Public Letters.* New York: Random House, 1965.

————. *Light in August.* New York: Modern Library, 1968.

Foote, Shelby. *The Civil War: A Narrative.* New York: Random House, 1958–1974.

Garrow, David J. *Bearing the Cross: Martin Luther King, Jr., and the Southern Christian Leadership Conference.* New York: Morrow, 1986.

Gates, Henry Louis Jr. *Colored People.* New York: Knopf, 1994.

Halberstam, David. *The Fifties.* New York: Villard Books, 1993.

————. *The Children.* New York: Ballantine, 1998.

Horwitz, Tony. *Confederates in the Attic.* New York: Random House, 1998.

Huie, William Bradford. *Three Lives for Mississippi.* New York: WCC Books, 1964.

Lee, Harper. *To Kill a Mockingbird.* New York: HarperCollins, 1988.

Lewis, David Levering. *W. E. B. DuBois, Biography of a Race: 1868–1919.* New York: Henry Holt & Co., 1993.

————. *W. E. B. DuBois, The Fight for Equality and the American Century: 1919–1963.* New York: Henry Holt & Co., 2000.

Loewen, James, and Charles Sallis. *Mississippi: Conflict and Change.* New York: Pantheon Books, 1974.

Malcolm, Andrew, and Roger Strauss III. *Mississippi Currents.* New York: William Morrow & Co., 1996.

Mars, Florence. *Witness in Philadelphia.* Baton Rouge: Louisiana State University Press, 1977.

Massengill, Reed. *Portrait of a Racist.* New York: St. Martin's Press, 1994.

McWhorter, Diane. *Carry Me Home: Birmingham and the Climactic Battle for Civil Rights.* New York: Simon & Schuster, 2001.

Moody, Anne. *Coming of Age in Mississippi.* New York: Dial Press, 1968.

Morris, Willie. *The Courting of Marcus Dupree.* Jackson: University Press of Mississippi, 1992.

Parmet, Herbert S. *Eisenhower and the American Crusades.* New York: Macmillan, 1972.

Silver, James. *Mississippi: The Closed Society.* New York: Harcourt, Brace & World, 1963.

Warren, Robert Penn. *The Legacy of the Civil War.* New York: Random House, 1961.

————. *All the King's Men.* New York: Harcourt Brace Jovanovich, 1984.

Welty, Eudora. *Losing Battles.* New York: Random House, 1970.

————. *The Collected Short Stories.* New York: Harcourt, Brace, Jovanovich, 1980.

Whitehead, Don. *Attack on Terror: The FBI vs. The Ku Klux Klan in Mississippi.* New York: Funk & Wagnalls, 1970.

Whitfield, Stephen J. *A Death in the Delta.* Baltimore: Johns Hopkins University Press, 1988.

Wilson, Charles Reagan, and William Ferris, eds. *An Encyclopedia of Southern Culture.* Chapel Hill: University of North Carolina Press, 1989.

Wright, Richard. *Black Boy.* New York: Perennial, 1966.

Yates, Gayle Graham. *Mississippi Mind.* Knoxville: University of Tennessee Press, 1990.

Essay

King, Martin Luther Jr. "Letter from Birmingham Jail," from *A World of Ideas.* Boston: Bedford Books, 1998.

Magazine and Newspaper Articles

———. "Climate of Fear," *Commonweal,* October 14, 1955.

———. "Death in Mississippi," *Commonweal,* September 23, 1955.

Goodman, Mrs. Robert, as told to Bernard Asbell. "My Son Didn't Die in Vain," *Good Housekeeping,* May 1965.

———. "Limpid Shambles of Violence," *Life,* July 3, 1964.

Mitchell, Jerry. "44 Days That Changed Mississippi," *Jackson Clarion-Ledger,* May 7, 2000–January 8, 2001.

Nevin, David. "A Strange Little Town Loath to Admit Complicity," *Life,* December 18, 1964.

———. "No Federal Case? Lynch Murders of Three Civil Rights Workers," *Newsweek,* March 8, 1965.

Government Documents

Prosecutive Summary of the Investigation of the Abduction and Murder of James Earl Chaney, Andrew Goodman and Michael Henry Schwerner on June 21, 1964. Federal Bureau of Investigation. (MIBURN).

United States of America vs. Cecil Ray Price et al., Criminal Action No. 5291, heard in Federal District Court for the Southern District of Mississippi in Meridian, October 11–21, 1967 (trial transcript).

Web Site

Linder, Doug. "Mississippi Burning Trial," Famous Trials Homepage, 2001. (www.law.umkc.edu/faculty/projects/ftrials/ftrials.htm)

Documentary Films

Burns, Ken, producer. *The Civil War.* Alexandria, Va.: PBS Video, 1989.

Hampton, Henry, editor. *Eyes on the Prize.* Alexandria, Va.: PBS Video, 1986.